LONG RANGE PLANNING

Cumulative Index

International Journal of Strategic Management
LONG RANGE PLANNING

The Journal of the Strategic Planning Society
and of the European Strategic Planning Federation

Editor:
Professor Bernard Taylor
North American Editor:
Professor John Grant
Japan and South-east Asia Editor:
Professor Toyohiro Kono

U.K. Editorial Office:

Professor Bernard Taylor
Henley—The Management College
Greenlands, Henley-on-Thames
Oxon RG9 3AU, U.K.

U.S. Editorial Office:

Professor John Grant
Joseph M. Katz Graduate School of Business
University of Pittsburgh
Pittsburgh
PA 15260, U.S.A.

Japan and South-east Asia Editorial Office:

Professor Toyohiro Kono
Department of Management
Faculty of Economics
Gakushuin University
1–5–1 Mejiro, Toshima-ku
Tokyo 171, Japan

LONG RANGE PLANNING

Cumulative Index
Volumes 1 to 22

PERGAMON PRESS
Member of Maxwell Macmillan Pergamon Publishing Corporation
OXFORD · NEW YORK · BEIJING · FRANKFURT
SÃO PAULO · SYDNEY · TOKYO · TORONTO

U.K.	Pergamon Press plc, Headington Hill Hall, Oxford OX3 0BW, England
U.S.A.	Pergamon Press, Inc., Maxwell House, Fairview Park, Elmsford, New York 10523, U.S.A.
PEOPLE'S REPUBLIC OF CHINA	Pergamon Press, Room 4037, Qianmen Hotel, Beijing, People's Republic of China
FEDERAL REPUBLIC OF GERMANY	Pergamon Press GmbH, Hammerweg 6, D-6242 Kronberg, Federal Republic of Germany
BRAZIL	Pergamon Editora Ltda, Rua Eça de Queiros, 346, CEP 04011, Paraiso, São Paulo, Brazil
AUSTRALIA	Pergamon Press Australia Pty Ltd., P.O. Box 544, Potts Point, N.S.W. 2011, Australia
JAPAN	Pergamon Press, 5th Floor, Matsuoka Central Building, 1-7-1 Nishishinjuku, Shinjuku-ku, Tokyo 160, Japan
CANADA	Pergamon Press Canada Ltd., Suite No. 271, 253 College Street, Toronto, Ontario, Canada M5T 1R5

First edition 1990

ISBN 0-08-040795-1 Hardcover

Printed in Great Britain by BPCC Wheatons Ltd, Exeter

Contents

Introduction vii
JOHN D. GRANT

Author Index 1

Subject Index 23

Introduction

When Robert Perrin, then Chairman of the Editorial Board, wrote the introduction to the first Cumulative Index he referred to *Long Range Planning* as being the first journal to specialise in strategic and corporate planning and its sources. Much has happened since then. Another five volumes, 30 issues and 350 articles have been added, making a new index necessary as guide to over 1200 papers on strategic matters in the collection.

Now we also have editorial offices in the U.S.A. and Japan supporting the Editor in the United Kingdom. Material is drawn from round the world. With the recent changes in Eastern Europe and discussions which have taken place we hope to see further development in the sourcing of articles.

A parallel development has been the production of the *Best of Long Range Planning* series, bringing out collections of articles on specific topics within the wide strategic field. This will improve accessibility since we often receive reports from libraries as to how well thumbed are copies of the Journal which are held. The joint investment by the Strategic Planning Society and Pergamon Press continues and we are always looking for ways to improve its practical value to a growing readership.

JOHN D. GRANT
Chairman, Editorial Board

Author Index

A

ABERNETHY W L. Corporate Planning—A Personal Viewpoint 1974 **7** (6), 49

ABT R *et al*. The Dangerous Quest for Certainty in Market Forecasting 1979 **12** (2), 52

ACKELSBERG R, ARLOW P. Small Businesses Do Plan and It Pays Off 1985 **18** (5), 61

ACKELSBERG R, HARRIS W C. How Danish Companies Plan 1989 **22** (6), 111

ACKOFF R. A Concept of Corporate Planning 1970 **3** (1), 2

ACKOFF R L. The Systems Revolution 1974 **7** (6), 2

ACZEL J, MORRIS G. Future Trends in World Trade (A Review of the Lima Target) 1978 **11** (2), 19

ADAMS F P, COX J F. Manufacturing Resource Planning: An Information Systems Model 1985 **18** (2), 86

ADAMS S *see* GRIFFIN A

ADEGBITE O. Planning in Nigerian Business 1986 **19** (4), 98

ADEYAMI K S, PETU A O. A Health Strategy for Nigeria 1989 **22** (6), 55

ADLER H S, SNEATH C G. Acquiring Companies in the U.S.A. 1987 **20** (2), 42

ADOLFSE J, VERVOORDELFONK F. Strategic Planning and Policy Making in Banks 1979 **12** (3), 73

ADRIAANS W, HOOGAKKER J T. Planning an Information System at Netherlands Gas 1989 **22** (3), 64

AGGARWAL R. International Business Through Barter and Countertrade 1989 **22** (3), 75

AHLQUIST C G. Turning Plans into Action—A Case Study 1974 **7** (6), 59

AHMAD I *see* MALIK M A K

AJIMAL K S. Force Field Analysis—A Framework for Strategic Thinking 1985 **18** (5), 55

AL-BAZZAZ S, GRINYER P M. How Planning Works in Practice—A Survey of 48 U.K. Companies 1980 **13** (4), 30

ALBALA A. A Model for New Product Planning 1977 **10** (6), 62

ALBALA A. Financial Planning for New Products. Part 1—Basis for Model Formulation 1977 **10** (4), 61

ALEXANDER L D. Successfully Implementing Strategic Decisions 1985 **18** (3), 91

ALLEN D. Establishing a Financial Objective—A Practical Approach 1979 **12** (6), 11

ALLEN D H. Credibility and the Assessment of R & D Projects 1972 **5** (2), 53

ALLEN D H. Linear Programming Techniques in R & D Project Planning 1974 **7** (1), 61

ALLEN D N, PLOSILA W H. Turnaround Strategies for Economic Development 1988 **21** (3), 59

ALLEN M. Strategic Management of Consumer Services 1988 **21** (6), 20

ALLESEN-HOLM J. Strategic Planning at the Copenhagen Telephone Company 1985 **18** (3), 68

ALLIO R J. The Corporate Road-Map—Planning at Babcock & Wilcox 1972 **5** (4), 9

ALLMEN E von. Setting up Corporate Planning 1969 **2** (1), 2

AMARA R. Strategic Planning in a Changing Corporate Environment 1979 **12** (1), 2

AMICK D *see* MORASKY R L

AMOS F J C. Ethics and Social Responsibility in Local Government 1982 **15** (2), 121

ANASTASSOPOULOS J-P, DUSSAUGE P. French '*Savoir-Faire*' in Selling Arms: A New Way of Doing Business? 1985 **18** (5), 13

ANDERSON G G. Planning for Restructured Competition 1985 **18** (1), 21

ANDREWS G S, FIRER C. Why Different Divisions Require Different Hurdle Rates 1987 **20** (5), 62

ANG J S, CHUA J H. Long Range Planning in Large United States Corporations—A Survey 1979 **12** (2), 99

ANSOFF H I. The Innovative Firm 1968 **1** (2), 26

ANSOFF H I *et al*. Does Planning Pay? The Effect of Planning on Success of Acquisitions in American Firms 1970 **3** (2), 2

ANTHONY W P *see* MADDOX N *et al*

ARAM J D, COWEN S S. The Directors' Role in Planning: What Information Do They Need? 1986 **19** (2), 117

ARCHER W R V. The R.T.Z. Financial Modelling Programme 1971 **3** (4), 32

ARGENTI J. Corporate Planning and Corporate Collapse 1976 **9** (6), 12

ARGENTI J. Defining Corporate Objectives 1969 **1** (3), 24

ARGENTI J. Strategic Planning in a Rapidly Changing Environment— Book Review Article 1979 **12** (5), 110

ARLOW P *see* ACKELSBERG R

ARMENAKIS A A, BURDG H B. Planning for Growth 1986 **19** (3), 93

ARMSTRONG K *see* LOCKETT A G

ARMSTRONG R H R, HOBSON M. The Use of Games in Planning 1972 **5** (1), 62

ARNOLD D *see* SCHOFIELD M

ARRINGTON C B, SAWAYA R N. Issues Management in an Uncertain Environment 1984 **17** (6), 17

ASHLEY W C *see* LAZARUS M

ASHRAFT R A *see* KELLER A Z *et al*

ATKINSON K N. National Programmes to Promote Youth Training 1985 **18** (3), 26

AVNER J *see* ANSOFF H I *et al*

AYAL I. Planning for a Professional Association 1986 **19** (3), 51

B

BABINGTON E A. Installing a Computerized Planning System in Ghana 1987 **20** (4), 110

BABSON C *see* SHUMAN J C

BACA H R *see* KNIGHT K E

BADEN-FULLER C, LONGLEY R. Predicting Plant Closures in European Industry 1988 **21** (1), 90

BADER G. Successful Strategies in French High Technology Companies 1986 **19** (6), 66

BAILEY D, SCHOTTA C. A Dynamic Programming Model for Long Range Educational Planning 1971 **4** (1), 45

BAILEY J. Winning Customers Through Employee Involvement 1984 **17** (4), 79

BAKER C R. Behavioral Aspects of Corporate Planning 1976 **9** (4), 72

BALASUBRAMANIAM R *see* SUBRAMANIAM S

BALIGH H H, BURTON R M. Marketing in Moderation—The Marketing Concept and the Organization's Structure 1979 **12** (2), 92

BALL D F, PEARSON A W. The Future Size of Process Plant 1976 **9** (4), 18

BALL R. Assessing Your Competitor's People and Organization 1987 **20** (2), 32

BALL R. Physical Distribution: A Suitable Case for Treatment 1980 **13** (1), 2

BAMBERGER I. Developing Competitive Advantage in Small and Medium-size Firms 1989 **22** (5), 80

BAMBERGER I. Portfolio Analysis for the Small Firm 1982 **15** (6), 49

BAMBERGER I *see* KEPPLER W *et al*

BAR-ZAKAY S N. A National Strategic Planning Model 1981 **14** (4), 76

BARBIR C *see* CHAMPAGNE F *et al*

BARCENA V A *see* LIVESEY F

BARHAM K *see* SADLER P

BARKDOLL G L. Making Planning Relevant to Public Agency Management 1976 **9** (1), 59

BARKSDALE H C, HARRIS C E. Portfolio Analysis and the Product Life Cycle 1982 **15** (6), 74

BARNETT G G. Identifying Managerial Potential for Manpower Planning 1975 **8** (5), 66

BARROWS D. Planning in the Ministry of Industry and Tourism 1979 **12** (6), 37

BARROWS D S, MORRIS S. Managing Public Policy Issues 1989 **22** (6), 66

BASTIANSEN E *see* NIELSEN K S *et al*

BATES C S. Mapping the Environment: an Operational Environmental Analysis Model 1985 **18** (5), 97

BATSON R G. Financial Planning, Using Goal Programming 1989 **22** (5), 112

BAVLY D. What is the Board of Directors Good For? 1986 **19** (3), 20

BAYLEY W J. Method Change at B.O.C. 1972 **5** (4), 86

BAYLISS D. Britain in the Year 2000: Some Issues for Planners 1971 **3** (3), 65

BEAN D G *see* GARE R J

BEASLEY J E, JOHNSON R. Forecasting Environmental Protection Legislation Using Cross Impact Analysis 1984 **17** (6), 132

BEATFIELD D. Energy Cost Saving Starts on the Shop Floor 1984 **17** (1), 73

BEAVAN P R *et al*. Developing a Strategy for an Industrial Training Board—a Participative Approach 1979 **12** (1), 41

BEAVIS B, ROWLEY C. The Control of Industrial Discharges to Tidal Rivers and Estuaries 1974 **7** (6), 53

BECK J. Accelerated Development for Women Managers 1988 **21** (3), 75

BECK P W. Corporate Planning for an Uncertain Future 1982 **15** (4), 12

BEEREL A C. Financial Modelling—A Tool for Raising Management Performance 1986 **19** (4), 47

BEGGS J M. Leadership—The NASA Approach 1984 **17** (2), 12

BELL D J. Manpower in Corporate Planning 1976 **9** (2), 31

BELL J A. Production Strategy Decisions—A Simulation Model Approach 1970 **2** (4), 62

BELL J A, KEUSCH R B. Comprehensive Planning for Libraries 1976 **9** (5), 48

BELLISARIO M. The Turnaround at Italtel 1985 **18** (6), 21

BEMELMANS T. Strategic Planning for Research and Development 1979 **12** (2), 33

BEN-SHAHAR H *et al*. Analytical Methods in Town Planning 1970 **3** (1), 42

BEN-YAACOV G Z. A Computer-Based Modelling System for Électric Utility Planning 1978 **11** (6), 30

BENESCH G N *see* MILLER W W *et al*

BENFITTO M T *et al*. Resource Management Schemes 1975 **8** (3), 46

BENFORD P. Tioxide: Computerization—The Key to the Future in Financial Planning 1985 **18** (3), 102

BENNETT B C. Economic Forecasting for a Television Company 1978 **11** (5), 63

BENWELL M. Public Participation in Planning—A Research Report 1980 **13** (4), 71

BERG M. Government Policy and its Impact on the Motor Industry 1985 **18** (6), 40

BERNARD G. A Method for Planning Long Term Strategy in Basic Industries 1977 **10** (2), 46

BERRY S J. Performance Review: Key to Effective Planning 1979 **12** (6), 17

BERSCHIN H H. Participation in Planning 1973 **6** (4), 25

BERTEAUX R. Selling Long Range Planning to Management 1969 **2** (2), 32

BETTIS R A, HALL W K. The Business Portfolio Approach—Where it Falls Down in Practice 1983 **16** (2), 95

BEZDEK R H. The State of the Art—Long Range Economic and Manpower Forecasting 1975 **8** (1), 31

BHARGAVA P K. Economic Planning in India: Failure or Success? 1982 **15** (1), 87

BHARGAVA P K. India: Can We Eliminate Poverty? 1987 **20** (2), 21

BHATTACHARYA P *see* NARCHAL R M *et al*

BHATTY E F. Corporate Planning in Medium-sized Companies in the U.K. 1981 **14** (1), 60

BINNING K G H. The Uncertainties of Planning Major Research and Development 1969 **1** (4), 48

BIRLEY S. Success and Failure in Management Buyouts 1984 **17** (3), 32

BIRLEY S, BRIDGE S. Promoting Small Business in Northern Ireland 1987 **20** (6), 71

BISHOP E B. Financial Planning and Control—Book Review Article 1983 **16** (1), 127

BISHOP E B. R.O.C.E. As a Tool for Planning and Control 1969 **2** (2), 80

BITONDO D *see* FROHMAN A L

BJORKLUND R L *see* KAHALAS H

BLACK M. The Function of Design in Long Range Planning 1972 **5** (2), 9

BLAKEMAN L T. Incomes, Productivity and Planning 1969 **1** (4), 10

BLANNING R W. How Managers Decide to Use Planning Models 1980 **13** (2), 32

BLASS W P. Ten Years of Business Planners 1983 **16** (3), 21

BLEACKLEY M *see* DEVLIN G

BLEICHER K, PAUL H. The External Corporate Venture Capital Fund—A Valuable Vehicle for Growth 1987 **20** (6), 64

BLISS M. The Impact of Retailers on Financial Services 1988 **21** (1), 55

BLOIS K J. Manufacturing Technology as a Competetive Weapon 1986 **19** (4), 63

BLOIS K J. Market Concentration—Challenge to Corporate Planning 1980 **13** (4), 56

BLUMBERG L F, COTTER L. Operations Research and Bank Planning 1975 **8** (5), 29

BLUMSTEM A. Systems Analysis and Planning for the Criminal Justice System 1972 **5** (4), 61

BOATFIELD D. Energy Cost Saving Starts on the Shop Floor 1984 **17** (1), 73

BOLLING R, KRAUTHOFF L C. National Policy Making in a Global Economy: The Case for U.S. Economic Planning 1983 **16** (3), 25

BOLWIJN P T, BRINKMAN S, Japanese Manufacturing: Strategy and Practice 1987 **20** (1), 25

BOOCKHOLDT J L *see* SEILER R E

BOOTH H J. Corporate Planning in an Engineering Business 1970 **3** (1), 67

BOOTHE R. Reducing Exposure to Exchange Rate Risk: A Case Study 1985 **18** (3), 98

BORJA M *see* ABT R *et al*

BOROVITS I, CAROL A. International Comparison of Industrial Structures Using Input-Output Analysis 1973 **6** (1), 63

BOSMAN J. Prospects for the British Hotel Industry 1976 **9** (6), 47

BOUAMRENE M A, FLAVEL R. Airline Corporate Planning—A Conceptual Framework 1980 **13** (1), 62

BOULDEN J B. Computerized Corporate Planning 1971 **3** (4), 2

BOULDEN J B. Multinational Planning Systems 1972 **5** (3), 25

BOULTON W R *et al*. How are Companies Planning Now?—A Survey 1982 **15** (1), 82

BOURANTAS D, MANDES Y. Does Market Share Lead to Profitability? 1987 **20** (5), 102

BOUTANTAS D. Avoiding Dependence on Suppliers and Distributors 1989 **22** (3), 140

BOWMAN D O. Long Range Planning in the Defense Equipment Business 1970 **2** (3), 66

BOWONDER B. The Energy Manager and His Corporate Role 1984 **17** (4), 74

BRADY R *see* SIMMIE J

BRAH S A *see* HUNSUCKER J L *et al*

BRANDENBURG R G *see* ANSOFF H I *et al*

BRANDT W K *et al*. Pitfalls in Planning for Multinational Operations 1980 **13** (6), 23

BRAUERS Prof Dr W K. Essay Review Article: Risk, Uncertainty and Risk Analysis 1986 **19** (6), 139

BRAY J. New Methods of Economic Management must be Developed 1968 **1** (1), 51

BRECH R. Creating Confidence about the Future: The Forecasting Business—Book Review Article 1978 **11** (5), 89

BREY A, GABSA G. Integrated Long Range Planning at Nestlé 1972 **5** (2), 44

BRIDGE S *see* BIRLEY S

BRIERS R. Analysing Business Opportunities in North Sea Oil 1976 **9** (1), 53

BRIGHT J R. Some Management Lessons from Technological Innovation Research 1969 **2** (1), 36

BRIGHTMAN H J, HARRIS S E. Is Your Information System Mature Enough for Computerized Planning? 1985 **18** (5), 68

BRIGSTOCKE T *see* WILSON P N

BRINKMAN S *see* BOLWIJN P T

BRISCOE G, HIRST M. A Further Appreciation of Demand Forecasting Models: Based on Survey Information 1975 **8** (1), 87

BRISCOE G, HIRST M. An Appreciation of Alternative Sales Forecasting Models: Recent Techniques Based on Historical Data 1973 **6** (3), 79

BROADBENT D A *see* NICHOLLS J R

BROMHEAD P A. The Effect of the Channel Tunnel on Europe 1974 **7** (2), 65

BROOKES L G. Energy and the Economy—A Reply to Smil and Kuz 1977 **10** (1), 54

BROOKES L G. Energy Resources and World Economic Growth 1973 **6** (3), 39

BROOKES L G *see* HILL K M *et al*

BROWN A. Everywhere, Planners are in Pain 1983 **16** (3), 18

BROWN A W *see* DUBE C S

BROWN C C. The Fading of an Ideology 1968 **1** (1), 34

BROWN G F, READ A R. Personnel and Training Policies—Some Lessons for Western Companies 1984 **17** (2), 48

BROWN J K *et al*. Long Range Planning in the U.S.A.—N.I.C.B. Survey 1969 **1** (3), 44

BROWN K, GREENWELL W. Appraising Financial Performance for Financial Institutions 1980 **13** (1), 82

BROWN L R. The World Food Prospect 1977 **10** (1), 26

BRUCE R *see* SCOTT M

BRUNNEN D J. Developing an Enterprise Culture at British Telecom 1989 **22** (2), 27

BRUNO A V *see* LEIDECKER J K

BRUNS J. Currency Problems in Multinational Long Range Planning 1970 **3** (2), 71

BRUZELIUS B *see* DELOMBRE J

BRYANT J. Assessing Company Strength Using Added Value 1989 **22** (3), 34

BRYSON J M. A Strategic Planning Process for Public and Non-profit Organizations 1988 **21** (1), 73

BUCKLEY A. Growth by Acquisition 1975 **8** (4), 53

BUCKLEY M R *see* REED R

BUGGIE F D. Strategies for New Product Development 1982 **15** (2), 22

BUIGUES P *see* MONTEBELLO M

BUIJ J. Strategic Planning and Product Innovation—Some Systematic Approaches 1979 **12** (5), 23

BUNN D, THOMAS H. Decision Analysis and Strategic Policy Formulation 1977 **10** (6), 23

BURDG H B *see* ARMENAKIS A A

BURGESS A R. Vertical Integration in Petrochemicals: Part 3. An Analysis of Ten Companies 1984 **17** (1), 54

BURGESS A R. Vertical Integration in Petrochemicals—1. The Concept and Its Measurement 1983 **16** (4), 55

BURGESS A R. Vertical Integration in Petrochemicals—2. Strategies and Problems 1983 **16** (6), 29

BURKATT A J. Tourism—Key Issues for the 1980's 1982 **15** (4), 91

BURKE T, WILSON L. Wither or Whither London? An Application of Industry Structure Analysis 1980 **13** (5), 79

BURROWS B C. Computer-Aided Design and Manufacturing—A Managers Guide 1986 **19** (5), 76

BURROWS B C. Information Technology—Its Impact on Property 1984 **17** (4), 60

BURROWS B C. Milton Keynes: A Model for Regenerating our Cities? 1987 **20** (1), 67

BURROWS B C. Planning, Information Technology and the Post-Industrial Society 1986 **19** (2), 79

BURROWS B C. Urban and Regional Planning—A Systems View 1980 **13** (2), 67

BURROWS B C. Venture Management—Success or Failure? 1982 **15** (6), 84

BURROWS B C *see* WHALEY R

BURT D N. Planning and Performance in Australian Retailing 1978 **11** (3), 62

BURTON R M *see* BALIGH H H

BUTLER D, COX G. The Programmable Society and the Individual as a Unit of Data 1974 **7** (5), 43

BUTTLE F. The Marketing Strategy Worksheet—A Practical Planning Tool 1985 **18** (4), 80

C

CAELDRIES F, VAN DIERDONCK R. How Belgian Businesses Make Strategic Planning Work 1988 **21** (2), 41

CALORI R. Designing a Business Scanning System 1989 **22** (1), 69

CALORI R. Effective Strategies in Emerging Industries 1985 **18** (3), 55

CALORI R, CESMA. How Successful Companies Manage Diverse Businesses 1988 **21** (3), 80

CALORI R, NOEL R. Successful Strategies in French High Technology Companies 1986 **19** (6), 54

CAMERON D. Appraising Companies for Acquisition 1977 **10** (4), 21

CAMERON D. Three Simple Steps to Determine Optimum Plant Capacity 1974 **7** (1), 40

CAMERON D A. Risk Analysis and Investment Appraisal in Marketing 1972 **5** (4), 43

CAMERON D A. Risk Analysis in Plant Design 1973 **6** (3), 30

CAMERON M J. Productivity Planning: a Central Issue for Australian Management 1982 **15** (3), 157

CAMILLUS J C. Designing a Capital Budgeting System that Works 1984 **17** (2), 103

CAMILLUS J C. Evaluating the Benefits of Formal Planning Systems 1975 **8** (3), 33

CAMPBELL A *see* GOOLD M

CAMPBELL N. Japanese Business Strategy in China 1987 **20** (5), 69

CANTLEY M F. Boning in on Biotechnology—Part II—Book Review Article 1982 **15** (3), 181

CANTLEY M F. Boning up on Biotechnology—Part I—Book Review Article 1982 **15** (1), 110

CANTLEY M F. The Choice of Corporate Objectives 1970 **3** (1), 36

CARDOZO R N, WIND J. Risk Return Approach to Product Portfolio Strategy 1985 **18** (2), 77

CARLISLE A E *see* MICHAEL S R

CARLSON T S. Long-Range Strategic Planning: Is it for Everyone? 1978 **11** (3), 54

CARMEL A M *see* TAYLOR D T

CARMICHAEL C *see* McEWEN N

CARNALL C A. Managing Strategic Change: An Integrated Approach 1986 **19** (6), 105

CAROL A *see* BOROVITS I

CARPENTER M A. Planning vs Strategy: Which will Win? 1986 **19** (6), 50

CARR C. Strategy Alternatives for Vehicle Component Manufacturers 1988 **21** (4), 86

CARROLL A B. Setting Operational Goals for Corporate Social Responsibility 1978 **11** (2), 35

CARROLL A B *see* NEWGREN K E

CARROLL B *see* LACZNIAK E R *et al*

CARROLL D S A. Managing Relations with Government and Society—The Business Perspective 1983 **16** (2), 10

CARSBERG B. Regulating Private Monopolies and Promoting Competition 1986 **19** (6), 75

CARTER A, FOY N. Will 1990 Mark the End of the Will to Work—Or the Right to Manage? 1981 **14** (2), 42

CARTER R D *et al*. Corporate Planning in Developing Economies 1973 **6** (2), 2

CARTWRIGHT J. Corporate Planning in Local Government— Implications for the Elected Member 1975 **8** (2), 46

CARTWRIGHT T J. The Lost Art of Planning 1987 **20** (2), 92

CATHERWOOD H F R. Should Government and Company Planners Influence Each Other? 1969 **1** (4), 72

CAUDLE P. U.K. Chemicals—Strategic Planning or Industrial Strategy 1977 **10** (6), 31

CAVUSGIL S T *see* SMITH L R

CECIL J B. Long Range Planning at Continental Oil 1971 **4** (1), 54

CESMA *see* CALORI R

CHABERT J. The European Cultural Foundation's Plan Europe 2000 1975 **8** (4), 23

CHAKRABORTY S. Strategic Planning for Telecommunications—A Systems Approach 1981 **14** (5), 46

CHALLEN P. Corporate Planning for Social Responsibility 1974 **7** (3), 38

CHAMPAGNE F *et al*. Strategic Planning for Hospitals—A Health-needs Approach 1987 **20** (3), 77

CHAMPION J R. Corporate Planning in CPC Europe 1970 **3** (2), 8

CHANDLER W J. Plans—Their Preparations and Implementation 1978 **11** (6), 14

CHANDRA G. The Cut-Off Rate for Investment Decisions in Growth Companies 1975 **8** (2), 95

CHANNON D. Industrial Structure 1982 **15** (5), 78

CHANNON D F. Prediction and Practice in Multinational Strategic Planning 1976 **9** (2), 50

CHAO H P *et al*. Analysing Complex Decisions for Electric Utilities 1985 **18** (2), 46

CHAPMAN A. From Organization Development to Corporate Development at Trebor 1985 **18** (4), 50

CHAPMAN P. Changing the Corporate Culture of Rank Xerox 1988 **21** (2), 23

CHAPMAN P F. A Method for Exploring the Future 1976 **9** (1), 2

CHAPMAN P F. Three Energy Scenarios for the United Kingdom 1976 **9** (2), 2

CHAPPELL P. Why Ownership Matters 1986 **19** (6), 130

CHARACH L *see* MOORE L F

CHARALAMBIDES L C. Designing Communication Support Systems for Strategic Planning 1988 **21** (6), 93

CHEN M *see* LIENTZ B P

CHEONG W K, KHEM G S. Strategies for Tourism in Singapore 1988 **21** (4), 36

CHESSHIRE J H, SURREY A J. World Energy Resources and the Limitations of Computer Modelling 1975 **8** (3), 54

CHING C T K *see* MILLER W W *et al*

CHISNALL P M. Marketing Planning in a Service Economy 1975 **8** (6), 43

CHOUET D *see* DEMB A *et al*

CHRISTENSEN R L *see* FORSTE R H

CHRISTODOULOU C. Australian Industry: Sophisticated Planning and Weak R & D? 1988 **21** (1), 82

CHRISTOPHER M. Logistics Systems Engineering—Solving the Distribution Planning Problem 1974 **7** (6), 72

CHRISTOPHER W F. Achievement Reporting—Controlling Performance Against Objectives 1977 **10** (5), 14

CHRISTOPHER W F. What the New GATT Trade Agreement Means for Plastics 1980 **13** (1), 77

CHUA J H *see* ANG J S

CLARK J *see* LEWIS G *et al*

CLARKE C J. Acquisitions—Techniques for Measuring Strategic Fit 1987 **20** (3), 12

CLARKE C J. Using Finance for Competitive Advantage 1988 **21** (2), 63

CLARKE C J, GALL, F. Planned Divestment—A Five-step Approach 1987 **20** (1), 17

CLARKE F J P. Alternative Technologies and the Rising Cost of Energy 1981 **14** (4), 51

CLARKE K C. The Future for Wool 1975 **8** (6), 70

CLARKE-HILL C *see* KENNY B *et al*

CLAXTON C. Federated Marketing—A Practical Approach to Export for the Smaller Company or Division 1979 **12** (6), 43

CLAXTON C. Planning Major International Projects 1978 **11** (2), 25

CLAY M J. Contingency Planning 1971 **3** (3), 70

CLEARY M J *see* NUTT A B *et al*

CLEAVER A B. The Future of Computers in Financial Institutions 1980 **13** (3), 12

CLELAND D I, KING W R. Developing a Planning Culture for More Effective Strategic Planning 1974 **7** (3), 70

CLELAND D I *see* KING W R

CLEMENHAGEN C *see* CHAMPAGNE F *et al*

CLIFFORD W. The Long Range Planning of Criminal Justice Systems 1979 **12** (4), 42

CLOWES G A, MARSHALL S A. A Control Engineering Framework for Planning 1975 **8** (4), 70

COATE M B. Pitfalls in Portfolio Planning 1983 **16** (3), 47

COATES J B. Productivity: What is it? 1980 **13** (4), 90

COCHRANE R L D *see* TYSON W J

COGHLAN D. Corporate Strategy in Catholic Religious Orders 1987 **20** (1), 44

COHEN A B. New Venture Development at Du Pont 1970 **2** (4), 7

COLEMAN A. Land-Use Planning in a World of Shrinking Resources 1978 **11** (1), 47

COLLIER D A. The Service Sector Revolution: The Automation of Services 1983 **16** (6), 10

COLLINS A C. A Management Strategy for Information Processing 1983 **16** (6), 21

COLLINS A C. A Management Strategy for Information Processing. 1—The Segas Case 1983 **16** (5), 29

COLLINS A C. A Managements Strategy for Information Processing 3—Management Information Requirements 1984 **17** (1), 33

COLLINS M R, MACGREGOR J M. Designing Computer Models that Work 1980 **13** (6), 60

CONSTABLE J. Diversification as a Factor in U.K. Industrial Strategy 1986 **19** (1), 52

CONTANDRIOPOULOS A-P *see* CHAMPAGNE F *et al*

CONTAS K *see* VICHAS R P

CONVERY F J. Forestry and Long Range Planning 1973 **6** (2), 27

COOMER J C *see* HILL K Q

COOPER A C. Strategic Management: New Ventures and Small; Business 1981 **14** (5), 39

COOPER F. Long Range Defence Planning in the U.K. 1970 **3** (2), 18

COOPER G L, DAVIDSON M J. The Female Manager—The Pressures and the Problems 1983 **16** (1), 10

COOPER M J *see* DAVIDSON M J

CORBY M E. How Will the British Post Office Cope with Technological Change 1982 **15** (6), 58

CORDELL A J. Innovation, The Multinational Corporation: Some Implications for National Science Policy 1973 **6** (3), 22

CORFIELD K. Translating Planning into Action 1984 **17** (4), 23

CORKE D K. Long Range Planning for Production 1970 **3** (2), 27

CORNELISSEN J A. Corporate Strategy in the Eighties 1977 **10** (5), 2

CORNISH F. Building a Customer-orientated Organization 1988 **21** (3), 105

CORRY C *see* DE VULPIAN A

COTTEE B. Road Transport and the Environment 1978 **11** (2), 39

COTTER L *see* BLUMBERG L F

COUSSEMENT A M. Investing and Financing in a New Era 1978 **11** (5), 2

COWEN S S, MIDDAUGH II J K. Designing an Effective Financial Planning and Control System 1988 **21** (6), 83

COWEN S S *see* ARAM J D

COWHERD D M, LUCHS H. Linking Organization Structures and Processes to Business Strategy 1988 **21** (5), 47

COWIE H. North Atlantic Free Trade Area—the Implications for British Industry 1969 **2** (2), 2

COWLEY P R. The Experience Curve and History of the Cellophane Business 1985 **18** (6), 84

COX G *see* BUTLER D

COX J. Manpower Planning at National and Company Level 1971 **3** (4), 27

COX J F *see* ADAMS F P

COX J G. A Framework of Decision Making for Technological Change 1978 **11** (1), 53

COX J G. Planning for Technological Innovation: Part II—Investment in Technological Change in Three Major Industries 1978 **11** (4), 70

COX J G. Planning for Technological Innovation—Part I. Investment in Technology 1977 **10** (6), 40

COYNE J *see* WRIGHT M *et al*

CRAIG G D. A Simulation System for Corporate Planning 1980 **13** (5), 43

CRAIG R S. Seeking Strategic Advantage with Technology?—Focus on Customer Value! 1986 **19** (2), 50

CRAVER J K. The Effect of the Future on Today's Decisions 1973 **6** (2), 29

CRAWFORD R L see GRAM H A

CRAWLEY F W. Competition in Retail Banking 1982 **15** (3), 71

CROFT W. Values and Future's Research 1977 **10** (6), 51

CROON P. Aids in Determining Strategy, the Internal Analysis 1979 **12** (4), 65

CROSS K. Manufacturing Planning with Companies at Honeywell 1984 **17** (6), 66

CRUM R L see DERKINDEREN F G J

CSATH M. Corporate Planning in Hungarian Companies 1989 **22** (4), 89

CSATH M. Strategic Planning—A New Arrival in Hungarian Industry 1983 **16** (2), 85

CUFF J D. Risk-Decision Analysis in Weapons Systems Acquisitions 1973 **6** (1), 49

CULLIGAN K, MURPHY J. The Future of Leisure 1989 **22** (6), 127

CURRIE W L. Investing in CAD: A Case of *ad hoc* Decision-making 1989 **22** (6), 85

CURRILL D L. Introducing Corporate Planning—A Case History 1977 **10** (4), 70

CURRILL D L. Technological Forecasting in Six Major U.K. Companies 1972 **5** (1), 72

CUTTING G D see McKAY C W

D

DALE B G. Quality Circles—Are they Working in British Factories 1984 **17** (6), 50

DALE B G, LEES J. Quality Circles: From Introduction to Integration 1987 **20** (1), 78

DALE B G see DUNCALF A J

DAM A van. Can Corporate Planning Invent the Future of the Third World? 1974 **7** (2), 8

DAM A van. Corporate Planning for Asia, Latin America and Africa 1972 **5** (4), 2

DAM A van. Future Demand Patterns in the Emerging World 1974 **7** (4), 34

DAM A van. Joint Planning in a World of Shrinking Resources 1975 **8** (6), 8

DAM A van. Planning for a New International Economic Order? 1976 **9** (5), 57

DAM A van. Strategic Planning for Corporate Growth in Developing Countries 1969 **2** (1), 9

DAM A van. The Business Environment in the 1980s 1977 **10** (4), 8

DAM A van. The Corporate Role in a North-South Dialogue 1979 **12** (6), 22

DAM A van. Water Supply—The Case for Joint Planning 1978 **11** (1), 69

DANIEL W W. The Social and Psychological Causes of Inflation 1977 **10** (3), 37

DANIELSSON C. A Complete Guide to Company Growth and Development 1982 **15** (6), 8

DARLING P. Food Manufacturing: The Future Prospect 1983 **16** (1), 26

DAS R, MOHANTY B. Choosing a Diversification Project in a Regulated Economy 1981 **14** (2), 78

DASTMALCHIAN A see JAVIDAN M

DAVID F R. How Companies Define Their Mission 1989 **22** (1), 90

DAVID F R. The Strategic Planning Matrix—A Quantitative Approach 1986 **19** (5), 102

DAVIDSON M J, COOPER G L. Working Women in the European Community—The Future Prospect 1983 **16** (4), 49

DAVIDSON M J see COOPER G L

DAVIES A H T. Strategic Planning in the Thomas Cook Group 1981 **14** (5), 27

DAVIES B C L see HARRIS D J

DAVIES J. Planning Participation in Public Decision Making 1970 **2** (4), 23

DAVIES J see EASTERBY-SMITH M

DAVIES O. The Marketing Approach to Purchasing 1974 **7** (3), 2

DAVIS D L. New Jobs in Energy Research and Development—A Survey 1977 **10** (4), 51

DAVIS J B. The Strategic Divestment Decision 1974 **7** (1), 15

DAY D. Towards 1992: A Strategy for Training 1989 **22** (6), 48

DAY L H. Long Range Planning in Bell Canada 1973 **6** (3), 44

DE NOBLE A F et al. Planning for Post-merger Integration—Eight Lessons for Merger Success 1988 **21** (4), 82

DE VULPIAN A, CORRY C. Social Futures: Individualism or Social Harmony 1986 **19** (5), 33

DECLERCK R P. The Management of Development—The Next Decade 1977 **10** (3), 59

DEGUELDRE J. Corporate Planning and Modelling in a Large Bank 1980 **13** (4), 43

DEKKER W. Managing a Global Electronics Company in Tomorrow's World 1986 **19** (2), 31

DELOMBRE J, BRUZELIUS B. Importance of Relative Market Share in Strategic Planning—A Case Study 1977 **10** (4), 2

DEMB A et al. Defining the Role of the Board 1989 **22** (1), 61

DENNING B W. Organizing the Corporate Planning Function 1969 **1** (4), 67

DENNING B W. Strategic Environmental Appraisal 1973 **6** (1), 22

DERKINDEREN F. Pre-Investment Planning 1977 **10** (1), 2

DERKINDEREN F G J, CRUM R L. Pitfalls in Using Portfolio Techniques—Assessing Risk and Potential 1984 **17** (2), 129

DERRICK P. Prospects for Industrial Co-operatives—An Alternative to Industrial Democracy? 1981 **14** (4), 106

DESAI D. Technology Management in Indian Companies 1972 **5** (4), 70

DESPICHT N. Long Range Planning and Regional Policy 1. Britain—A European Pioneer 1970 **2** (4), 28

DESPICHT N. Long Range Planning and Regional Policy 2. France and Italy—Latecomers to the Industrial Urban Scene 1970 **3** (1), 75

DETMOLD P. Optimising Railway Strategies 1969 **1** (3), 74

DETRIE J-P, RAMANANTSOA B. Diversification—the Key Factors for Success 1986 **19** (1), 31

DEVLIN G, BLEACKLEY M. Strategic Alliances—Guidelines for Success 1988 **21** (5), 18

DICKIE R see POST J E et al

DIFFENBACH J. Corporate Environmental Analysis in Large U.S. Corporations 1983 **16** (3), 107

DIFFENBACH J see HIGGINS R B

DIGMAN L A see YOO S

DILL W R. Integrating Planning and Management Development 1975 **8** (5), 8

DILL W R. Public Participation in Corporate Planning—Strategic Management in a Kibitzer's World 1975 **8** (1), 57

DIMSON E. Financing the Smaller Company 1978 **11** (6), 9

DIMSON E, MARCH P. Calculating the Cost of Capital 1982 **15** (2), 112

DOBBIE J W. Formal Approaches to Setting Long-Range Goals 1974 **7** (3), 75

DOBBINS R, GREENWOOD M. The Future Pattern of U.K. Share Ownership 1975 **8** (4), 81

DOBROV G M. Scientific-Technological Forecasting in the U.S.S.R. 1971 **3** (3), 13

DOBROV G M. The Strategy for Organized Technology in the light of Hard-, Soft-, and Org-Ware Interaction 1979 **12** (4), 79

DOBSON S M, SHORROCK J E T. Planning and Control of Purchasing Performance: A New Concept 1980 **13** (3), 30

DOBSON S see SHORROCK J

DOHRN P J, SALKIN G R. The Use of Financial Models in Long Range Planning 1969 **2** (2), 27

DOLOGITE D G see MOCKLER R J

DOMINIAN J. Marital Breakdown and the Future of Marriage 1984 **17** (2), 77

DOMSCH M. Personnel Planning and Information Systems 1971 **4** (2), 12

DOMSCH M. The Organization of Corporate R & D Planning 1978 **11** (3), 67

DONALD B L. Planning and Health Care—The Approach in a Reorganized NHS 1974 **7** (6), 33

DONALDSON J A. Foreign Exchange Risk Management 1979 **12** (3), 22

DOR P see LEFEBVRE M et al

DORWIN K. Re-positioning a Leading Stockbroker 1988 **21** (6), 13

DOUGHARTY L A. Developing Corporate Strategy Through Planning, Programming and Budgeting 1970 **2** (3), 24

DOUGLAS J V *see* PENROD J I

DOUMA S. Towards a New Industrial Policy 1984 **17** (4), 16

DOWDY W L, NIKOLCHEV J. Can Industries De-Mature—Applying New Technologies to Mature Industries 1986 **19** (2), 38

DOWLING G. Buying is Marketing Too—Japan's Influence on the Australian Coal Trade 1987 **20** (1), 35

DOYLE P, FENWICK I. Sales Forecasting—Using a Combination of Approaches 1976 **9** (3), 60

DOYLE P, LYNCH J E. Long Range Planning for Universities 1976 **9** (6), 39

DOYLE P *see* WONG V *et al*

DUBE C S, BROWN A W. Strategic Assessment—A Rational Response to University Cutbacks 1983 **16** (2), 105

DUDINSKY I. COMECON—The Prospects to 1975 1973 **6** (1), 69

DUGDALE I. Corporate Planning and Control Systems in Williams & Glyn's Bank 1978 **11** (5), 41

DUNCALF A J, DALE B G. How British Industry is Making Decisions on Product Quality 1985 **18** (5), 81

DUNCOMBE H L. The Dangers of Centralized Economic Planning 1976 **9** (3), 16

DUSSAUGE P *see* ANASTASSOPOULOS J-P

DWIVEDI R S. Increasing Trust Improves Productivity 1985 **18** (3), 82

DYSON R G. Participation in Planning—A Study of Two Organizations in The Netherlands 1978 **11** (4), 61

DYSON R G, FOSTER M J. Making Planning More Effective 1983 **16** (6), 68

E

EAST R J. Comparison of Strategic Planning in Large Corporations and Government 1972 **5** (2), 2

EAST R J. Improving Government Expenditure Decisions through Programme Analysis and Review 1973 **6** (1), 2

EASTERBY-SMITH M, DAVIES J. Developing Strategic Thinking 1983 **16** (4), 39

EDDIE G C. A Future for Fishing 1975 **8** (5), 76

EDEN C *see* SIMS D

EDFELT R *see* TRONDSEN E

EDWARDES M. A New Industrial Strategy for the United Kingdom 1977 **10** (3), 14

EDWARDS J P, HARRIS D J. Planning in a State of Turbulence 1977 **10** (3), 43

EDWARDS M J. Market Planning at the National Coal Board 1986 **19** (3), 46

EHRLEMARK U. Design Your Own Management Information Systems 1984 **17** (2), 85

EL-NAMAKI M S S. Business Planning in Tanzanian State Enterprises 1977 **10** (5), 52

EL-NAMAKI M S S. Encouraging Entrepreneurs in Developing Countries 1988 **21** (4), 98

ELBING A O. Forecasting Organizational Changes 1974 **7** (6), 43

ELLEN E R. Long Range Planning for London Transport 1973 **6** (3), 10

EMERSON R V. Corporate Planning: A Need to Examine Corporate Style 1985 **18** (6), 29

ENGLEDOW J L, LENZ R T. Whatever Happened to Environmental Analysis? 1985 **18** (2), 93

EPPINK D J. Futures Research—Is it Used? 1981 **14** (2), 33

EPPINK D J. Planning for Strategic Flexibility 1978 **11** (4), 9

EPPINK D J *et al*. Corporate Planning in the Netherlands 1976 **9** (5), 30

EPPINK D J, VAN RHIJN B M. International Strategies of Dutch Insurance Companies 1989 **22** (1), 41

EPPINK D J, VAN RHIJN B M. The Internationalization of Dutch Insurance Companies 1988 **21** (5), 54

EPPINK J. Competitive Strategies in the Dutch Insurance Industry 1987 **20** (4), 30

ERBE J P. The Consumer and Change 1973 **6** (4), 13

ERICKSON D *et al*. Water Rights Conservation and Recreation Planning 1975 **8** (1), 75

EUGSTER C. Diversification in the Swiss Chemical Industry 1969 **2** (1), 42

EVERED R. So What is Strategy? 1983 **16** (3), 57

EWUSI-MENSAH K. Developing a Competitive Intelligence System for IT 1989 **22** (5), 121

EWUSI-MENSAH K. Information Systems for Planning 1984 **17** (4), 111

EZRA D. Long-Term Planning for Coal 1974 **7** (6), 21

F

FAHEY L *et al*. Environmental Scanning and Forecasting in Strategic Planning—The State of the Art 1981 **14** (1), 32

FAHEY W R *see* GRATWICK J *et al*

FAIRTLOUGH G. Can we Plan for New Technology? 1984 **17** (3), 14

FALK N. Planning for Job Creation 1980 **13** (2), 20

FANNIN W R, GILMORE C B. Developing a Strategy for International Business 1986 **19** (3), 81

FANNIN W R, RODRIGUES A F. National or Global?—Control vs Flexibility 1986 **19** (5), 84

FARLEY J U *see* HOU WEE C *et al*

FARMER D. Competitive Analysis—Its Role in Purchasing 1984 **17** (3), (3), 72

FARMER D. The Impact of Supply Markets on Corporate Planning 1972 **5** (1), 10

FARMER D *see* FORD D

FARUQUI A. Marketing Electricity—A Military Approach 1987 **20** (4), 67

FEIGENBAUM E A. Towards the Library of the Future 1989 **22** (1), 118

FELDBERG M. Defining Social Responsibility 1974 **7** (4), 39

FELLS I. Energy Options to 2030 1982 **15** (4), 76

FENWICK I *see* DOYLE P

FERRO L *see* TAYLOR B

FILDES R *et al*. Forecasting in Conditions of Uncertainty 1978 **11** (4), 29

FINIZZA A J. How the Rip Van Winkle Approach Helps Oil Executives Plan 1985 **18** (1), 59

FINLAY A W. Swedish Industrial Policy Planning—A Workshop Report, Stockholm, 6–7 March 1980 1980 **13** (6), 55

FINLAY P. Essay Review: Porter on Strategy 1988 **21** (3), 108

FINLAY P N. Classes of Financial Planning Package—A Management Perspective 1985 **18** (6), 94

FINLEY P N. Introducing Corporate Planning in a Medium-Size Company—A Case History 1982 **15** (2), 93

FINN R *see* HIGGINS J C

FIRER C *see* ANDREWS G S

FIRNBERG D. Future Trends in Computing 1978 **11** (6), 58

FISHER G H. The World of Program Budgeting 1969 **2** (1), 50

FISHER S T. The Hazards of Nuclear Power Generation—The Case for Survival 1983 **16** (1), 77

FITZGERALD G. Planning in Ireland 1971 **4** (2), 30

FITZPATRICK J. Why Textile and Clothing Industries are Shifting to the Third World 1983 **16** (6), 42

FLAVELL R *see* BOUAMRENE M A

FLECK V *see* SMITH J G

FLEMIN J E. The Future of U.S. Government—Corporate Relations 1979 **12** (4), 20

FLETCHER J G. Planning a Computer Network: The Octopus Experience 1975 **8** (3), 72

FLETCHER W. Advertising: Trends and Prospects 1978 **11** (6), 37

FONTELA E. Industrial Applications of Cross-Impact Analysis 1976 **9** (4), 29

FORBES A M. Long Range Planning for the Small Firm 1974 **7** (2), 43

FORD D. Develop Your Technology Strategy 1988 **21** (5), 85

FORD D, FARMER D. Make or Buy—A Key Strategic Issue 1986 **19** (5), 54

FORD H P. Long Range Planning of Managers 1968 **1** (1), 18

FORD T M. Strategic Planning—Myth or Reality?—A Chief Executive's View 1981 **14** (6), 9

FORMAN R. Strategic Planning and the Chief Executive 1988 **21** (4), 57

FORREST C. Economic Trends 1982 **15** (5), 6

FORSTE R H, CHRISTENSEN R L. Economic Analysis of Public Water Supply in the Piscataqua River Watershed 1971 **3** (4), 75

FOSTER D. Planning in the Smaller Company 1971 **4** (1), 71

FOSTER D W. Developing a Product Market Strategy 1970 **2** (3), 70

FOSTER M J see DYSON R G

FOTTLER M D. Improving Health Care Planning—Some Lessons from Immunization 1984 **17** (4), 88

FOXALL G R. Forecasting Developments in Consumerism and Consumer Protection 1980 **13** (1), 29

FOY N see CARTER A

FRANC J-D Le. The Future for European Business-Strategies for Growth 1980 **13** (4), 18

FRANKENHOFF W P, GRANGER C H. Strategic Management: A New Managerial Concept for an Era of Rapid Change 1971 **3** (3), 7

FRANKLIN S G see BOULTON W R et al

FRANKO L G. Strategic Planning for Internationalization—The European Dilemma and some Possible Solutions 1973 **6** (2), 58

FRAZER P see MORISON I

FREDERICK G D. The State of Private Sector Strategic Planning in Canada 1983 **16** (3), 40

FRIEDMAN Y, SEGEV E. Horizons For Strategic Planning 1976 **9** (5), 84

FRIEDRICH A, HOESCH A G. Planning in a German Steel Company 1972 **5** (4), 78

FRIEDRICH A, LAND A van't. Organization of the Planning Department in a Divisionalized Concern 1974 **7** (2), 27

FRIEND J K. The Dynamics of Policy Change 1976 **9** (5), 40

FRIPP J. Management and Management for the 1980s, Much the Same, but More So!—Book Review Article 1981 **14** (1), 104

FROHMAN A L, BITONDO D. Coordinating Business Strategy and Technical Planning 1981 **14** (6), 58

FROST F. Strategic Alternatives for Australian Iron-Ore Producers 1986 **19** (1), 89

FUBARA B A. Corporate Planning in Nigeria 1986 **19** (2), 125

G

GABELE E see KEPPLER W et al

GABSA G see BREY A

GALER G, KASPER W. Scenario Planning for Australia 1982 **15** (4), 50

GALIMBERTI F. Getting FIAT Back on the Road 1986 **19** (1), 25

GALL F see CLARKE C J

GANSLER J S. Resource Planning for Technology-Oriented Companies 1973 **6** (4), 17

GARDE V D, PATEL R R. Technological Forecasting for Power Generation—A Study Using the Delphi Technique 1985 **18** (4), 73

GARDINER P see ROTHWELL R

GARE R J, BEAN D G. The Future Prospects in Commodity Markets 1975 **8** (3), 2

GARRETT J, HOME N. A Planning System for the British Prison Department 1972 **5** (3), 36

GARUZZO G. Trucks and Road Transport Towards 1992 1988 **21** (4), 45

GEARY N R. Strategic Planning for British Nuclear Fuels 1973 **6** (3), 2

GECHELE G B. Evaluating Industrial Technological Forecasting 1976 **9** (4), 76

GEDRICH S F. Business Planning at Sperry Rand 1976 **9** (2), 38

GELZER J see MENKE M M et al

GERADIN L A. Exploratory Planning in an Electronics Industry 1973 **6** (3), 74

GERMAY J see LEFEBVRE M et al

GHOSH B C, NEE A Y C. Strategic Planning—A Contingency Approach—Part 1. The Strategic Analysis 1983 **16** (4), 93

GHOSH B C, NEE A Y C. Strategic Planning—A Contingency Approach—Part 2. The Plan 1983 **16** (6), 46

GILMORE C B see FANNIN W R

GINTER P M, RUCKS A C. Can Business Learn from Wargames? 1984 **17** (3), 123

GLADSTONE E J. The Interaction of Systems Analysis and Marketing Planning 1971 **4** (1), 35

GLUECK W F see SNYDER N

GODET M. Creative Crisis: New Patterns of Growth and Employment 1981 **14** (5), 12

GODIWALLA Y H. Multinational Planning—Developing a Global Approach 1986 **19** (2), 110

GODIWALLA Y M et al. Corporate Planning and The Chief Executive 1979 **12** (2), 2

GODIWALLA Y M et al. Corporate Planning—A Functional Approach 1978 **11** (5), 47

GODIWALLA Y M et al. Environmental Scanning—Does it Help the Chief Executive? 1980 **13** (5), 87

GODSE V T. Planning for Banking—The Indian Experience 1986 **19** (1), 105

GOHL J, OPPELLAND H J. Manpower Planning and Individual Goals 1979 **12** (6), 29

GOLDFARB D L, HUSS W R. Building Scenarios for an Electric Utility 1988 **21** (2), 78

GOLDSTEIN S G M. Involving Managers in System-improvement Planning 1981 **14** (1), 93

GOODALL A J. Corporate Planning at Batchelors Foods Limited: A Case Study 1974 **7** (5), 47

GOODMAN J. Television in the Seventies 1973 **6** (4), 63

GOOLD M, CAMPBELL A. Managing the Diversified Corporation: The Tensions Facing the Chief Executive 1988 **21** (4), 12

GOOLD M, CAMPBELL A. Managing Diversity: Strategy and Control in Diversified British Companies 1987 **20** (5), 42

GOPAL R. Turnaround of a Cable Company 1989 **22** (1), 98

GORB P see WILSON P

GOTCHER J W. Strategic Planning in European Multinationals 1977 **10** (5), 7

GOTCHER J W. Strategic Planning for Multinationals—The Views of Government and Scientists 1981 **14** (1), 23

GOUY M. Strategic Decision Making in Large European Firms 1978 **11** (3), 41

GRACE R P see TURNER R K

GRAM H A, CRAWFORD R L. Corporate Strategies for Political Action 1979 **12** (5), 62

GRANGER C H see FRANKENHOFF W P

GRANT R M. Competing Against Low Cost Cutlery Imports 1989 **22** (5), 59

GRATWICK J et al. A Role for Transportation in Canada 1976 **9** (1), 38

GRAY E R. Planning for Corporate Social Programs—Problems and Guidelines 1981 **14** (2), 49

GREANIAS G see WINDSOR D

GREEN G J L, JONES E G. Strategic Management Step by Step 1982 **15** (3), 61

GREEN G J L see BEAVAN P R et al

GREEN H see MAY G

GREEN J F. Management Information Systems 1970 **2** (4), 74

GREEN J, JONES T. Strategic Development as a Means of Organizational Change: Four Case Histories 1981 **14** (3), 58

GREEN N P see KELLER A Z et al

GREEN S. Strategy, Organizational Culture and Symbolism 1988 **21** (4), 121

GREEN S. The Incentive Effects of Ownership and Control in Management Buy-outs 1988 **21** (1), 26

GREENLEY G E. Does Strategic Planning Improve Company Performance 1986 **19** (2), 101

GREENLEY G E. Where Marketing Planning Fails 1983 **16** (1), 106

GREENWELL W see BROWN K

GREENWOOD M see DOBBINS R

GREWE T et al. Participative Planning for a Public Service 1989 **22** (1), 110

GRIFFIN A, ADAMS S. Shared Services—A Recipe for Cost-cutting in Hospitals 1981 **14** (6), 76

GRIMM U see KREIKEBAUM H

GRINYER P H. Designing Effective Organizations—Book Review Article 1984 **17** (2), 151

GRINYER P H. Financial Modelling for Planning in the U.K. 1983 **16** (5), 58

GRINYER P H. Organizational Structure: The Aston Programmes I, II and III. Advances in Organization Theory—An Overview of Some Recent Literature—Book Review Article 1978 **11** (6), 89

GRINYER P H, NORBURN D. Strategic Planning in 21 U.K. Companies 1974 **7** (4), 80

GRINYER P H, WOOLLER J. Computer Models for Corporate Planning 1975 **8** (1), 14

GRINYER P M *see* AL-BAZZAZ S

GRONROOS C. Designing a Long Range Marketing Strategy for Services 1980 **13** (2), 36

GROSSFIELD K *see* LOCKE H B *et al*

GROVES D L *et al*. Planning—Satisfaction and Productivity 1976 **9** (4), 52

GROVES D L, McCART G D. Land Use Planning and the Community 1976 **9** (2), 83

GROVES D L *see* ERICKSON D L *et al*

GROVES D L *see* KAHALAS H

GRUNEWALD H-G, VELLMANN K. Integrating Regional and Functional Plans at Henkel 1981 **14** (2), 19

GUMMESSON E. Organizing for Strategic Management—A Conceptual Model 1974 **7** (2), 13

GUMMESSON E. The New Marketing—Developing Long-term Interactive Relationships 1987 **20** (4), 10

GUOY M. Strategic Decision Making in Large European Firms 1978 **11** (3), 41

GUP B E. Portfolio Theory—A Planning Tool 1977 **10** (3), 10

GUP B E, WHITEHEAD D D. Strategic Planning in Banks—Does it Pay? 1989 **22**(1), 124

GUPTA Y P, TORKZADEH G. Re-designing Bank Service Systems for Effective Marketing 1988 **21** (6), 38

GUSTAFSON L T *see* DE NOBLE A F *et al*

H

HACKMAN N. Planning in a German Engineering Business 1971 **3** (4), 54

HAGER R B *see* BENFITTO M T *et al*

HAGGERTY P E. Corporate Self Renewal 1969 **1** (3), 9

HAHN D. The Control Function in Major German Companies 1982 **15** (3), 21

HAINES W R. Corporate Planning and Management by Objectives 1977 **10** (4), 13

HAINES W R. Making Corporate Planning Work in Developing Countries 1988 **21** (2), 91

HAKE B. Strategies for Diversification 1972 **5** (2), 65

HALAL W E. Big Business vs Big Government—A New Social Contract 1984 **17** (4), 30

HALAL W E. Business and Government—A New Partnership? 1987 **20** (1), 123

HALL W K. Changing Perspectives on the Capital Investment Process 1979 **12** (1), 37

HALL W K. Why Risk Analysis Isn't Working 1975 **8** (6), 25

HALL W K *see* BETTIS R A

HAMELMAN P W *see* MAZZE E M *et al*

HAMILTON J G *see* CARTER R D *et al*

HAMMER R M *et al*. Privatization—A Cure for all Ills? 1989 **22** (6), 19

HANAGAN P. What is to be Done About Unemployment? 1982 **15** (2), 46

HANDY C. Careers for the 21st Century 1988 **21** (3), 90

HANER F T. Risk Management in Corporate Planning 1981 **14** (6), 12

HANKINSON G A. Energy Scenarios—The Sizewell Experience 1986 **19** (5), 94

HANSEN S-O *see* MALASKA P *et al*

HARDIE M C. What Should we Spend on Health Care? 1974 **7** (1), 2

HARDING A. The Effect of Technological Change on Planning for International Transport 1969 **2** (1), 30

HARDING B, HOULDEN B T. Using Input-Output Models for Planning in Groups with Considerable Inter-Company Trading 1980 **13** (3), 35

HARDY K G, MAGRATH A J. Planning for Better Channel Management 1988 **21** (6), 30

HARGREAVES B J A. Sociological and Cultural Forecasting 1978 **11** (3), 49

HARGREAVES D. Corporate Planning—A Chairman's Guide 1969 **1** (3), 28

HARMAN R *see* TAITZ L

HARRELL G D, MURRAY G O. New Venture Management in a Electric Utility 1986 **19** (2), 57

HARRIGAN K R. Strategic Planning for Endgame 1982 **15** (6), 45

HARRIS C E *see* BARKSDALE H C

HARRIS D J, DAVIES B C L. Corporate Planning as a Control System in United Kingdom Nationalized Industries 1981 **14** (1), 15

HARRIS D J *see* EDWARDS J P

HARRIS D J *see* WILLIAMS D G

HARRIS S E *see* BRIGHTMAN H J

HARRIS W C *see* ACKELSBERG R

HARRISON F L. How Corporate Planning Responds to Uncertainty 1976 **9** (2), 88

HARRISON F L. Microcomputers—The Breakthrough in Computer Modelling 1983 **16** (5), 94

HARRISON J S. Alternatives to Merger—Joint Ventures and Other Strategies 1987 **20** (6), 78

HARTLEY W C F. Critical Decision Areas in Corporate Financial Policy 1970 **2** (4), 54

HARVEY J W, McCROHAN K F. Strategic Issues for Charities and Philanthropies 1988 **21** (6), 44

HAVEMANN E. Organization for Business Objectives 1969 **2** (2), 14

HAWKINS K *see* KEMPNER T *et al*

HAWKINS K, TARR R J. Corporate Planning in Local Government—A Case Study 1980 **13** (2), 43

HAYEN R L. How to Design a Financial Planning Model 1983 **16** (5), 111

HAYES R L, RADOSEVICH R. Designing Information Systems for Strategic Decisions 1974 **7** (4), 45

HAYWARD R G. Developing an Information Systems Strategy 1987 **20** (2), 100

HEALY D F. Environmental Pressures and Marketing in the 1970's 1975 **8** (3), 41

HEANY D F *see* STONE W R

HEARNDEN K. Computer Crime: Multi-million Pound Problem? 1986 **19** (5), 18

HECKMAN N. Planning in a German Engineering Business 1971 **3** (4), 54

HEDLEY B. A Fundamental Approach to Strategy Development 1976 **9** (6), 2

HEDLEY B D. Strategy and the Business Portfolio 1977 **10** (1), 9

HEGARTY W H, HOFFMAN R C. Who Influences Strategic Decisions? 1987 **20** (2), 61

HELPS I G. A Critique of some Techniques of Manpower Forecasting at National and Sectoral Levels 1973 **6** (2), 75

HELPS I G, SKITMORE P M. Discrimination Against Women in Employment 1975 **8** (1), 3

HENDRY I C. The Three-Parameter Approach to Long Range Forecasting 1972 **5** (1), 40

HENRY E W. An Input-Output Model of the Irish Economy 1973 **6** (3), 64

HENRY H W. Formal Planning in Major U.S. Corporations 1977 **10** (5), 40

HERDAN B L. Civil Spin-off from Defence Research: A Fresh Approach 1987 **20** (1), 84

HERGERT M *see* DE NOBLE A F *et al*

HERTZ D B, THOMAS H. Evaluating the Risks in Acquisition 1982 **15** (6), 38

HETRICK J C. A Formal Model for Long Range Planning: 1. Relating the Company to the Economy 1969 **1** (3), 16

HETRICK J C. A Formal Model for Long Range Planning: 2. The Assessment of Opportunity and Risk 1969 **1** (4), 54

HETRICK J C. A Formal Model for Long Range Planning: 3. Allocating and Appraising Capital Investment 1969 **1** (3), 16

HETRICK J C. Towards a Global Economy 1972 **5** (3), 46

HICHENS R E *see* ROBINSON S J Q *et al*

HICKEY K D *see* SETHI N K *et al*

HIGGINS J C. The Value of Accuracy in Information for Planning and Control 1974 **7** (4), 67

HIGGINS J C, FINN R. Managerial Attitudes Towards Computer Models for Planning and Control 1976 **9** (6), 107

HIGGINS J C, FINN R. The Organisation and Practice of Corporate Planning in the U.K. 1977 **10** (4), 88

HIGGINS J C, ROMANO D. Social Forecasting: An Integral Part of Corporate Planning? 1980 **13** (2), 82

HIGGINS R B. Creating a Climate Conducive to Planning 1981 **14** (1), 49

HIGGINS R B. Reunite Management and Planning 1976 **9** (4), 40

HIGGINS R B, DIFFENBACH J. Communicating Corporate Strategy—The Payoffs and the Risks 1989 **22** (3), 133

HIGGINS R B, DIFFENBACH J. Strategic Credibility—The Basis of a Strong Share Price 1989 **22** (6), 10

HILL K M *et al*. How Much Basic Research is Enough?—A Problem in Resource Allocation 1969 **1** (3), 38

HILL K Q, COOMER J C. Local Politicians and Their Attitudes to Planning 1977 **10** (6), 57

HILLIER T J. Market Research for 'Out of Town' Shopping Centres 1972 **5** (3), 53

HILLMAN M. Keeping People Alive—The Implications for Planning 1977 **10** (1), 48

HININGS B *et al*. Policy Planning and Central-Local Relations 1985 **18** (2), 38

HINOMOTO H. Projecting Consumptions of Competing Products 1977 **10** (5), 46

HINOMOTO H, REDDY J M. Corporate Planning Using Government Information Systems 1977 **10** (6), 79

HINTERHUBER H H *see* HAMMER R M *et al*

HINTERHUBER H, POPP W. Strategy as a System of Expedients 1988 **21** (4), 107

HIRSCHHEIM R A. Database—A Neglected Corporate Resource? 1983 **16** (5), 79

HIRSCHHEIM R A. Managing the Growth of Electronic Office Information Systems 1983 **16** (6), 59

HIRST M *see* BRISCOE G

HITT M A *et al*. Building Competitive Strength in International Markets 1987 **20** (1), 115

HOBSON M *see* ARMSTRONG R H R

HODGES S, KENNETT D. Practical Problems of Gravity Modelling 1973 **6** (4), 41

HOESCH A G *see* FRIEDRICH A

HOFFMAN R C *see* HEGARTY W H

HOHN S. Economic Development and Ecological Equilibrium—A Target Conflict in Modern Industrial Enterprises 1982 **15** (4), 22

HOHN S. How Information Technology is Transforming Corporate Planning 1986 **19** (4), 18

HOHN S. Key Strategic Issues for German Companies 1986 **19** (6), 38

HOHN S. The European Automobile Industry—Three Possible Scenarios 1980 **13** (4), 12

HOLLIS J D. The Future of the Stock Exchange 1975 **8** (6), 65

HOLLOWAY C. Developing Planning Models 1974 **7** (1), 52

HOLLOWAY C. Does Futures Research Have a Corporate Role? 1978 **11** (5), 17

HOLLOWAY C. Strategic Management and Artificial Intelligence 1983 **16** (5), 89

HOLLOWAY C Developing Planning Models 1974 **7** (1), 52

HOLLOWAY C, JONES G T. Planning at Gulf—A Case Study 1975 **8** (2), 27

HOLLOWAY C, KING W R. Evaluating Alternative Approaches to Strategic Planning 1979 **12** (4), 74

HOLLOWAY C, PEARCE J A. Computer Assisted Strategic Planning 1982 **15** (4), 56

HOLMBERG S R. Monitoring Long-Range Plans 1974 **7** (3), 63

HOLMBERG S R. Regional Planning Regulations in the United States 1978 **11** (5), 72

HOLROYD P. Futures Research: New Directions—Book Review Article 1980 **13** (1), 90

HOLROYD P. Is There a Future for Social Forecasting? 1980 **13** (5), 29

HOLT S C. A System of Government for the Seventies 1969 **2** (1), 61

HOME N *see* GARRETT J

HONTON E J *see* HUSS W R

HOOGAKKER J T *see* ADRIAANS W

HOORN Th P van. Strategic Planning in Small and Medium-sized Companies 1979 **12** (2), 84

HORIKOSHI H *see* KUWAHARA Y *et al*

HORNE A. The Journal Readership Survey 1980 **13** (3), 40

HORNER R W. The Thames Tidal Flood Prevention Scheme 1976 **9** (5), 78

HOROVITZ J H. Strategic Control: A New Task for Top Management 1979 **12** (3), 2

HORWITZ R. Corporate Planning—A Conceptual Critique 1979 **12** (1), 62

HOU WEE C *et al*. Corporate Planning Takes off in Singapore 1989 **22** (2), 78

HOULDEN B T. Data and Effective Corporate Planning 1980 **13** (5), 106

HOULDEN B T. Developing a Company's Strategic Management Capacity 1986 **19** (5), 89

HOULDEN B T. Survival of the Corporate Planner 1985 **18** (5), 49

HOULDEN B T *see* HARDING B

HOUSE W C. Dynamic Planning for the Smaller Company—A Case History 1979 **12** (3), 38

HOUSTON J. Massey-Ferguson's Diversification into Industrial and Construction Equipment 1970 **2** (3), 30

HOWARD E F. Strategic Thinking in Insurance 1989 **22** (5), 76

HOWARD K, WAGLE B V. A Modelling System for Local Government Resource Planning 1978 **11** (4), 77

HOWELL J M. Regional Development—Alternatives for New England 1976 **9** (5), 72

HOYLE M H, STUBBS R J. Management Stocktaking: An Approach to Manpower Planning in Banking 1970 **2** (3), 18

HUELLMANTEL A *see* ZABRISKIE N

HUFF A S, RANNEY J M. Assessing the Environment for an Educational Institution 1981 **14** (3), 107

HUFFMIRE D W. Strategies of the United States Airlines 1975 **8** (2), 72

HULBERT J M *see* BRANDT W K *et al*

HUMBLE J, JONES G. Creating a Climate for Innovation 1989 **22** (4), 46

HUMBLE J W. Corporate Planning and Management by Objectives 1969 **1** (4), 36

HUMPHREY A S. Getting Management Commitment to Planning a New Approach 1974 **7** (1), 45

HUMPHREYS R G. Decisions, Decisions—Book Review Article 1981 **14** (4), 129

HUNSUCKER J L *et al*. How NASA moved from R & D to Operations 1989 **22** (6), 38

HUNT H *see* HILL K M *et al*

HUSS W R, HONTON E J. Scenario Planning—What Style Should You Use? 1987 **20** (4), 21

HUSS W R *see* GOLDFARB D L

HUSSEY D. Brief Case: A Portfolio of Commentary and Opinion 1988 **21** (2), 104

HUSSEY D E. Corporate Planning at Fyffes Group 1969 **2** (1), 22

HUSSEY D E. Corporate Planning for a Church 1974 **7** (2), 61

HUSSEY D E. Implementing Corporate Strategy: Using Management Education and Training 1985 **18** (5), 28

HUSSEY D E. Multinational Corporate Planning: Is it Really Different?—Book Review Article 1980 **13** (2), 105

HUSSEY D E. Planning for Ovaltine: Introducing Corporate Planning at A. Wander Ltd 1971 **3** (3), 41

HUSSEY D E. Portfolio Analysis: Practical Experience with the Directional Policy Matrix 1978 **11** (4), 2

HUSSEY D E. Strategic Management: Lessons from Success and Failure 1984 **17** (1), 43

HUSSEY D E. Strategic Planning and Inflation 1976 **9** (2), 24

HUSSEY D E. Strategic Planning for International Business 1972 **5** (2), 16

HUSSEY D E. The Corporate Appraisal: Assessing Company Strengths and Weaknesses 1968 **1** (2), 19

HUSSEY D E. Who Says Planners Don't 1977 **10** (5), 83

HUSSEY D E *see* YOUNG R

HUTCHINSON A C. Planned Euthanasia for Old Projects 1971 **4** (2), 17

HUTCHINSON C. People and Pollution: The Challenge to Planning 1970 **2** (3), 2

HYUN Y, LEE J. Can Hyundai Go It Alone? 1989 **22** (2), 63

I

IBRAHIM S M A. Energy Resources and the Impact of New Technologies 1980 **13** (4), 63

IMUNDO L V *see* LANFORD H W
IRELAND R D *see* HITT M A *et al*
IRVING P *see* TAYLOR B
IRWIN P H. Towards Better Strategic Management 1974 **7** (6), 64
ISHIKURE K. Achieving Japanese Productivity and Quality Levels at a U.S. Plant 1988 **21** (5), 10
IVERSTINE J *see* WRIGHT P *et al*

J

JACKSON C. Building a Competitive Advantage Through Information Technology 1989 **22** (4), 29
JACKSON C M. Society for Long Range Planning—The Diary Page 1977 **10** (6), 84
JACKSON R. Decentralized Administration and Citizen Participation in Community Planning 1972 **5** (1), 16
JACKSON W U. Assessing Performance in Local Government 1984 **17** (3), 24
JACOBS K *see* SHAMA A
JAIN A K *see* MAHAJAN V *et al*
JAIN P K. Assessing the Performance of a Development Bank 1989 **22** (6), 100
JAIN S C. Effect of Economic Planning on Business Decisions 1977 **10** (4), 42
JAIN S C. Environmental Scanning in U.S. Corporations 1984 **17** (2), 117
JAIN S C, SINGHVI S S. Environmental Forecasting and Non-Profit Professional Organizations 1977 **10** (3), 50
JALLAND M *see* FILDES R *et al*
JAMES B G. The Theory of the Corporate Life Cycle 1974 **7** (2), 49
JAMES B G. Alliance: The New Strategic Focus 1985 **18** (3), 76
JAMES B G. Social Impact: The Pharmaceutical Industry 1978 **11** (1), 2
JAMES J R. The Crisis of Urban Living 1971 **3** (4), 44
JANTSCH E. Technological Forecasting in Corporate Planning 1968 **1** (1), 40
JANZEN L T. Company Rescue—An Example 1983 **16** (6), 88
JANZEN L T. Systematic Planning and Re-organization 1971 **4** (2), 58
JARRETT M *see* RHODES D *et al*
JAUCH L R, WILSON H K. A Strategic Perspective for Make or Buy Decisions 1979 **12** (6), 56
JAVIDAN M. Where Planning Fails—An Executive Survey 1985 **18** (5), 89
JAVIDAN M, DASTMALCHIAN A. Why Planning in State Enterprises Doesn't Work 1988 **21** (3), 98
JECKOVICH S. Technological Forecasting as a Guide for Managerial Planning 1971 **4** (1), 29
JENSTER Per V. Using Critical Success Factors in Planning 1987 **20** (4), 102
JOHNSON R J. Food Packaging 1974–1984 1975 **8** (1), 52
JOHNSON R *see* BEASLEY J E
JOHNSON W B. The Transformation of a Railroad 1976 **9** (6), 18
JOHNSTON D R. Forest Policy—Formulation and Implementation 1975 **8** (6), 30
JOHNSTONE R D. Project Selection and Evaluation 1972 **5** (3), 40
JOLLIFFE J K. Failings in U.K. Transport Planning 1977 **10** (1), 73
JONES E G *see* GREEN G J L
JONES G T *see* HOLLOWAY C
JONES H. Planning and the Chief Executive—Book Review Article 1978 **11** (3), 80
JONES H G. Scenarios for Industrial Relations: Sweden Evolves a New Consensus 1987 **20** (3), 65
JONES H G. Tetra Pak—A Model for Successful Innovation 1982 **15** (6), 31
JONES P. Energy Policy: Government vs Industry 1987 **20** (1), 12
JONES P M S. Energy Choices for the Future 1980 **13** (6), 18
JONES T *see* GREEN J
JONG K de *see* EPPINK D J *et al*
JONSSON S, PETZALL I. Forecasting Political Decisions and Their Impact on Business 1982 **15** (4), 98
JOSEPH K. Measuring Unemployment 1976 **9** (3), 12

JOYNT P. Planning for the Older Manager—Collaborative Research in Norwegian Business 1987 **20** (3), 35
JUDD B R *see* CHAO H P *et al*

K

KAHALAS H. A Look at Major Planning Methods: Development, Implementation Strengths and Limitations 1978 **11** (4), 84
KAHALAS H. Decision Making in the Public Sector—A Logical Model 1976 **9** (3), 75
KAHALAS H. Long Range Planning—An Open Systems View 1977 **10** (5), 78
KAHALAS H. Planning for Research and Development—The Impact on Society 1975 **8** (6), 37
KAHALAS H, BJORKLUND R L. An Environmental Decision Model for Dynamic Planning 1976 **9** (1), 81
KAHALAS H, GROVES D L. Ecology, Pollution and Business: A Proposed Planning Solution 1978 **11** (6), 62
KAHALAS H, LEININGER W E. A Manpower Planning Model for Organizational Effectiveness 1975 **8** (4), 85
KAHALAS H *see* ERRICKSON D L *et al*
KAHALAS H *see* GROVES D L *et al*
KALFF H. How is Competition Performing? 1979 **12** (3), 16
KALLMAN E A, SHAPIRO H J. The Motor Freight Industry—A Case against Planning 1978 **11** (1), 81
KAMI M J. Gap Analysis: Key to Super Growth 1969 **1** (4), 44
KANE J *see* THOMSPON W *et al*
KANE N J A. Marketing the Telephone in a De-regulated Environment 1986 **19** (4), 59
KAPOOR M C, SINGH J D. Marketing Planning in India—A Survey 1981 **14** (3), 97
KARAGOZOGLU N, SEGLUND R. Strategic Planning for a Public Sector Enterprise 1989 **22** (2), 121
KARGER D W. Economic and Industrial Development—A New Ingredient 1976 **9** (5), 90
KARGER D W. Integrated Formal Long Range Planning and How to Do it 1973 **6** (4), 31
KARGER D W, MALIK Z A. Long Range Planning and Organizational Performance 1975 **8** (6), 60
KARGER D W, VORA J A. Integrated Planning for Health Care Organizations Especially Hospitals 1979 **12** (1), 91
KARUNARATNE N D. Assessing Performance in Libraries 1978 **11** (2), 66
KASHYAP R N. Introducing Management Information Systems for Corporate Planning and Control 1973 **6** (1), 28
KASHYAP R N. Management Information Systems for Corporate Planning Control 1972 **5** (2), 25
KASPER W *see* GALER G
KASTENS M L. How Much is an Acquisition Worth? 1973 **6** (2), 52
KATZ A. Planning in the IBM Corporation 1978 **11** (3), 2
KAY H. Psychological Perspectives on the Future 1975 **8** (2), 51
KEARNEY A T *see* STOTLAND J A
KEATING B P, KEATING M O. Goal Setting and Efficiency in Social Service Agencies 1981 **14** (1), 40
KEATING M O *see* KEATING B P
KEEGAN W J. Productivity: Lessons from Japan 1975 **8** (2), 61
KEENEY R L, NAIR K. Setting Goals in a Professional Service Firm 1976 **9** (3), 54
KELCEY J G. Environmental Impact Assessment—Their Development And Application 1986 **19** (1), 67
KELLER A Z *et al.* Forecasting Expenditure on Capital Project 1984 **17** (4), 110
KEMP R L. Planning for Local Government—A Grass-Roots Approach 1985 **18** (6), 91
KEMPNER T *et al.* The Role of Business in Society 1970 **2** (4), 2
KENDALL K E. Multiple Objective Planning for Regional Blood Centres 1980 **13** (4), 98
KENDALL K E. Planning for Innovation in Health Care: A Breakthrough in Blood Banking 1984 **17** (6), 127
KENDRICK D W. The Future of London as an International Financial Centre 1980 **13** (1), 42
KENNEDY C. The Transformation of AT & T 1989 **22** (3), 10

KENNEDY C. How Marriott Corporation Grew Five-fold in Ten Years 1988 **21** (2), 10

KENNEDY C. Planning Global Strategies for 3M 1988 **21** (1), 9

KENNEDY C. Xerox Charts a New Strategic Direction 1989 **22** (1), 10

KENNETT D see HODGES S

KENNINGTON D. Long Range Planning for Public Libraries—A Delphi Study 1977 **10** (2), 73

KENNY B et al. Planning for the Physically Handicapped 1989 **22** (2), 91

KENYON P H A. Currency Exposure Management 1980 **13** (3), 21

KEPPLER W et al. Organization for Long Range Planning—A Survey of German Companies 1979 **12** (5), 69

KERN D. The Evaluation of Country Risk and Economic Potential 1985 **18** (3), 17

KERN D. The Medium-Term Currency Outlook 1980 **13** (2), 2

KERN D. Financial Trends 1982 **15** (5), 18

KETTLEWELL P J. A European Bibliography of Corporate Planning, 1972 1974 **7** (1), 72

KEUNING D see EPPINK D J et al

KEUSCH R B see BELL J A

KHAKEE A. Town Planning in Sweden: National Officials Versus Local Politicians 1984 **17** (6), 82

KHAN A M. Realistic Planning for Transportation—A Flexible Approach 1989 **22** (5), 128

KHARBANDA O P, STALLWORTHY E A. Planning for Emergencies—Lessons From the Chemical Industry 1989 **22** (1), 83

KHEM G S see CHEONG W K

KIDEL A. Techniques and Methodology of the French Fifth Plan 1969 **1** (3), 60

KIESER P J. Planning for Heavy Industry in South Africa 1972 **5** (1), 78

KINARD J see WRIGHT P et al

KING A. Whales and the Whaling Industry 1975 **8** (2), 89

KING Lord. Lessons for Privatization 1987 **20** (6), 18

KING M, SMITH D K. Planning the Deployment of Clergy 1982 **15** (2), 104

KING S. Conflicts Between Public and Private Opinion 1981 **14** (4), 90

KING W R. How Effective is Your Information Systems Planning? 1988 **21** (5), 103

KING W R. Planning for Strategic Decision Support Systems 1983 **16** (5), 73

KING W R. Using Strategic Issue Analysis 1982 **15** (4), 45

KING W R, CLELAND D I. Information for More Effective Strategic Planning 1977 **10** (1), 59

KING W R see CLELAND D I

KING W R see FAHEY L et al

KING W R see HOLLOWAY C

KING W R see RODRIGUEZ J I

KINGSHOTT A L. Financial Forecasting for Corporate Planning 1968 **1** (2), 28

KINGSHOTT A L. Planning in a Nationalised Industry 1975 **8** (5), 58

KINGSMAN B G. Forecasting and Research for Supply Markets—Commodity Buying Systems 1974 **7** (5), 24

KIRPALANI V H. Product Regrouping can Aid MNE Planning 1978 **11** (3), 16

KIRTON M J. Adaptors and Innovators—Why New Initiatives Get Blocked 1984 **17** (2), 137

KITCHING D W C. Rationalizing Branch Banking 1982 **15** (1), 53

KITTAPPA K see NARCHAL R M et al

KLEIN H E, LINNEMAN R E. The Use of Scenarios in Corporate Planning—Eight Case Histories 1981 **14** (5), 69

KLEIN H E see LINNEMAN R E

KLOEZE H J et al. Strategic Planning and Participation: A Contradiction in Terms 1980 **13** (5), 10

KLUYVER C A de, MCNALLY G M. Developing a Corporate Planning Model for a Small Company 1982 **15** (1), 97

KNEE D see WALTERS D

KNIGHT K E, BACA H R. The Role of Government in Industrial Innovation 1978 **11** (6), 79

KNOEPFEL R W. The Politics of Planning: Man in the Decision Process 1973 **6** (1), 17

KNOEPFEL R W. Establishing Corporate Objectives at Solvay 1970 **2** (4), 11

KNOWLSON P. The Society for Long-Range Planning: Challenges in Corporate Planning—Third International Conference on Corporate Planning—Brussels, September 1973 1974 **7** (1), 69

KOBAYASHI N. Strategic Alliances with Japanese Firms 1988 **21** (2), 29

KOERNER E. GE's High-tech Strategy 1989 **22** (4), 11

KOERNER E. Technology Planning at General Motors 1989 **22** (2), 9

KOHL J P. Strategies for Growth: Intervention in a Church 1984 **17** (6), 76

KOHL J P, STEPHENS D B. Reducing Personnel Turnover and Improving Morale 1989 **22** (4), 125

KOLAJA J. A Move Towards Greater Satisfaction—Book Review Article 1981 **14** (3), 118

KONO T. Japanese Management Philosophy: Can it be Exported? 1982 **15** (3), 90

KONO T. Long Range Planning of U.K. and Japanese Corporations—A Comparative Study 1984 **17** (2), 58

KONO T. Long Range Planning—Japan—USA—A Comparative Study 1976 **9** (5), 61

KONO T see NAKAJO T

KOPELMAN J B, WEAVER N L. Energy Modeling as a Tool for Planning 1978 **11** (1), 25

KOTOV F. Long-Term Planning in the U.S.S.R. 1975 **8** (4), 61

KRANNET H C see PESSEMIER E A

KRAUSHAR C A A. Product Planning at Perkins Engines Group 1968 **1** (2), 15

KRAUSHAR P M. Organization for Corporate Development 1976 **9** (3), 43

KRAUTHOFF L C see BOLLING R

KREIKEBAUM H, GRIMM U. Planning in a Free Market Economy 1982 **15** (3), 103

KRIEBEL C H. The Strategic Dimension of Computer Systems Planning 1968 **1** (1), 7

KRIJNEN H G. The Flexible Firm 1979 **12** (2), 63

KRIJNEN H G. Formulating Corporate Objectives and Strategies 1977 **10** (4), 78

KRISTENSEN N E see NIELSEN K S et al

KRUGER W. Patterns of Success in German Business 1989 **22** (2), 106

KUCHMEN W H see MAZZE E M et al

KUDLA R J. The Components of Strategic Planning 1978 **11** (6), 48

KUDLA R J. The Current Practice of Bank Long-Range Planning 1982 **15** (3), 132

KUDLA R J. Elements of Effective Corporate Planning 1976 **9** (4), 82

KUDO H et al. How U.S. and Japanese CEO's Spend Their Time 1988 **21** (6), 79

KUMAR R VRAT P. Using Computer Models in Corporate Planning 1989 **22** (2), 114

KUMAR S P. Long-Term Planning for Indian Shipping 1976 **9** (6), 63

KUWAHARA Y et al. Research and Development at Hitachi 1989 **22** (3), 54

KUZ T see SMIL V

KYLE B S. Business Planning in Europe 1981 **14** (5), 2

L

LA LONDE B J. Integrated Distribution Management—The American Perspective 1969 **2** (2), 61

LA LONDE B J. Strategic Planning for Distribution 1971 **4** (2), 23

LA LONDE B J, ZINSER P H. Managing in Uncertain Economic Times: The Case for Planning 1975 **8** (5), 18

LABROUKOS N S, LIOUKAS S. Planning for Esso Greece—The Impact of Nationalization 1989 **22** (4), 98

LACHMANN O. Personnel Administration in 1980: A Delphi Study 1972 **5** (2), 21

LACZNIAK E R et al. A Tough Future for Australian Business 1989 **22** (1), 48

LaFORGE L, WOOD D R. Corporate Planning and Operations Research: Do They Go Together? 1982 **15** (3), 152

LAHR M L. Interactive Planning—The Way to Develop Commitment 1983 **16** (4), 31

LAMB F see GROVES D L et al

LAMBERT D M, STOCK J R. The Corporate Energy Policy: A Management Planning Perspective 1979 **12** (2), 45

LANCIONI R A. Reorganisation for Physical Distribution 1975 **8** (4), 46

LAND A van't *see* FRIEDRICH A

LANFORD H W, IMUNDO L V. Approaches to Technological Forecasting as a Planning Tool 1974 **7** (4), 49

LANFORD H W, McCANN T M. Effective Planning and Control of Large Projects—Using Work Breakdown Structure 1983 **16** (2), 38

LANFORD H W *see* NUTT A B *et al*

LANGLEY A. The Roles of Formal Strategic Planning 1988 **21** (3), 40

LANGRISH J. Technological Change: Theory and Practice—Book Review Article 1983 **16** (4), 106

LANZENAUER C H von, SPRUNG M R. Developing Inflation Scenarios 1982 **15** (4), 37

LAPOINTE F A *see* BENFITTO M T *et al*

LAROUCHE D *see* CHAMPAGNE F *et al*

LASSERRE P. Selecting a Foreign Partner for Technology Transfer 1984 **17** (6), 43

LASSERRE P. The New Industrializing Countries of Asia—Perspectives and Opportunities 1981 **14** (3), 36

LASSERRE P. Training: Key to Technological Transfer 1982 **15** (3), 52

LASSERRE P. Why Europeans are Weak in Asia—An Organizational Perspective 1988 **21** (4), 25

LAUGLAUG A S. A Framework for the Strategic Management of Future Tyre Technology 1987 **20** (5), 21

LAWRENCE J. Manpower and Unemployment in the U.K. 1979 **12** (5), 16

LAWSON F. Telecommunications and the Customer—Prospects for the 1980s 1980 **13** (6), 70

LAWSON R W. Marketing the Key to Organizational Effectiveness 1983 **16** (4), 90

LAZARUS M, ASHLEY W C. Transportation After Deregulation 1985 **18** (1), 42

LE FRANC J-D. The Future for European Business—Strategies for Growth 1990 **13** (4), 18

LEACH S *see* HININGS B *et al*

LEAVY B. Assessing Country Risk for Foreign Investment Decisions 1984 **17** (3), 141

LECKIE A H. Measuring Manufacturing Performance—The DAP Concept 1973 **6** (4), 52

LEDERER T F. Relocation or Dislocation?—A Planned Approach to Location 1980 **13** (6), 10

LEDERMAN L L. Foresight Activities in the U.S.A.: Time for a Re-Assessment 1984 **17** (3), 41

LEDGERWOOD G. Alternative Plans for London Dockland: Not Force but Seduction 1980 **13** (6), 46

LEE J *see* HYUN Y

LEE S K *see* HOU WEE C *et al*

LEE S M, SHIM J P. Zero-Base Budgeting—Dealing with Conflicting Objectives 1984 **17** (5), 103

LEEMHUIS J P. Setting Investment Criteria for Government and Industry 1985 **18** (3), 33

LEEMHUIS J P. Using Scenarios to Develop Strategies 1985 **18** (2), 30

LEES J *see* DALE B G

LEFEBVRE M *et al*. The New Environment of European Corporations 1978 **11** (1), 15

LEHNER F. The Software Life Cycle in Computer Applications 1989 **22** (5), 38

LEHR M F *see* MERRETT A J

LEI D. Strategies for Global Competition 1989 **22** (1), 102

LEIDECKER J K, BRUNO A V. Identifying and Using Critical Success Factors 1984 **17** (1), 23

LEIGH A *see* WHITE M

LEININGER W E *see* KAHALAS H

LENZ R C *see* NUTT A B *et al*

LENZ R T, LYLES M A. Paralysis by Analysis: Is Your Planning System Becoming Too Rational? 1985 **18** (4), 64

LENZ R T, LYLES M A. Tackling the Human Problems in Planning 1981 **14** (2), 72

LENZ R T *see* ENGLEDOW J L

LEONTIADES J. Going Global—Global Strategies vs National Strategies 1986 **19** (6), 96

LEONTIADES J. Planning Strategy for World Markets 1970 **3** (2), 40

LEONTIADES J C. Plant Location—The International Perspective 1974 **7** (1), 10

LEONTIADES M. Planning for Changes in Stages of Corporate Development 1979 **12** (6), 70

LEONTIADES M. What Kind of Corporate Planner Do You Need? 1977 **10** (2), 56

LETOURNEUR J S. The Pechiney Ugine Kuhlmann Plan 1973 **6** (1), 9

LEWIS G *et al*. BPH Reorganizes for Global Competition 1988 **21** (3), 18

LEYSHON A M. Marketing Planning and Corporate Planning 1976 **9** (1), 29

LIDSTONE J. Market Segmentation for Pharmaceuticals 1989 **22** (2), 54

LIENTZ B P, CHEN M. Assessing the Impact of New Technology in Information Systems 1981 **14** (6), 44

LIENTZ B P, CHEN M. Long Range Planning for Information Services 1980 **13** (1), 55

LINDSAY W M *see* BOULTON W R *et al*

LINNEMAN R E, KLEIN H E. The Use of Multiple Scenarios by U.S. Industrial Companies 1979 **12** (1), 83

LINNEMAN R E, KLEIN H E. The Use of Multiple Scenarios by U.S. Industrial Companies: A Comparison Study, 1977—1981 1983 **16** (6), 94

LINNEMAN R E *see* KLEIN H E

LINNEMAN R E, THOMAS M J. A Commonsense Approach to Portfolio Planning 1982 **15** (2), 77

LIOUKAS S *see* LABROUKOS N S

LISTON D J. Politics, Government and Company Planning: The New Perspective 1980 **13** (5), 57

LITSCHERT R J, NICHOLSON E A. Corporate Long-Range Planning Groups—Some Different Approaches 1974 **7** (4), 62

LITSCHERT R J, NICHOLSON E A. Staffing Long Range Planning Groups 1972 **5** (1), 37

LITTLER D A, SWEETING R C. Corporate Development—Preferred Strategies in U.K. Companies 1987 **20** (2), 125

LIVESEY F. A Note on Forecasting the Market Demand for Waste Paper 1978 **11** (1), 87

LIVESEY F. Waste Paper and the Market Mechanism 1975 **8** (3), 17

LIVESEY F, BARCENA V A. Waste Paper and the Market Mechanism 1975 **8** (3), 17

LLOYD B. Are We Taking the World Development Problems Seriously?—An Overview of Recent Reports and Publications—Book Review Article 1979 **12** (3), 97

LLOYD B. The Identification and Assessment of Political Risk in the International Environment 1974 **7** (6), 24

LLOYD-JACOB D. The Use of Simulations for Market Forecasting—A Case Study in the Mining Industry 1969 **2** (1), 76

LOCKE B. Investment and Planning in R & D 1974 **7** (3), 12

LOCKE B. Materials Developments and Planning—Future Implications in the Engineering and Chemical Industries 1969 **2** (1), 66

LOCKE H B. Innovation by Design 1976 **9** (4), 34

LOCKE H B. Planning Innovation 1978 **11** (6), 21

LOCKE H B *et al*. Planning for Innovation 1974 **7** (2), 19

LOCKETT A G, ARMSTRONG K. Throwing Away Millions—Long Range Planning for Disposables 1971 **4** (1), 15

LOFTHOUSE S. Strategy, Cross Subsidization and the 'Business Portfolio' 1978 **11** (4), 58

LOFTHOUSE S. Strategy and Tactics for Resisting Take-Over 1984 **17** (4), 38

LONG G. A Businessman's Guide to the Media 1983 **16** (2), 15

LONG R A. Planning in British Railways 1969 **2** (2), 72

LONGFORD D M. Can Bureaucracies Become More Flexible and Responsive 1986 **19** (1), 99

LONGLEY R C M *see* WILLIAMSON E I

LONGLEY R *see* BADEN-FULLER C

LORAINE J A. Population Policies and the Contemporary Political Scene 1975 **8** (6), 2

LORANGE P. A Framework for Strategic Planning in Multinational Corporations 1976 **9** (3), 30

LORANGE P. The Planner's Dual Role—A Survey for U.S. Companies 1973 **6** (1), 13

LORENTZ J *see* HAMMER R M *et al*

LOSSIUS T *see* DEMB A *et al*

LOVELL R G. From Food to Freezes to Freight, Marketing is Vital 1986 **19** (5), 40
LOVERIDGE D J. Decisions, Judgement and Style 1979 **12** (1), 22
LOW N. Urban Management—Some Models for Policy Making 1979 **12** (5), 91
LUCHS H see COWHERD D M
LUCHS R. Successful Businesses Compete on Quality—Not Costs 1986 **19** (1), 12
LUMSDEN C see PAYNE A
LUNDBERG D. Pluralist Organization and Consensus in Swedish Planning 1976 **9** (6), 69
LUQMANI M et al. Corporate Strategy and Public Policy in Saudi Arabia 1989 **22** (4), 79
LYLES M A see LENZ R T
LYNCH J E see DOYLE P
LYONS T P. Personnel Policy and Manpower Planning in Banking 1979 **12** (5), 2

M

McCANN J E. Analyzing Industrial Trends—A Collaborative Approach 1985 **18** (5), 116
McCANN T M see LANFORD H W
McCART R T see GROVES D L
McCONNELL J D. Strategic Planning: One Workable Approach 1971 **4** (2), 2
McCROHAN K F see HARVEY J W
MACDONALD I. How Singapore Makes Central Planning Work 1986 **19** (1), 38
McEWEN N et al. Managing Organizational Change—A Strategic Approach 1988 **21** (6), 71
McGILL R. Planning for Strategic Performance in Local Government 1988 **21** (5), 77
MACGREGOR J M. What Users Think About Computer Models 1983 **16** (5), 45
MACGREGOR J M see COLLINS M R
MACGREGOR J M see POWER P D
MACHIN J L J, WILSON L S. Closing the Gap between Planning and Control 1979 **12** (2), 16
McHUGH M see McNAMEE P
McKAY C W, CUTTING G D. A Model for Long Range Planning in Higher Education 1974 **7** (5), 58
McKENNEY J L. An Approach to Simulation Model Development for Improved Planning 1970 **2** (3), 56
McKINNON L M B. The Corporate Library as a Source of New Technology 1980 **13** (2), 102
MACKINTOSH I M. Integrated Circuits: The Coming Battle 1979 **12** (3), 28
McLAUGHLIN J B. Controlling the Urban System 1970 **3** (2), 61
MacLAURIN I. Food Retailing in the Eighties—Technological Opportunities and Social Constraints 1982 **15** (1), 40
MACMILLAN I C. Strategy and Flexibility in the Smaller Business 1975 **8** (3), 62
MACMILLAN K see KEMPNER T et al
McNALLY G M see KLUYVER C A de
McNAMEE P. Competitive Analysis Using Matrix Displays 1984 **17** (3), 98
McNAMEE P B. The V-Matrix—A New Tool for Plotting Earnings 1984 **17** (1), 19
McNAMEE P, McHUGH M. Competitive Strategies in the Clothing Industry 1989 **22** (4), 63
McNAMEE P, McHUGH M. Mapping Competitive Groups in the Clothing Industry 1989 **22** (5), 89
MacNULTY C A R. Social Forecasting for Company Planning—Book Review Article 1983 **16** (2), 118
MacNULTY C see MITCHELL A
McPHETERS I R, STRONG W B. Some Law Enforcement Operations Implications of Crime Seasonality 1974 **7** (2), 57
MADDOX N et al. Creative Strategic Planning Using Imagery 1987 **20** (5), 118
MADU C N. Transferring Technology to Developing Countries— Critical Factors for Success 1989 **22** (4), 115

MAGRATH A J see HARDY K G
MAHAJAN V et al. A New Product Growth Model with a Dynamic Market Potential 1979 **12** (4), 51
MAHAJAN V see RICKS D A
MAHAJAN V, WIND Y. Business Synergy Does Not Always Pay Off 1988 **21** (1), 59
MAHON J F, KELLEY P C. Managing Toxic Wastes—After Bhopal and Sandoz 1987 **20** (4), 50
MAHON J F see POST J E et al
MAINELLI M R, MILLER D R. Strategic Planning for Information Systems at British Rail 1988 **21** (4), 65
MAJANI B, MAKRIDAKIS S. Can Recessions be Predicted? 1977 **10** (2), 31
MAKRIDAKIS S. If we Cannot Forecast How Can we Plan? 1981 **14** (3), 10
MAKRIDAKIS S. Management in the 21st Century 1989 **22** (2), 37
MAKRIDAKIS S see MAJANI B
MAKRIDAKIS S, WHEELWRIGHT S. Integrating Forecasting and Planning 1973 **6** (3), 53
MALASKA P et al. Scenarios in Europe—Who Uses Them and Why? 1984 **17** (5), 45
MALHOTRA N see MAHAJAN V et al
MALIK M A K, AHMAD I. Forecasting Demand for Food in Libya— Using Confidence Limits 1981 **14** (5), 90
MALIK Z A see KARGER D W
MALMIVIRTA M see MALASKA P et al
MALMLOW E G. A Systematic Approach to Diversification 1973 **6** (4), 2
MALMLOW E G. Corporate Strategic Planning in Practice 1972 **5** (3), 2
MANDES Y see BOURANTAS D
MANN C W. The Use of a Model in Long Term Planning—A Case History 1978 **11** (5), 55
MANSFIELD M J see NAYLOR T H
MARCH P see DIMSON E
MARCUS A A. Airline Deregulation: Why the Supporters Lost Out 1987 **20** (1), 90
MARCUS A A. U.S. Firms' Responses to Regulation: Stonewalling and Opportunism 1987 **20** (3), 98
MARCUS A A, MEVORACH B. Planning for the U.S. Political Cycle 1988 **21** (4), 50
MARLEY-CLARKE B. The Delphi Method and Urbanization 1974 **7** (6), 81
MARLEY-CLARKE B W G. Policy Planning for Environmental Management 1976 **9** (5), 2
MARLEY-CLARKE B W G see PUCCINI D S
MARMUSE C. Minimum Level of Activity—A Quick Method of Assessing Growth Potential in the Smaller Business 1983 **16** (1), 84
MAROTI E. Corporate Planning in the Canadian National Railways 1970 **3** (1), 21
MARQUAND J. Government Economic Planning in the United Kingdom 1978 **11** (6), 2
MARSHALL I. Strategic Issues for the Trustee Savings Banks 1985 **18** (4), 39
MARSHALL J see GREWE T et al
MARSHALL R. Sector Policy in Government 1974 **7** (4), 2
MARSHALL S A see CLOWES G A
MARTIN J. Business Planning: The Gap Between Theory and Practice 1979 **12** (6), 2
MARTIN W H, MASON S. Leisure 1980 and Beyond 1976 **9** (2), 58
MARTYN A S. Some Problems in Managing Complex Development Projects 1975 **8** (2), 13
MARWOOD D C L. ICL Crisis and Swift Recovery 1985 **18** (2), 10
MASCARENHAS B. Planning for Flexibility 1981 **14** (5), 78
MASON J. Developing Strategic Thinking 1986 **19** (3), 72
MASON J B, MAYER M L. Bank Management and Strategic Planning for the 1980s 1979 **12** (4), 35
MASON J B, RESNIK A. Marketing: the Prospects for the 1980s 1982 **15** (1), 34
MASON S see MARTIN W H
MAST H J. Industrial Investment and Financial Requirements 1978 **11** (6), 42
MASUD E. Advanced Concepts for Bulk Power Systems Studies 1977 **10** (5), 25

MATHIESON R F. The Planning Function and Input-Output Analysis 1972 **5** (4), 73

MATHOT G B M. How to get New Products to Market Quicker 1982 **15** (6), 20

MATHUR S S. Competitive Industrial Marketing Strategies 1984 **17** (4), 102

MATT H. An Effective Tool for the Optimization of Distribution Systems 1972 **5** (4), 48

MATTSON B E. Spotting a Market Gap for a New Product 1985 **18** (1), 87

MAY G, GREEN H. Planning for Job Creation 1984 **17** (1), 100

MAY R. Pricing Policies and Corporate Strategy 1970 **2** (4), 49

MAYCOCK P D see ZIEMER D R

MAYER M L see MASON J B

MAYS W A see HITT M A

MAZOR A see BEN-SHAHAR H et al

MAZZE E M. University Planning: An Organization Model 1971 **4** (2), 55

MAZZE E M et al. Corporate Product Planning: A Vector Analysis Approach 1973 **6** (2), 35

MAZZOLINI R. How Strategic Decisions are Made 1981 **14** (3), 85

MEDLEY G J. Strategic Planning for the World Wildlife Fund 1988 **21** (1), 46

MEINHART W A see GODIWALLA Y M et al

MELIN L. Strategies in Managing Turnaround 1985 **18** (1), 80

MELVILLE-ROSS T. Home Ownership in the U.K. in the 1980s 1981 **14** (4), 43

MENDELOW A L. Setting Corporate Goals and Measuring Organizational Effectiveness—A Practical Approach 1983 **16** (1), 70

MENKE M M. Strategic Planning in an Age of Uncertainty 1979 **12** (4), 27

MENKE M M et al. Evaluating Basic Research Strategies 1981 **14** (3), 44

MENKE M M see ABT R et al

MEREDITH J R. Strategic Control of Factory Automation 1987 **20** (6), 106

MERISTO T see MALASKA P et al

MERRETT A J, LEHR M F. Financial Evaluation of Corporate Plans 1970 **2** (3), 37

MERRITT T P, Forecasting the Future Business Environment: The State of the Art, 1974 **7** (3), 54

MERWE A van der, MERWE S van der. Strategic Leadership and the Chief Executive 1985 **18** (1), 100

MERWE S van der see MERWE A van der

METZ C K C. How Much Customer Service Do You Need? 1978 **11** (4), 39

MEVORACH B see MARCUS A A

MICHAEL R J see PEARSON J V

MICHAEL S R. Guidelines for Contingency Approach to Planning 1979 **12** (6), 62

MICHAEL S R. National Planning in the United States 1976 **9** (3), 21

MICHAEL S R. Tailor-made Planning: Making Planning Fit for the Firm 1980 **13** (6), 74

MICHAEL S R, CARLISLE A E. National Planning in the United States 1976 **9** (3), 21

MIDDAUGH II J K see COWEN S S

MIESING P. Integrating Planning with Management 1984 **17** (5), 118

MIGLIORE R H. Planning and Management by Objectives 1976 **9** (4), 58

MILBORROW G C. The View from the Bridge—Book Review Article 1983 **16** (5), 125

MILISAVLJEVIC M. Business Planning and Employee Democracy in Yugoslavia 1983 **16** (4), 84

MILLER D R see MAINELLI M R

MILLER W W et al. Framework for Making Resource Use Decisions: An Application to Subdivisions Development 1978 **11** (1), 72

MILLETT S M. How Scenarios Trigger Strategic Thinking 1988 **21** (5), 61

MILLS G. Who Controls the Board? 1989 **22** (3), 125

MILLS L. The Role of Trade Unions in Strategic Planning 1978 **11** (5), 78

MILLS R W. Capital Budgeting—The State of the Art 1988 **21** (4), 76

MILLS R W see ROBERTSON J

MILLSON P C. The International Scene Towards 1980 1971 **4** (2), 36

MITCHELL A, MacNULTY C. Changing Values and Lifestyles 1981 **14** (2), 37

MITCHELL D. 1992: The Implications for Management 1989 **22** (1), 32

MOCK E see WALSH C

MOCKLER R J, DOLOGITE D G. Developing Knowledge-based Systems for Strategic Corporate Planning 1988 **21** (1), 97

MOHANTY B see DAS R

MOHANTY R P. Strategic Planning for Water—A Case History 1984 **17** (4), 79

MOLENKAMP A see KLOEZE H J et al

MOLZ R. How Leaders Use Goals 1987 **20** (5), 91

MONTEBELLO M, BUIGUES P. How French Industry Plans 1982 **15** (3), 116

MOORE C S. Rate of Return on New Invested Capital—Its Relationship to Corporate Earnings Growth Rate and Equity Market Values 1972 **5** (4), 33

MOORE J J. Corporate Long Range Planning for Ocean Oriented Industries 1971 **4** (2), 7

MOORE L F, CHARACH L. Planning for University: Using Interactive Forecasting 1980 **13** (3), 109

MOORE P G. Demography and Planning 1969 **2** (2), 18

MOORE V. The Control of Bank Exposure to Risk 1979 **12** (5), 35

MORASKY R L. Defining Goals—A Systems Approach 1977 **10** (2), 85

MORASKY R L, AMICK D. Social System Needs Assessment 1978 **11** (2), 47

MORGAN J I. Putting Modularity in Business Planning and Control 1971 **4** (1), 24

MORISON I, FRAZER P. Shaping the Future of Retail Banking 1982 **15** (4), 105

MORLEY W B. The Privatization of British Telecom—Its Impact on Management 1986 **19** (6), 124

MORRELL J. Forecasting the Economic and Business Environment 1972 **5** (1), 52

MORRIS G K. Forecasting the Impact of Social Change 1975 **8** (3), 64

MORRIS G K. The Use of Futures Research in Product Planning 1982 **15** (6), 67

MORRIS G see ACZEL J

MORRIS J F. The Brain, the Heart and the Big Toe—Book Review Article 1982 **15** (4), 138

MORRIS P A see CHAO H P et al

MORRIS S see BARROWS D S

MORSE C W. The Delusion of Intrapreneurship 1986 **19** (6), 92

MOSS A. Developing a Manpower Strategy for an Industry 1980 **13** (3), 69

MOSS B see LEWIS G et al

MOULINS J-L. Strategies for International Growth in the Automobile Industry 1978 **11** (1), 34

MOULTON J L. Defence Planning: The Uncertainty Factor 1971 **3** (4), 50

MOVSESIAN B see SETHI N K et al

MOYER R. The Futility of Forecasting 1984 **15** (4), 91

MREMA E L. Strategic Planning in Tanzania 1987 **20** (3), 105

MULLER R. Corporate Crisis Management 1985 **18** (5), 38

MURAKAMI T. Recent Changes in Long Range Corporate Planning in Japan 1978 **11** (2), 2

MURPHY J J. Identifying Strategic Issues 1989 **22** (2), 101

MURPHY J see CULLIGAN K

MURPHY T. Pay for Performance—An Instrument of Strategy 1989 **22** (4), 40

MURRAY E A see POST J E et al

MURRAY G O see HARRELL G D

MURRAY J A. Strategic Marketing 1979 **12** (2), 76

MUSHKAT M. Implementing Public Plans: The Case for Social Marketing 1980 **13** (4), 24

MUSHKAT M. Improving the Prospects for Plan Acceptance in Public Organizations 1987 **20** (1), 52

MUSHKAT M. Planners and Bureaucrats—Developing the Consultant Client Relationship 1984 **17** (2), 111

MUTHER R. Long Range Planning of Industrial Facilities 1969 **2** (2), 58

N

NADLER G. Corporate Planning—A System View 1978 **11** (6), 67

NAGAL A. Strategy Formulation for the Smaller Firm—A Practical Approach 1981 **14** (4), 115

NAGASHIMA Y. Response of Japanese Companies to Environmental Changes 1976 **9** (1), 20

NAGEL A. Organizing for Strategic Management 1984 **17** (5), 71

NAGEL A. Strategy Formulation for the Smaller Firm—A Practical Approach 1981 **14** (4), 115

NAIR K, SARIN R L. Generating Future Scenarios—Their Use in Strategic Planning 1979 **12** (3), 57

NAIR K see KEENEY R L

NAKAJO T, KONO T. Success Through Culture Change in a Japanese Brewery 1989 **22** (6), 29

NAKAMURA G-I. Strategic Management in Major Japanese Hightech Companies 1986 **19** (6), 82

NANUS B. QUEST—Quest Environmental Scanning Technique 1982 **15** (2), 39

NAOR J. A New Approach to Corporate Planning 1978 **11** (2), 55

NARAYANAMURTHY S G see RAO B B

NARAYANAN V K see FAHEY L et al

NARCHAL R M et al. An Environmental Scanning System for Business Planning 1987 **20** (6), 96

NAYLOR M E. Regaining Your Competitive Edge 1985 **18** (1), 30

NAYLOR T H. Experience with Corporate Simulation Models—A Survey 1976 **9** (2), 94

NAYLOR T H. How to Integrate Strategic Planning into your Management Process 1981 **14** (5), 56

NAYLOR T H. Integrating Models into the Planning Process 1977 **10** (6), 11

NAYLOR T H, MANSFIELD M J. The Design of Computer-Based Planning and Modeling Systems 1977 **10** (1), 16

NEAL L. The Next Decade in Industrial Relations 1974 **7** (4), 7

NEE A Y C see GHOSH B C

NEILSEN R P. Piggybacking for Business and Nonprofits: A Strategy for Hard Times 1984 **17** (2), 96

NEUBAUER F F, SOLOMON N. A Managerial Approach to Environmental Assessment 1977 **10** (2), 13

NEUBAUER F see DEMB A et al

NEUBURGER K. Assessing the Risks in Acquisitions—The Risk-Chance Analysis 1986 **19** (3), 41

NEUMANN Y see PIZMAN A

NEWGREN K E, CARROLL A B. Social Forecasting in U.S. Corporations—A Survey 1979 **12** (4), 59

NEWTON D. Controlling and Evaluating Personnel Strategy 1969 **1** (4), 24

NEWTON J K. Acquisitions: A Directional Policy Matrix Approach 1981 **14** (6), 51

NEWTON J K. Market Share—Key to Higher Profitability? 1983 **16** (1), 37

NICHOLLS J R. The Impact of the EEC on the U.K. Food, Drink and Tobacco Processing Industry 1979 **12** (3), 82

NICHOLLS J R. The Role of Marketing in Evaluating Acquisitions 1979 **12** (1), 67

NICHOLLS J R, BROADBENT D A. The Role of Marketing in Evaluating Acquisitions 1979 **12** (1), 67

NICHOLSON E A see LITSCHERT R J

NIEDERHAUSERN W von. Planning for Executive Development at J.R. Geigy, SA 1970 **3** (1), 63

NIELSEN K S et al. Forecasting the Market for Ships 1982 **15** (4), 70

NIELSEN R P. Balancing Total System Growth with Special Interests Protections—Book Review Article 1984 **17** (3), 153

NIELSEN R P. Generic Win-Win Negotiating Solutions 1989 **22** (5), 137

NIELSEN R P. Industrial Policy: The Case for National Strategies for World Markets 1984 **17** (5), 50

NIELSEN R P. Strategic Planning and Consensus Building for External Relations—Five Cases 1983 **16** (6), 74

NIKOLCHEV J see DOWDY W L

NISHIKAWA T. New Product Planning at Hitachi 1989 **22** (4), 20

NKOMO S M. Strategic Planning for Human Resources—Let's Get Started 1988 **21** (1), 66

NOEL R see CALORI R

NORBURN D. The British Boardroom: Time for a Revolution? 1984 **17** (5), 35

NORBURN D see GRINYER P H

NORBURN D see WRAY M

NORDEN R F. The Norwegian State Railways—Profit Motivated Enterprise or a Community Service? 1978 **11** (2), 13

NORRIS W C. Developing Corporate Policies for Innovation: A Program of Action 1981 **14** (4), 34

NORSE D. The U.K. and its OECD Competitors 1982 **15** (5), 131

NOYA L E De. How to Evaluate a Long-Range Plan 1978 **11** (3), 36

NOYA L E De. The Federal Government as a Source of Strategic Planning Information 1980 **13** (5), 100

NUENO P, OOSTERVELD J. Managing Technology Alliances 1988 **21** (3), 11

NURMI R. Developing a Climate for Planning 1976 **9** (3), 48

NUTT A B et al. Data Sources for Trend Extrapolation in Technological Forecasting 1976 **9** (1), 72

NUTT B. The Strategic Design of Buildings 1988 **21** (4), 130

NUTT W O. A Future for the Corporate Planner 1977 **10** (2), 90

NUTT W O. Computer Based Corporate Modelling—Book Review Article 1984 **17** (1), 114

NUTT W O. Corporate Information Planning—Book Review Article 1978 **11** (2), 77

NUTT W O. Entering the 21st Century: The Global 2000 Report to the President—Book Review Article 1983 **16** (3), 120

NUTT W O, TANI S N. Readers' Comments 1980 **13** (2), 109

NUTT W O. The Management Phoenix—Essay Review 1982 **15** (2), 128

O

OBERKAMPF V. Technology Assessment: Need and Motivation of Industry 1978 **11** (4), 48

ODELL P R. Third World Oil and Gas—Underexplored and Underdeveloped 1981 **14** (1), 10

ODERMATT H K. Participative Planning at Swiss Reinsurance 1978 **11** (5), 11

OKADA O see KUWAHARA Y et al

O'KEEFE P, WESTGATE K. Preventive Planning for Disasters 1977 **10** (3), 25

O'NEILL H M. How Entrepreneurs Manage Growth 1983 **16** (1), 116

O'NEILL H M. Turnaround and Recovery: What Strategy do You Need? 1986 **19** (1), 80

OOSTERVELD J see NUENO P

OPPELLAND H J see GOHL J

ORSINI J-F. Artificial Intelligence: A Way Through the Strategic Planning Crisis? 1986 **19** (4), 71

OSMOND C N. Corporate Planning: Its Impact on Management 1971 **3** (3), 34

O'TOOLE D E see GREWE T et al

OVERBURY R E. Technological Forecasting—a Criticism of the Delphi Technique 1969 **1** (4), 76

OVERLAND T. Creating a Successful Marketing Strategy for UNI Insurance 1989 **22** (4), 25

P

PACKER J P L. The Projection of Financial Results 1971 **3** (3), 49

PADEVET K, SKALINA P. Technical Progress and the Work Force in Czechoslovakia 1969 **1** (4), 20

PAINE R E. Corporate Planning for a Town—A Case History 1975 **8** (5), 39

PALMA F. Computerized Analysis of Capital Projects by DCF Techniques 1972 **5** (4), 53

PALMER C. Using IT for Competitive Advantage at Thomson Holidays 1988 **21** (6), 26

PASS C. The Industrial Reorganisation Corporation—A Positive Approach to the Structure of Industry 1971 **4** (1), 63

PASS C L, SPARKES J R. U.K. Competition Policy Evaluated 1983 **16** (4), 76

PATEL P, YOUNGER M. A Frame of Reference for Strategy Development 1978 **11** (2), 6
PATEL R R. Planning for Electricity Generation in India 1983 **16** (4), 61
PATEL. R R see GARDE V D
PATERSON R R. Reorganization for Export at Ideal Standard 1970 **3** (2), 65
PATTAKOS A N. Growth in Activist Groups: How Can Business Cope? 1989 **22** (3), 98
PATTEN A J Van. Planning for Business with China 1974 **7** (4), 27
PAUL H see BLEICHER K
PAVITT K. Technological Innovation in European Industry: The Need for a World Perspective 1969 **2** (2), 8
PAYNE A, LUMSDEN C. Strategy Consulting—A Shooting Star? 1987 **20** (3), 53
PEARCE J A see HOLLOWAY C
PEARSON A. Planning of Research and Development 1972 **5** (1), 56
PEARSON A W see BALL D F
PEARSON B. A Business Development Approach to Planning 1976 **9** (6), 54
PEARSON G. The Strategic Discount—Protecting New Business Projects Against DCF 1986 **19** (1), 18
PEARSON G J. Promoting Entrepreneurship in Large Companies 1989 **22** (3), 87
PEARSON G J. Setting Corporate Objectives as a Basis for Action 1979 **12** (4), 13
PEARSON J V, MICHAEL R J. Zero-based Budgeting—A Technique for Planned Organizational Decline 1981 **14** (3), 68
PEARSON R. Avoiding Skill Shortages in the New Technologies 1985 **18** (4), 33
PECK S C see CHAO H P et al
PECOTICH A see LACZNIAK E R et al
PEEL D A. The Political Business Cycle—Have we Seen the End of it? 1982 **15** (1), 30
PENDLEBURY A J. Creating a Manufacturing Strategy to Suit Your Business 1987 **20** (6), 35
PENNINGTON M W. Why Has Planning Failed? 1972 **5** (1), 2
PENROD J I, DOUGLAS J V. How Belgian Businesses Make Strategic Planning Work 1988 **21** (2), 41
PERETZ D. R & D and Corporate Planning in Government 1972 **5** (4), 67
PERLITZ M. Country-Portfolio Analysis—Assessing Country Risk and Opportunity 1985 **18** (4), 11
PERRET D. Planning for Water Resources 1977 **10** (2), 65
PERRIN H F R. Management Training Film on Long Range Planning 1971 **4** (2), 67
PERRIN R. Long Range Planning: The Concept and the Need 1968 **1** (1), 3
PERRIN-PELLETIER F. 1992: A European Market for Cars? 1988 **21** (3), 27
PERRY P T. Organizational Implications for Long Range Planning 1975 **8** (1), 26
PERUTZ P. Implications of Qualitative Growth for a Business 1976 **9** (5), 42
PESSEMIER E A, KRANNET H C. Financial Planning and Control of Industrial Research and Development 1970 **3** (2), 32
PETERSON R A see MAHAJAN V et al
PETRONI G. Business Policy and Management Development in Large American and European Concerns 1978 **11** (3), 26
PETRONI G. Controlling Overseas Insurance Subsidiaries 1989 **22** (4), 106
PETRONI G. Strategic Planning and Research and Development—Can we Integrate Them? 1983 **16** (1), 15
PETRONI G. The Strategic Management of R & D, Part II—Organizing for Integration 1983 **16** (2), 51
PETRONI G. Who Should Plan Technological Innovation? 1985 **18** (5), 108
PETTIGREW A see WHIPP R et al
PETU A O see ADEYAMI K S
PETZALL I see JONSSON S
PEZIER J P. Turning Uncertainty to Advantage—Book Review Article 1980 **13** (3), 128
PEZIER J P see ABT R et al
PEZIER J P see MENKE M M et al

PILDITCH J. Product Planning—We're Still Getting it Upside Down 1981 **14** (5), 20
PINES D see BEN-SHAHAR H et al
PINK A I H. Strategic Leadership through Corporate Planning at ICI 1988 **21** (1), 18
PINNELL B. Changement: Understanding and Managing Business Change—Book Review Article 1980 **13** (5), 112
PINNELL B. Keeping Corporate Planning Relevant—A Key Task for the Planning Department 1986 **19** (1), 45
PINNELL B. The Role of the Board in Corporate Planning 1986 **19** (5), 27
PINNELL L B. The Development of Long Term Corporate Planning at Pilkington 1969 **1** (4), 14
PIPER J A. Classifying Capital Projects for Top Management Decision-Making 1980 **13** (3), 45
PIZMAN A, NEUMANN Y. Planning of Medical Manpower 1976 **9** (1), 44
PLOSILA W H see ALLEN D N
POCOCK B M. Futurology and Planning 1975 **8** (1), 64
POLLOCK A J. Banking: Time to Unbundle the Services? 1985 **18** (1), 36
POPP W see HINTERHUBER H
PORTER F E see ANSOFF H I et al
PORTER L H see WILEMON D L
PORTER R S. Private Investment in Developing Countries 1971 **4** (1), 58
PORWAL L S, SINGHVI S S. A Comparative Study of Capital Expenditure Evaluation 1978 **11** (5), 25
POST J E et al. The Public Affairs Function in American Corporations: Development and Relations with Corporate Planning 1982 **15** (2), 12
POTTS G W. Raising Productivity in Customer Services 1988 **21** (2), 15
POULSEN A. Planning for Personal Development 1977 **10** (5), 86
POWER P D. Computers and Financial Planning 1975 **8** (6), 53
POWER P D, MACGREGOR J M. Modelling for Corporate Planning—Book Review Article 1980 **13** (3), 125
PREBLE J F. Future Forecasting with LEAP 1982 **15** (4), 64
PRENTICE J. Competing with the Japanese Approach to Technology 1984 **17** (2), 25
PRICE D H R, THILLAINATHAN V. Policy Experiments with a Paper Industry Model 1981 **14** (1), 73
PUCCINI D S, MARLEY-CLARKE B W G. The Management of Offshore Resources—Some Implications of the 200-Mile Limit 1979 **12** (5), 8

Q

QUANLI C see YUJI W
QUINN J J. How Companies Keep Abreast of Technological Change 1985 **18** (2), 69
QURAESHI Z A see LUQMANI M et al

R

RABINO S. Foreign Competition for the U.S. Banking World 1984 **17** (3), 115
RADE N L see SMIT J D E
RADFORD G D. How Sumitomo Transformed Dunlop Tyres 1989 **22** (3), 28
RADOSEVICH R. Designing Innovating Systems 1977 **10** (2), 79
RADOSEVICH R see ANSOFF H I et al
RADOSEVICH R see HAYES R L
RAFFERTY J. Exit Barriers and Strategic Position in Declining Markets 1987 **20** (2), 86
RAMAMURTI R. Strategic Planning in Government-Dependent Businesses 1986 **19** (3), 62
RAMANANTSOA B see DETRIE J-P
RAMSEY J E. Selecting R & D Projects for Development 1981 **14** (1), 83
RANNEY J M see HUFF A S

RANSON S *see* HININGS B *et al*

RAO B B. Housing the Deprived and Underprivileged: India's Experience 1979 **12** (1), 75

RAO B B, NARAYANAMURTHY S G. Research and Planning Inputs to Metropolitan Development System 1977 **10** (5), 71

RAO R. India—The Plan for Steel 1978 **11** (4), 22

RAO T R. Scenarios for the Indian Iron and Steel Industry 1984 **17** (4), 91

RAPHAEL D E. Betting The Bank on Technology—Technology Strategic Planning at Bank of America 1986 **19** (2), 23

RAY G F. Development and Planning of Infra Structure 1971 **4** (2), 47

RAY G F. Energy: Long Term Prospects, On Some Recent Significant Energy Publications—Book Review Article 1978 **11** (2), 71

RAY G.F. Energy and Primary Materials 1982 **15** (5), 95

RAY G F. Energy Resources and Demand in This Century and Beyond 1973 **6** (1), 56

RAY G F. Innovation as the Source of Long Term Economic Growth 1980 **13** (2), 9

RAY G F. Raw Materials, Shortages and Producer Power 1975 **8** (4), 2

RAY K. Managerial Manpower Planning—A Systematic Approach 1977 **10** (2), 21

RAZELL E J. Planning in Whitehall—Is it Possible?—Will it Survive? 1980 **13** (1), 34

READ A R *see* BROWN G F

READ C N. Information Technology in Banking 1983 **16** (4), 21

REDDY J M *see* HINOMOTO H

REDDY Y R K. Cost-Benefit Analysis of Training—An Appraisal 1979 **12** (6), 50

REDMOND W H. Values in Forecasting and Planning 1978 **11** (3), 22

REDWOOD H. Setting Corporate Objectives 1977 **10** (6), 2

REDWOOD H. The Fisons Shareholder Survey 1971 **3** (3), 2

REDWOOD H. The Future for Pharmaceuticals in a Health Care Crisis 1989 **22** (1), 18

REED R, BUCKLEY M R. Strategy in Action—Techniques for Implementing Strategy 1988 **21** (3), 67

REGAN A C, REICHEL A. 'Shark Repellents' How to Avoid Hostile Takeovers 1985 **18** (6), 60

REGAN D E. Rationality in Policy Making: Two Concepts Not One 1978 **11** (5), 83

REICHEL A *see* REGAN A C

REICHERT SMITH K. Competing with AT & T 1985 **18** (1), 47

REID A. Seventh World Planning Congress—A Report 1979 **12** (2), 114

REILLY D N. Bringing Planning Systems to the Manager 1974 **7** (3), 45

REIMANN B C. Creating Value to Keep the Raiders at Bay 1989 **22** (3), 18

REINHARDT W A. An Early Warning System for Strategic Planning 1984 **17** (4), 25

RENDEIRO J O. How the Japanese Came to Dominate the Machine Tool Business 1985 **18** (3), 62

RENFRO W L. Forecasting the Impact of Public Policies 1980 **13** (4), 80

RESNIK A *see* MASON J B

RHODES D *et al*. Management Control for Effective Corporate Planning 1984 **17** (4), 115

RHODES J D, THAME S. Accelerating Innovation Through Real-time Workshops 1988 **21** (5), 41

RHYS G. Smaller Car Firms—Will They Survive? 1989 **22** (5), 22

RIBON B. The Experience Effect and Pricing for Agricultural Products 1981 **14** (4), 65

RICHARDS G *see* KENNY B *et al*

RICHERS R *see* BRANDT W K *et al*

RICHETTO J P. The Breakdown in Rural Communities—Can We Stop it? 1983 **16** (1), 97

RICHETTO J P. U.S. Industry: Decline and Fall? 1988 **21** (1), 35

RICKARDS T *see* STANDER A

RICKS D A, MAHAJAN V. Blunders in International Marketing: Fact or Fiction 1984 **17** (1), 78

RIDER R W. Making Strategic Planning Work in Local Government 1983 **16** (3), 73

RINGBAKK K-A. Organised Planning in Major U.S. Companies 1969 **2** (2), 46

RINGBAKK K-A. Strategic Planning in a Turbulent International Environment 1976 **9** (3), 2

RINGBAKK K-A. The Corporate Planning Life Cycle—An International Business Point of View 1972 **5** (3), 10

RINGGARD L. The Long-Term Business Strategy of a Danish Savings Bank 1985 **18** (6), 25

RISELEY M. A Current Awareness Service for Long Range Planning 1976 **9** (2), 109

ROBBIE K *see* WRIGHT M *et al*

ROBERTS K J. How to Define Market Segment 1986 **19** (4), 53

ROBERTSON J, MILLS R W. Company Failure or Company Health?— Techniques for Measuring Company Health 1988 **21** (2), 70

ROBINSON C. The Energy Market and Energy Planning 1976 **9** (6), 30

ROBINSON D F. Human Asset Accounting 1974 **7** (1), 58

ROBINSON J. Paradoxes in Planning 1986 **19** (6), 21

ROBINSON S J Q. Strategies for Declining Industrial Markets 1986 **19** (2), 72

ROBINSON S J Q. What Growth Rate Can You Achieve? 1979 **12** (4), 7

ROBINSON S J Q *et al*. The Directional Policy Matrix—Tool for Strategic Planning 1978 **11** (3), 8

RODRIGUES A F *see* FANNIN W R

RODRIGUEZ J I, KING W R. Competitive Information Systems 1977 **10** (6), 45

ROE P A. Modelling a Make or Buy Decision at ICI 1972 **5** (4), 21

ROELOFS F J W *see* KLOEZE H J *et al*

ROMAN Z. Long-Term Planning in Hungarian Industry 1970 **3** (2), 23

ROMANO D *see* HIGGINS J C

ROMPUY V van. Government Policies and Private Enterprise—Some Fundamental Trends 1975 **8** (4), 41

RONCHI L. The Decision-Making Process for Strategic Adaptation 1980 **13** (1), 48

RONDINELLI D A. Planning Development Projects: Lessons from Developing Countries 1979 **12** (3), 48

RONDINELLI D A. Public Planning and Political Strategy 1976 **9** (2), 75

ROPER D A. Planning Developments in British Nuclear Fuels Ltd 1978 **11** (5), 32

ROSE D. Woolworth's Drive for Excellence 1989 **22** (1), 28

ROSEN S. The Future from the Top: Presidential Perspectives on Planning—Part One 1974 **7** (2), 2

ROSEN S. The Future from the Top: Presidential Perspectives on Planning—Part Three 1974 **7** (4), 73

ROSEN S. The Future from the Top: Presidential Perspectives on Planning—Part Two 1974 **7** (3), 34

ROSENBERG R. Branch Banking in the Year 2000 1980 **13** (5), 65

ROSENBLOOM B, TRIPURANENI R V. Strategic Planning Catches on in U.S. Retailers 1985 **18** (4), 55

ROSENFIELD R *see* WHIPP R *et al*

ROSENSTEIN J. Why Don't U.S. Boards Get More Involved in Strategy? 1987 **20** (3), 30

ROSS J E, SHETTY Y K. Making Quality a Fundamental Part of Strategy 1985 **18** (1), 53

ROSS M H. Automated Manufacturing—Why is it Taking so Long? 1981 **14** (3), 28

ROSSITER P M. Corporate Planning at Dunlop 1979 **12** (1), 17

ROTHKOPF M H. An Economic Model of World Energy 1900—2020 1973 **6** (2), 43

ROTHWELL R, GARDINER P. Design and Competition in Engineering 1984 **17** (3), 78

ROTHWELL S. Productivity Improvement Through Reduced Labour Turnover 1982 **15** (2), 67

ROWLANDS D G. Technological Forecasting and the Delphi Technique—A Reply 1969 **2** (2), 78

ROWLEY C *see* BEAVIS B

ROY A. Acquiring Firms With Higher PE Ratios 1988 **21** (5), 96

ROZMAN R. Developing a Practical Planning System for a Steel Business 1986 **19** (2), 90

RUCKS A C *see* GINTER P M

RUE L W. Tools and Techniques of Long-Range Planners 1974 **7** (5), 61

RUE L W *see* BOULTON W R *et al*

RUFFAT J. Strategic Management of Public and Non-Market Corporations 1983 **16** (2), 74

RUGGLES R L. Developing Systems for Strategic Planning 1971 **3** (4), 39

RUGMAN A M. Strategies for National Competitiveness 1987 **20** (3), 92

RUGMAN C A. Corporate Planning in Local Government 1973 **6** (3), 17

RUSH K. Business Planning at Union Carbide 1968 **1** (2), 10

RUSSELL Colonel W N. Strategic Planning for the Armed Forces 1986 **19** (4), 41

RUSSELL J G R see BEAVAN P R et al

RUTENBERG D P. Planning for a Multi-National Synergy 1969 **2** (2), 24

RUTGERSWERKE A G see KEPPLER W et al

S

SACHDEV J C. Dilution of Ownership in Multinational Concerns 1977 **10** (5), 33

SACHDEVA P S. Development Planning—An Adaptive Approach 1984 **17** (5), 96

SADLER P. Management and The Social Environment 1975 **8** (4), 18

SADLER P, BARHAM K. Demographic and Social Trends 1970—1980 1982 **15** (5), 52

SALKIN G R see DOHRN P J

SALLENAVE J-P. The Uses and Abuses of Experience Curves 1985 **18** (1), 64

SALVESON M E. The Management of Strategy 1974 **7** (1), 19

SANDS S S see BROWN J K et al

SANTOS D L see HUNSUCKER J L et al

SARIN R L see NAIR K

SAUNDERS C B, TUGGLE F D. Why Planners Don't 1977 **10** (3), 19

SAUNDERS J see WONG V et al

SAVILLE J see SCHWARTZ P

SAWAYA R N see ARRINGTON C B

SAWYER G C. Innovation in Organizations 1978 **11** (6), 53

SCHERPENJUIJSEN ROM W E. Policy Making at Nederlandsche Middenstandsbank (NMB), Amsterdam 1980 **13** (5), 36

SCHMID G. International Security and the World Economy 1981 **14** (3), 21

SCHNAARS S P. How to Develop and Use Scenarios 1987 **20** (1), 105

SCHNEE J E see YAVITZ B

SCHNEIDER K R. Planning Without Vision—Roots of the Urban Disaster 1977 **10** (3), 71

SCHNEIDERMAN A see GRATWICK J et al

SCHOFIELD D A. Integration—The Key to Success with CAD/CAM 1987 **20** (3), 84

SCHOFIELD M, ARNOLD D. Strategies for Mature Business 1988 **21** (5), 69

SCHOLLHAMMER H. National Planning and the French Business Executive 1971 **3** (3), 22

SCHOLLHAMMER H see STEINER G A

SCHOLZ C. Corporate Culture and Strategy—The Problem of Strategic Fit 1987 **20** (4), 78

SCHOLZ C. Planning Procedures in German Companies—Findings and Consequences 1984 **17** (6), 94

SCHOTTA C see BAILEY D

SCHWANINGER M. A Practical Approach to Strategy Development 1987 **20** (5), 74

SCHWARTZ P, SAVILLE J. Multinational Business in the 1990s—A Scenario 1986 **19** (6), 31

SCHWENK C R. Management Illusions and Biases: Their impact on Strategic Decisions 1985 **18** (5), 74

SCORER R S. Air Pollution: its Implications for Industrial Planning 1970 **3** (2), 46

SCOTT M, BRUCE R. Five Stages of Growth in Small Business 1987 **20** (3), 45

SEABRIGHT J W. Turnaround at MFI—From a Troubled Mail-Order Firm to a Leading Furniture Retailer 1985 **18** (4), 27

SEDGWICK A. Keeping it Simple: A Case Study in Corporate Planning 1978 **11** (1), 10

SEGEV E see FRIEDMAN Y

SEGLUND R see KARAGOZOGLU N

SEILER R E, BOOCKHOLDT J L. Creative Development of Computerized Information Systems 1983 **16** (5), 100

SEMISTER L. Planning and Economics 1971 **4** (2), 63

SEPULVEDA C R. Systemic Health Planning 1979 **12** (3), 62

SERIZAWA Y. Planning for Growth in a Japanese Business 1989 **22** (2), 20

SETHI N K. Management Information Systems in Planning 1978 **11** (3), 75

SETHI N K. Strategic Planning System for Multinational Companies 1982 **15** (3), 80

SETHI N K et al. Can Technology be Managed Strategically? 1985 **18** (4), 89

SETHI S P. Opportunities and Pitfalls for Multinational Corporations in a Changed Political Environment 1987 **20** (6), 45

SEYNA E J. MBO: The Fad That Changed Management 1986 **19** (6), 116

SHAGORY G E. Development of Corporate Planning Staff 1975 **8** (1), 70

SHAH R K D. Strategic Planning for Power Equipment Manufacture 1989 **22** (5), 98

SHAMA A, JACOBS K. Solar Energy: Where Policy-makers and Conservationists Disagree 1982 **15** (1), 63

SHANKS M. 2000 or Bust!—Book Review Article 1979 **12** (1), 97

SHANKS M. Social Trends: Urgent Issues for Management 1982 **15** (1), 12

SHAPIRO H J see KALLMAN E A

SHARMA C K see SUBRAMANIAM S

SHARP E. The Relationship between Land Use and Economic Planning in the United Kingdom 1970 **3** (1), 16

SHAW B, STONE M. Competitive Superiority Through Data Base Marketing 1988 **21** (5), 24

SHAW J J see SHUMAN J C et al

SHAW R R. Safety in Commercial Aviation—The Long-Term Trends 1976 **9** (6), 24

SHAW S. The Crisis in the Jails 1986 **19** (3), 27

SHELLEY R, The Second Decade—The Economic Outlook for a Developing Nation 1976 **9** (4), 66

SHEPHERDSON P. Some Hints on Financing New Technologies 1985 **18** (6), 34

SHETTY Y K see ROSS J E

SHIM J K see SIEGEL J G

SHIM J P see LEE S M

SHIPPER F, WHITE C S. Linking Organizational Effectiveness and Environmental Change 1983 **16** (3), 99

SHIRLEY R C. Identifying the Levels of Strategy for a College or University 1983 **16** (3), 92

SHIRLEY R C. The Human Side of Merger Planning 1977 **10** (1), 35

SHIRLEY S. Corporate Strategy and Entrepreneurial Vision 1989 **22** (6), 107

SHORROCK J, DOBSON S. Economic Impact Reports—Management Controls for the 1980's 1979 **12** (6), 26

SHORROCK J E T see DOBSON S M

SHORT D see McEWEN N

SHRIVASTAVA P. Strategic Planning for MIS 1983 **16** (5), 19

SHRIVASTAVA P see SIOMKOS G

SHUMAN J C. Corporate Planning in the U.S. Regional Airline Industry 1973 **6** (4), 35

SHUMAN J C, BABSON C. Marketing and Airline Corporate Planning 1974 **7** (6), 68

SHUMAN J C et al. Strategic Planning in Smaller Rapid Growth Companies 1985 **18** (6), 48

SHUMAN J G. Corporate Planning in Small Companies—A Survey 1975 **8** (5), 81

SHURIG R. Morphology: A Tool for Exploring New Technology 1984 **17** (3), 129

SIEGEL J G, SHIM J K. Quality of Earnings: A Key Factor in Financial Planning 1981 **14** (6), 68

SIFFERT C see TENDAM H

SILLAR W. Planning for Disasters 1975 **8** (5), 2

SIMEONS C. Health and Safty Regulations—A Key Issue for the Board 1986 **19** (3), 86

SIMMIE J, BRADY R. Middle Class Decline in Post-industrial Society 1989 **22** (4), 52

SIMMONS W W. Corporate Planning: The Keystone of the Management System 1968 **1** (2), 2

SIMMONS W W. Practical Planning 1972 **5** (2), 32

SIMS D, EDEN C. Future Research—Working with Management Teams 1984 **17** (4), 51

SINGER A. Planning for Giro 1976 **9** (3), 38

SINGH J D see KAPOOR M C

SINGH K. Successful Strategies—The Story of Singapore Airlines 1984 **17** (5), 17

SINGHVI S S. A Practical Approach to Risk and Sensitivity Analyses 1980 **13** (1), 12

SINGHVI S S. Financial Planning in a Divisionalized Firm 1972 **5** (4), 15

SINGHVI S S. Game Theory Technique in Investment Planning 1974 **7** (4), 59

SINGHVI S S see JAIN S C

SINGHVI S S see PORWAL L S

SIOMKOS G, SHRIVASTAVA P. Strategies for Declining Businesses—Survival in the Fur Business 1987 **20** (6), 84

SIZER R. Key Issues in Managing Information 1983 **16** (5), 10

SKALINA P see PADEVET K

SKELCHER C see HININGS B et al

SKELTON J D. Investment Strategies for Pension Funds (in an Age of Inflation) 1973 **6** (4), 47

SKIPTON M D. Helping Managers to Develop Strategies 1985 **18** (2), 56

SKITMORE P M see HELPS I G

SKYTTE P see NIELSEN K S et al

SLATER A G. Developing Materials Management 1979 **12** (1), 28

SLATER A G. The Changing Pattern of Distribution 1977 **10** (4), 29

SLATTER S St P. Strategic Planning for Public Relations 1980 **13** (3), 57

SMALTER D J. Analytical Techniques in Planning 1968 **1** (1), 25

SMALTER D J. Anatomy of a Long Range Plan 1969 **1** (3), 2

SMIL V. Energy and the Environment—A Delphi Forecast 1972 **5** (4), 27

SMIL V, KUZ T. Energy and the Economy—A Global and National Analysis 1976 **9** (3), 65

SMITH C N. Predicting the Political Environment of International Business 1971 **4** (1), 7

SMITH D K see KING M

SMITH F M. Innovation: The Way Out of the Recession? 1982 **15** (1), 19

SMITH G. Planning for Productivity 1980 **13** (2), 52

SMITH J de, RADE N L. Rational and Non-Rational Planning 1980 **13** (2), 87

SMITH J G. Strategy—The Key to Planning in the Public Corporation 1981 **14** (6), 24

SMITH J G, FLECK V. Strategies of New Biotechnology Firms 1988 **21** (3), 51

SMITH L R, CAVUSGIL S T. Marketing Planning for Colleges and Universities 1984 **17** (6), 104

SNEATH C G see ADLER H S

SNEDDON L M. Decision Analysis for Top Management 1970 **3** (1), 50

SNOWDON M. Measuring Performance in Capital Project Management 1980 **13** (4), 51

SNYDER N, GLUECK W F. How Managers Plan—The Analysis of Managers' Activities 1980 **13** (1), 70

SOLOMON N see NEUBAUER F F

SOMBART N. Long-Term Planning and Forecasting in Europe 1972 **5** (2), 47

SONTHIEMER K C, THORN R S. Competitive Strategies in U.S. Banking 1986 **19** (1), 113

SPARKES J R see PASS C L

SPEKMAN R E. Competitive Procurement Strategies: Building Strength and Reducing Vulnerability 1985 **18** (1), 94

SPORN D L. Designing an ADP Planning Process 1978 **11** (1), 43

SPRUNG M R see LANZENAUER C H von

STACEY N A H. Mergers and British Industry 1968 **1** (1) 13

STAIT N H. Long Range Planning in a Fast Changing Fashion Market 1970 **3** (2), 55

STALLWORTHY E A see KHARBANDA O M

STANBRIDGE P J. Long Range Planning in Under-Developed Countries—A Case History 1969 **2** (2), 38

STANDER A, RICKARDS T. The Oracle that Failed 1975 **8** (5), 13

STEEL A see McEWEN N et al

STEELE D W. Alcohol: Is it Time to Say 'When'? 1987 **20** (5), 86

STEINER G A. Formal Strategic Planning in the United States Today 1983 **16** (3), 2

STEINER G A. Pitfalls in Multi-National Long-Range Planning 1975 **8** (2), 2

STEINER G A. The New Class of Chief Executive Officer 1981 **14** (4), 10

STEINER G A. Top Management's Role in Planning 1969 **1** (4), 2

STEINER G A, SCHOLLHAMMER H. Pitfalls in Multi-National Long-Range Planning 1975 **8** (2), 2

STEPHENS D B see KOHL J P

STEWART J D. Corporate Planning in Local Government 1973 **6** (2), 18

STIWENIUS O. Planning for a Rapidly Changing Environment in SAS 1985 **18** (2), 22

STOCK J R see LAMBERT D M

STONE M. Competing with Japan—The Rules of the Game 1984 **17** (2), 33

STONE M. Strategies for Marketing New Computer Products 1985 **18** (3), 41

STONE M see SHAW B

STONE M, SHAW R. Database Marketing for Competitive Advantage 1987 **20** (2), 12

STONE W R, HEANY D F. Dealing with a Corporate Identity Crisis 1984 **17** (1), 10

STOPFORD J M. Understanding Corporate Strategy 1982 **15** (6), 104

STOTLAND J A. Planning Acquisitions and Mergers 1976 **9** (1) 66

STRIGEL W H. Forecasting and the Business Cycle in an Uncertain Environment 1980 **13** (5), 21

STRIGEL W H. Planning in West German Industry 1970 **3** (1), 9

STRONG W B see McPHETERS I R

STUART C. Long Range Planning for Transport 1968 **1** (2), 38

STUART C F. Planning for Pensions in Inflation 1975 **8** (6), 13

STUBBART C. Are Environmental Scanning Units Effective? 1982 **15** (3), 139

STUBBART C. Why we Need a Revolution in Strategic Planning 1985 **18** (6), 68

STUBBS R J see HOYLE M H

SUBRAMANIAM S. Corporate Planning in Indian Railways—A Case Study 1979 **12** (3), 91

SUBRAMANIAM S. Engineering Manpower Planning in an Airline 1977 **10** (4), 56

SUBRAMANIAM S. Planning Problems of State Road Transport—India 1976 **9** (1), 77

SUBRAMANIAM S, BALASUBRAMANIAM R. Key Strategic Issues for Public Corporations 1974 **7** (5), 39

SUBRAMANIAM S, BALASUBRAMANIAM R. Urban Planning in India. A Case Study 1974 **7** (2), 39

SUBRAMANIAM S, SHARMA C K. Corporate Planning in Domestic Airlines—An Indian Case Study 1975 **8** (4), 64

SURREY A J see CHESSHIRE J A

SUSSMAN G see SHUMAN J C et al

SUTCLIFFE R. Financial Models in Corporate Planning—Book Review Article 1979 **12** (4), 91

SUZUKI N see KUDO H et al

SWAMIDASS P M. Planning for Manufacturing Technology 1987 **20** (5), 125

SWAN R T. A Concept of an Integrated Transport Model 1974 **7** (5), 17

SWANNACK A R. Should You Have a Payment System Based on Added Value? 1982 **15** (1), 76

SWART J M M de. Personnel Planning—A Strategic View 1979 **12** (3), 8

SWEETING R C see LITTLER D A

SZAKASITS G D. Selection of Mission Oriented Technical Programmes 1972 **5** (3), 58

SZEWCZAK E J. Building a Strategic Data Base 1988 **21** (2), 97

T

TACHIKAWA T see KUDO H et al

TAITZ L, HARMAN R. Assessing Trunk Roads—The Conservationist Viewpoint 1979 **12** (1), 56

TANBURN J. The Influence of Retailing Trends on the Food Industry 1975 **8** (3), 10

TARGETT D. Marketing Strategies for Scotch Whisky 1983 **16** (2), 65

TARR R J *see* HAWKINS K

TAYLOR B. Conflict of Values—The Central Strategy Problem 1975 **8** (6), 20

TAYLOR B. Corporate Planning for the 1990s: The New Frontiers 1986 **19** (6), 13

TAYLOR B. Introducing Strategic Management 1973 **6** (3), 34

TAYLOR B. Key Social Issues for European Business 1983 **16** (1), 42

TAYLOR B. Managing the Process of Corporate Development 1976 **9** (3), 81

TAYLOR B. New Dimensions in Corporate Planning 1976 **9** (6), 80

TAYLOR B. Strategic Planning for Resources 1974 **7** (4), 12

TAYLOR B. Strategic Planning for Social and Political Change 1974 **7** (1), 33

TAYLOR B. Strategic Planning—Which Style do you Need? 1984 **17** (3), 51

TAYLOR B. Strategies for Planning 1975 **8** (4), 27

TAYLOR B, FERRO L. Key Social Issues for European Business 1983 **16** (1), 42

TAYLOR B, IRVING P. Organized Planning in Major U.K. Companies 1971 **3** (4), 10

TAYLOR D E. Strategic Planning as an Organizational Change Process—Some Guidelines from Practice 1979 **12** (5), 43

TAYLOR D T, CARMEL A M. Dealing with Uncertainty in the Oil Industry 1981 **14** (2), 12

TAYLOR R N. Psychological Aspects of Planning 1976 **9** (2), 66

TAYLOR R N. Psychological Perspectives on the Future 1975 **8** (2), 51

TAYLOR W B. The Use of Life Cycle Costing in Acquiring Physical Assets 1981 **14** (6), 32

TEAGER R H. Shirt-Sleeved Approach to Long Range Planning for the Smaller Growing Corporation—Book Review Article 1980 **13** (6), 83

TEELING-SMITH G. Medicines in the 1990's: Experience with a Delphi Forecast 1971 **3** (4), 69

TENDAM H. Strategic Management in a Government Agency 1986 **19** (4), 78

TENDAM H, SIFFERT C. Strategic Management in a Firm of Consulting Engineers 1984 **17** (4), 21

TERRY P T. Mechanisms for Environmental Scanning 1977 **10** (3), 2

TEZIER J P *see* ABT R *et al*

THAKUR M. Planning for Hospitals: No Focus, No Strategy 1985 **18** (6), 77

THAME S *see* RHODES J D

THILLAINATHAN V *see* PRICE D H R

THOMAS C H. Product Forecasting: The BAC 3–11 Airliner 1970 **2** (4), 36

THOMAS F A. Corporate Planning in an International Environment 1974 **7** (5), 13

THOMAS H. Risk Analysis and the Formulation of Acquisition/Diversification Strategies 1983 **16** (2), 28

THOMAS H A. The Planned Marketing of Textiles 1971 **3** (3), 54

THOMAS H *see* BUNN D

THOMAS H *see* HERTZ D B

THOMAS J. Force Field Analysis: A New Way to Evaluate your Strategy 1985 **18** (6), 54

THOMAS M J *see* LINNEMAN R E

THOMAS P S. Environmental Scanning—The State of the Art 1980 **13** (1), 20

THOMAS R. Corporate Strategic Planning in a University 1980 **13** (5), 70

THOMPSON G C *see* BROWN J K *et al*

THOMPSON Sir P. The NFC Buy-Out—A New Form of Industrial Enterprise 1985 **18** (5), 19

THOMPSON W *et al.* Canadian Industrial Policy—Simulation and Analysis 1973 **6** (4), 66

THORBURN A. The Modern Approach to Sub-Regional Planning 1970 **2** (3), 60

THORN R S *see* SONTHIEMER K C

THORNLEY I A. Creating a Productive Culture at Shell Chemicals 1988 **21** (3), 34

THOROMAN D G. Strategic Planning in IBM 1971 **4** (1), 1

THRING M W. Automation in Coal Mining 1983 **16** (4), 66

TIBBITS G L. Establishing Goals 1979 **12** (2), 97

TIELEMAN T M. Portfolio Planning at Akzo 1981 **14** (6), 17

TOBE E I. Planning for Leisure in Sweden 1971 **4** (1), 50

TOLL R. Analytical Techniques for New Product Planning 1969 **1** (3), 52

TOLLEY L. Management in the 1980s—Key Issues and Priorities 1981 **14** (1), 55

TOMLINSON D S. Developing a Data Base for Planning—A Shipping Industry Case 1980 **13** (6), 42

TOPFER A. Corporate Planning and Control in German Industry 1978 **11** (1), 59

TORKZADEH G *see* GUPTA Y P

TOWNSEND D *see* WRIGHT P *et al*

TOZER E E. Developing Strategies for Management Information Systems 1986 **19** (4), 31

TREVOR M. Quality Control—Learning From the Japanese 1986 **19** (5), 46

TRIPURANENI R V *see* ROSENBLOOM B

TRONDSEN E, EDFELT R. New Opportunities in Global Services 1987 **20** (5), 53

TROWBRIDGE A V. 'Titanic Planning' in an Uncertain Environment 1988 **21** (2), 86

TUGGLE F D *see* SAUNDERS C B

TURBIL J-P. How Elf Aquitaine Provides Technological Assistance to Small Businesses 1986 **19** (3), 59

TURNBULL P. Planning for Leisure 1975 **8** (5), 55

TURNER D. Corporate Planning Within the British Airports Authority 1986 **19** (3), 35

TURNER G. A New Strategy at Barclays 1985 **18** (3), 12

TURNER G. GEC's Pragmatic Planners 1985 **18** (1), 12

TURNER G. How GKN Plans Now 1984 **17** (4), 12

TURNER G. How Top Management is Changing Dutch Business 1987 **20** (6), 10

TURNER G. ICI Becomes Proactive 1984 **17** (6), 12

TURNER G. Inside Europe's Giant Companies: Cultural Revolution at Philips 1986 **19** (4), 12

TURNER G. Inside Europe's Giant Companies: Nestlé Finds a Better Formula 1986 **19** (3), 12

TURNER G. Inside Europe's Giant Companies: Olivetti Goes Bear-hunting 1986 **19** (2), 13

TURNER G. Inside Europe's Giant Companies—Daimler-Benz Goes Top of the Leauge 1986 **19** (5), 12

TURNER G. The Future Ambitions of Japan's Financial Giants 1987 **20** (5), 11

TURNER R K, GRACE R P. Forecasting the Market Demand for Waste Paper 1977 **10** (3), 30

TWISS B C. Developing and Implementing a Strategy for Production 1974 **7** (2), 31

TWISS B C. Management and the Micro-Electronic Revolution—Part 1—Book Review Article 1981 **14** (5), 101

TWISS B C. Management and the Micro-Electronic Revolution—Part II—Book Review Article 1981 **14** (6), 83

TWISS B C. Recent Trends in Long Range Forecasting for Technology-Based Organizations—Book Review Article 1979 **12** (2), 120

TWISS B C. Strategy for Research and Development 1970 **3** (1), 57

TYSON W J, COCHRANE R L D. Corporate Planning and Project Evaluation in Urban Transport 1981 **14** (5), 62

TZANNATOS Z. Narrowing the Gap—Equal Pay in Britain 1970–1986 1987 **20** (2), 69

U

UNGER L. Strategic Planning for Commodities and Specialities 1983 **16** (4), 12

UNNI V K. The Role of Strategic Planning in Small Businesses 1981 **14** (2), 54

URI N D. Forecasting Mexico's Oil Potential 1982 **15** (4), 86

V

VALENTINE S. The Stock Exchange After the Big Bang 1988 **21** (2), 35

van DAM A. Joint Planning for an Interdependent World 1975 **8** (6), 8

van DAM A. Water Supply—The Case for Joint Planning 1978 **11** (1), 69

van Den KROONENBERG H H. Getting a Quicker Pay-off From R & D 1989 **22** (5), 51

van DIERDONCK R *see* CAELDRIES F

van GUNSTEREN L A. Planning for Technology as a Corporate Resource 1987 **20** (2), 51

van HAM K, WILLIAMS R. The Quest for Quality at Philips 1986 **19** (6), 25

van RHIJN B M *see* EPPINK D J

VANDERMERWE S. Strategies for a Pan European Market 1989 **22** (3), 45

VANDORFFY J. Mathematical Models in National Planning 1973 **6** (1), 42

VARADARAJAN P R. Marketing in Developing Countries: The New Frontier 1984 **17** (6), 118

VARADARAJAN P R. Vaulting Trade Barriers: The Japanese Approach 1985 **18** (1), 73

VASCONCELLOS E SA J. The Impact of Key Success Factors on Company Performance 1988 **21** (6), 56

VELLMANN K *see* GRUNEWALD H-G

VENNING M. Manpower Studies for Industrial Sectors 1974 **7** (3), 27

VENU S. Corporate Planning in a Developing Economy: Indian Experience 1972 **5** (3), 29

VENU S. Energy Planning in India 1982 **15** (3), 146

VENU S. Environmental Pollution and Economic Growth: Implications for Corporate Planning With an Indian Case Study 1974 **7** (3), 49

VERHULST M. Planning for Industrial Development in Newly Independent Countries—An Operational Approach 1975 **8** (3), 79

VERRAVER J *see* LEFEBVRE M *et al*

VERTINSKY I *see* THOMPSON W *et al*

VERVOORDELFONK F *see* ADOLFSE J

VESPER V D. Strategic Mapping—A Tool for Corporate Planners 1979 **12** (6), 75

VICHAS R P, CONTAS K. Public Planners and Business Investors—Why Can't They Collaborate? 1981 **14** (3), 77

VICKERS G. Community Without Consensus?—Book Review Article 1981 **14** (2), 90

VINCENT J D. Long Range Planning of Paper and Board Supplies 1980 **13** (2), 60

VORA J A *see* KARGER D W

VOSSBERG H. Bayer Reorganizes in Response to Growth 1985 **18** (6), 13

VRAT P *see* KUMAR R

W

WADE D P *see* ROBINSON S J Q *et al*

WAGLE B. Management Science and Strategic Planning 1971 **3** (3), 26

WAGLE B V *see* HOWARD K

WAGNER G R. Strategic Thinking Supported by Risk Analysis 1980 **13** (3), 61

WAKERLY R G. PIMS: A Tool for Developing Competitive Strategy 1984 **17** (3), 92

WALDING P. Planning and Social Change 1974 **7** (5), 51

WALKER R F. Portfolio Analysis in Practice 1984 **17** (3), 63

WALLER R A. Assessing the Impact of Technology on the Environment 1975 **8** (1), 43

WALLEY K H. The Prospect for Petrochemicals—Merger and Rationalization? 1982 **15** (1), 47

WALSH C, MOCK E. Setting Corporate Objectives Using Market Required Earnings 1979 **12** (5), 54

WALTERS D, KNEE D. Competitive Strategies in Retailing 1989 **22** (6), 74

WARD E P. Focusing Innovative Effort Through a Convergent Dialogue 1980 **13** (6), 32

WARD E P. Organization for Technological Change 1981 **14** (4), 121

WARD E P. Planning for Technological Innovation 1981 **14** (2), 59

WARD J M. Integrating Information Systems into Business Strategies 1987 **20** (3), 79

WARD S C. How to Computerize Your Personnel Planning 1987 **20** (4), 88

WARDE W D *see* GODIWALLA Y M *et al*

WARNER F. Design and Location of Plant—A Case Study 1969 **1** (3), 68

WARRINGTON M B. Will Hong Kong's Entrepreneurs Move to Planning? 1982 **15** (3), 168

WASDELL D. Long Range Planning and the Church 1980 **13** (3), 99

WEAVER N I *see* KOPELMAN J B

WEBER C E. Strategic Thinking—Dealing with Uncertainty 1984 **17** (5), 60

WEBER J A. Planning Corporate Growth with Inverted Product Life Cycles 1976 **9** (5), 12

WEDLEY W C. New Uses of Delphi in Strategy Formulation 1977 **10** (6), 70

WEEKS J. Planning for Physical Distribution 1977 **10** (3), 64

WEIHRICH H. The TOWS Matrix—A Tool for Situational Analysis 1982 **15** (2), 54

WEIR G A. Developing Strategies: A Practical Approach 1974 **7** (5), 7

WELCH J B. Strategic Planning Could Improve Your Share Price 1984 **17** (2), 144

WELLS G E. The Revolution in Building Societies 1989 **22** (5), 30

WELLS J D. Computerised Industrial Forecasting for Planning in Central Government 1971 **4** (2), 41

WELTER P. Financial Aspects of Company Planning 1973 **6** (1), 36

WERNHAM R. Bridging the Awful Gap Between Strategy and Action 1984 **17** (6), 34

WESSEMA J A. How to Assess the Strategic Benefit of a Capital Investment 1984 **17** (6), 25

WESTGATE K *see* O'KEEFE P

WESTON F C. An Organizational Study Approach to Planning Problems in an Industrial-Military Activity 1973 **6** (4), 58

WHALEY R. Data Bank on the Future Business Environment 1984 **17** (4), 83

WHALEY R, BURROWS B C. How Will Technology Impact Your Business? 1987 **20** (5), 109

WHEALE P R. The Future of the British Breakfast Cereals Industry 1978 **11** (2), 60

WHEATLEY JR W *see* MADDOX N *et al*

WHEELWRIGHT S *see* MAKRIDAKIS S

WHIPP R *et al*. Managing Strategic Change in a Mature Business 1989 **22** (6), 92

WHIPPLE III W. Evaluating Alternative Strategies Using Scenarios 1989 **22** (3), 82

WHITE C S *see* SHIPPER F

WHITE M, LEIGH A. Diagnosing Long-Term Information Problems 1974 **7** (1), 27

WHITEHEAD D D *see* GUP B E

WHITING P L. Waste Paper-Case for Government Action 1975 **8** (5), 23

WIEDEMANN P. PINCO: Personal Information and Confidentiality Controls 1983 **16** (5), 107

WILEMON D L, PORTER L H. A Systems Approach to Corporate Development 1972 **5** (1), 46

WILKES M V. Forecasting the Future—Developments in Computers 1970 **2** (3), 15

WILLDER S. Directing Technological Development—The Role of the Board 1985 **18** (4), 44

WILLIAMS D G, HARRIS D J. Corporate Management and Planning in Local Government 1976 **9** (4), 46

WILLIAMS P J *see* CARTER R D

WILLIAMS R *see* Van HAM K

WILLIAMS S. The Frontiers of Government 1972 **5** (3), 21

WILLIAMSON E I, LONGLEY R C M. Alternative Fuels for Automobiles—the Medium-Term Realities 1982 **15** (2), 32

WILLS G. The Preparation and Deployment of Technological Forecasts 1970 **2** (3), 44

WILMOT R. Computer Integrated Management—The Next Competitive Breakthrough 1988 **21** (6), 65

WILMOT R W. Change in Management and the Management of Change 1987 **20** (6), 23

WILSON A C B. Human and Organization Problems in Corporate Planning 1972 **5** (1), 67

WILSON A C B. The Annual Planning Cycle 1971 **3** (4), 62

WILSON A *see* LOCKE H B *et al*

WILSON B. Towards More Productive Industrial Relations 1983 **16** (6), 35

WILSON D G. The Future of the Bicycle—Its Problems and Its Potentialities 1975 **8** (2), 81

WILSON H K *see* JAUCH L R

WILSON I. Competitive Strategies for Service Businesses 1988 **21** (6), 10

WILSON I. Restructuring of Competition: The New Strategic Imperative 1985 **18** (1), 19

WILSON I. The Current State of Planning in North America: Introduction to the Special Issue 1983 **16** (3), 2

WILSON I. The Stategic Management of Technology: Corporate Fad or Strategic Necessity 1986 **19** (2), 21

WILSON I H. Future Forecasting for Strategic Planning at General Electric 1973 **6** (2), 39

WILSON I H. Reforming the Strategic Planning Process: Integration of Social and Business Needs 1974 **7** (5), 2

WILSON L S. A Unique Event and Delphi Technique 1977 **10** (1), 79

WILSON L S. Managing in the Competitive Environment 1984 **17** (1), 59

WILSON L S. The World's Changing Climate—Some Issues for Planners 1981 **14** (5), 83

WILSON L S *see* MACHIN J L J

WILSON L *see* BURKE T

WILSON P, GORB P. How Large and Small Firms Can Grow Together 1983 **16** (2), 19

WILSON P N, BRIGSTOCKE T. Energy and U.K. Agriculture 1977 **10** (5), 64

WIND J *see* CARDOZO R N

WIND Y *see* MAHAJAN V

WINDSOR D, GREANIAS G. Long Range Planning in a Politicized Environment 1983 **16** (3), 82

WINKEL J M M van de *see* WISSEMA J G

WISEMAN C. Strategic Planning in the Scottish Health Service—A Mixed-Scanning Approach 1979 **12** (2), 103

WISSEMA J G. Futures Research—Is it Useful? 1981 **14** (2), 29

WISSEMA J G. How to Assess the Strategic Value of a Capital Investment 1984 **17** (6), 25

WISSEMA J G. The Modern Prophets—How Can They Help Us? 1982 **15** (4), 126

WISSEMA J G, WINKEL J M M van de. Management in the Eighties: How is the Job Changing? 1981 **14** (4), 21

WITHERS R M J. Planning for Increased Productivity 1978 **11** (4), 16

WONG V *et al*. Japanese Marketing Strategies in the United Kingdom 1987 **20** (6), 54

WOOD D R. Long Range Planning in Large United States Banks 1980 **13** (3), 91

WOOD D R *see* LaFORGE L

WOOD D *see* FILDES R *et al*

WOOD E G. Industrial Performance Analysis—Book Review Article 1978 **11** (4), 91

WOOD E G. Setting Objectives in Terms of Added Value 1979 **12** (4), 2

WOOD P. The Use of Computers in Town Planning 1971 **3** (3), 59

WOODBURN T I. Corporate Planning in South African Companies 1984 **17** (1), 84

WOOLLER J *see* GRINYER P H

WORCESTER R M. Managing Change 1970 **3** (1), 31

WORCESTER R M. Planning for Growth in Leading U.S. Companies 1970 **2** (3), 8

WORCESTER R M. The Thatcher Revolution—Radical Policies in a Changing Society 1989 **22** (4), 72

WRAY M, NORBURN D. Japan's Drive for the European Car Market—Lessons from U.S. Experience 1987 **20** (4), 60

WRIGHT D. New Zealand—a Newcomer to Planning 1982 **15** (3), 122

WRIGHT M *et al*. Management Buy-outs in Britain—A Monograph 1987 **20** (4), 38

WRIGHT M *see* RHODES D *et al*

WRIGHT P. Corporate Strategy at Admiram Manufacturing Company: An Iranian Case Study 1980 **13** (3), 115

WRIGHT P *et al*. The Developing World to 1990: Trends and Implications for Multinational Business 1982 **15** (4), 116

WRIGHT R W, Planning the Future Raw Material Supply 1976 **9** (1), 12

WRIGHT V C. Corporate Planning in the Mineral Industry 1976 **9** (2), 19

WUBBENHORST K L. Life Cycle Costing for Construction Projects 1986 **19** (4), 87

Y

YAMAMOTO S. Japan's New Industrial Era—I. Restructuring Traditional Industries 1986 **19** (1), 61

YAMAMOTO S. Japan's New Industrial Era—II. The New Information and Services Industries 1986 **19** (2), 65

YAMANOUCHI T. Breakthrough: The Development of the Canon Personal Copier 1989 **22** (5), 11

YAVAS U *see* LUQMANI M *et al*

YAVITZ B, SCHNEE J E. Managing the Impacts of Large Public Programs 1977 **10** (1), 65

YELLE L E. Adding Life Cycles to Learning Curves 1983 **16** (6), 82

YOO S. An Information System for Just-In-Time 1989 **22** (6), 117

YOO S, DIGMAN L A. Decision Support System: A New Tool for Strategic Management 1987 **20** (2), 114

YOSHIHARA H. The Japanese Multinational 1977 **10** (2), 41

YOUNG R, HUSSEY D E. Corporate Planning at Rolls-Royce Motors Limited 1977 **10** (2), 2

YOUNGER M. Assessing Opportunities for Diversification—An Analytical Approach 1984 **17** (4), 10

YOUNGER M *see* PATEL P

YUJI W, QUANLI C. Regional Planning in China—A Systems Engineering Approach 1987 **20** (1), 99

Z

ZABRISKIE N, HUELLMANTEL A. Implementing Strategies for Human Resources 1989 **22** (2), 70

ZENTNER R D. Scenarios, Past, Present and Future 1982 **15** (3), 12

ZETTERGREN L. Financial Issues in Strategic Planning 1975 **8** (3), 23

ZIEMER D R. Quantifying Level of Investment in Growth and Renewal 1976 **9** (4), 2

ZIEMER D R, MAYCOCK P D. A Framework for Strategic Analysis 1973 **6** (2), 6

ZIMMERMAN F M. Managing a Successful Turnaround 1989 **22** (3), 105

ZIMMERMAN F M. Turnaround—A Painful Learning Process 1986 **19** (4), 104

ZINSER P H *see* LA LONDE B J

ZOPPOTH R C. The Use of Systems Analysis in New Product Development 1972 **5** (1), 23

ZVEGINTZOV M. Technological Innovation and Long Range Planning 1968 **1** (2), 46

Subject Index

A

ACCOUNTING
The Use of Life Cycle Costing in Acquiring Physical Assets (Taylor W B, Kent County Council) 1981 **14** (6), 32

ACQUISITIONS
Acquiring Companies in the U.S.A. (Adler H S, Peat Marwick Group New York; Sneath C G, Peat Marwick London) 1987 **20** (2), 42

Acquiring Firms With Higher PE Ratios (Roy A) 1988 **21** (5), 96

Acquisitions—Techniques for Measuring Strategic Fit (Clarke C J, Smith Trust) 1987 **20** (3), 12

Appraising Companies for Acquisition (Cameron D, Consultant) 1977 **10** (4), 21

Assessing the Risks in Acquisitions—The Risk-Chance Analysis (Neuburger K) 1986 **19** (3), 41

Does Planning Pay? The Effect of Planning on Success of Acquisitions in American Firms (Ansoff H I, Avner J, Brandenburg R G, Porter F E, Radosevich R, Vanderbilt U) 1970 **3** (2), 2

Growth by Acquisition (Buckley A, Redland) 1975 **8** (4), 53

How much is an Acquisition Worth? (Kastens M L, Consultant) 1973 **6** (2), 52

The NFC Buy-Out—A New Form of Industrial Enterprise (Thompson Sir P, Nat Freight Consortium) 1985 **18** (5), 19

Planning Acquisitions and Mergers (Stotland J A, A.T. Kearney) 1976 **9** (1), 66

The Role of Marketing in Evaluating Acquisitions (Nicholls J R, Bath U; Broadbent D A, Royal Melbourne Inst of Technology) 1979 **12** (1), 67

'Shark Repellents': How to Avoid Hostile Takeovers (Regan A C, Reichel A, New York U) 1985 **18** (6), 60

Strategy and Tactics for Resisting Take-Over (Lofthouse S, Industrial Economist) 1984 **17** (4), 38

Success and Failure in Management Buyouts (Birley S, Notre Dame U) 1984 **17** (3), 32

see also **MERGERS**

ADDED VALUE *see* **VALUE ADDED**

ADVERTISING
Long Range Planning and Advertising (Doyle P, Bradford U) 1977 **10** (6), 16

Trends and Prospects (Fletcher W, Fletcher Shelton) 1978 **11** (6), 37

AEROSPACE INDUSTRY
The NASA Approach (Beggs J M, NASA) 1984 **17** (2), 12

Planning for a Rapidly Changing Environment in SAS (Stiwenius O, Consultant) 1985 **18** (2), 22

AFRICA
Corporate Planning for Asia, Latin America, and Africa (Dam A van, CPC International Inc) 1972 **5** (4), 2

AGRICULTURAL INDUSTRY
Energy and U.K. Agriculture (Wilson P N, Brigstocke T, BOCM Silcock) 1977 **10** (5), 64

The Experience Effect and Pricing for Agricultural Products (Ribon B, Consultant) 1981 **14** (4), 65

AIR POLLUTION
Air Pollution: its Implications for Industrial Planning (Scorer R S, Imperial Coll) 1970 **3** (2), 46

AIRCRAFT INDUSTRY
Product Forecasting: The BAC 3–11 Airliner (Thomas C H, BAC) 1970 **2** (4), 36

AIRLINES
Airline Corporate Planning—A Conceptual Framework (Bouamrene M A, Flavel R, Imperial Coll of Science and Technology) 1980 **13** (1), 62

Airline Deregulation: Why the Supporters Lost Out (Marcus A A, U of Minnesota Sch of Mgt) 1987 **20** (1), 90

Corporate Panning in Domestic Airlines—An Indian Case Study (Subramaniam S, Sharma C K, Indian Inst of Mgt) 1975 **8** (4), 64

Corporate Planning in the U.S. Regional Airline Industry (Shuman J C, Babson Coll) 1973 **6** (4), 35

Engineering Manpower Planning in an Airline (Subramaniam S, Indian Inst of Mgt) 1977 **10** (4), 56

Lessons of Privatization (Lord King) 1987 **20** (6), 18

Marketing and Airline Corporate Planning (Shuman J C, Babson Coll) 1974 **7** (6), 68

Safety in Commercial Aviation—The Long-Term Trends (Shaw R R, IATA) 1976 **9** (6), 24

Strategies of the United States Airlines (Huffmire D W, Connecticut) 1975 **8** (2), 72

ARTIFICIAL INTELLIGENCE
Artificial Intelligence: A Way Through the Strategic Planning Crisis? (Orsini J-F, Consultant) 1986 **19** (4), 71

Developing Knowledge-based Systems for Strategic Corporate Planning (Mockler R J, Dologite D G) 1988 **21** (1), 97

Strategic Management and Artificial Intelligence (Holloway C, Coll of Business Admin) 1983 **16** (5), 89

Towards the Library of the Future (Feigenbaum E A) 1989 **22** (1), 118

ASIA
Corporate Planning for Asia, Latin America, and Africa (Dam A van, CPC International Inc) 1972 **5** (4), 2

The New Industrializing Counties of Asia—Perspectives and Opportunities (Lasserre P, INSEAD) 1981 **14** (3), 36

Why Europeans are Weak in Asia—An Organizational Perspective (Lasserre P) 1988 **21** (4), 25

AUSTRALIA
BHP Reorganizes for Global Competition (Lewis G, Clark J, Moss B) 1988 **21** (3), 18

Buying is Marketing Too—Japan's Influence on the Australian Coal Trade (Dowling G, U of New South Wales) 1987 **20** (1), 35

Planning and Performance in Australian Retailing (Burt D N, Naval Postgraduate Sch) 1978 **11** (3), 62

Productivity Planning: A Central Issue for Australian Management (Cameron M J, Australian Paper Manufacturers) 1982 **15** (3), 157

Scenario Planning for Australia (Galer G, Shell; Kasper W, New South Wales U) 1982 **15** (4), 50

Strategic Alternatives for Australian Iron-Ore Producers (Frost F, Australian Inst of Technology) 1986 **19** (1) 89

A Tough Future for Australian Business (Laczniak E R, Pecotich A, Carroll B) 1989 **22** (1), 48

AUSTRALIAN
Australian Industry: Sophisticated Planning and Weak R & D? (Christodoulou C) 1988 **21** (1), 82

AUTOMATION
Automated Manufacturing—Why is it Taking so Long (Ross M H, Arthur D. Little) 1981 **14** (3), 28

Automation in Coal Mining (Thring M W, Queen Mary Coll) 1983 **16** (4), 66

The Service Sector Revolution: The Automation of Services (Collier D A, Virginia U) 1983 **16** (6), 10

Strategic Control of Factory Automation (Meredith J R) 1987 **20** (6), 106

B

BANKING
Assessing the Performance of a Development Bank (Jain P K) 1989 **22** (6), 100

Bank Management and Strategic Planning for the 1980s (Mason J B, Mayer M L, Alabama U) 1979 **12** (4), 35

Banking: Time to Unbundle the Services? (Pollock A J, Continental Illinois) 1985 **18** (1), 36

Betting The Bank on Technology—Strategic Planning at Bank of America (Raphael D E, Bank of America) 1986 **19** (2), 23

Branch Banking in the Year 2000 (Rosenberg R, Wells Fargo Bank) 1980 **13** (5), 65

Building a Customer-orientated Organization (Cornish F) 1988 **21** (3), 105

Competition in Retail Banking (Crawley F W, Lloyds Bank) 1982 **15** (3), 71

Competitive Strategies in U.S. Banking (Sontheimer C K, Thorn R S, U of Pittsburgh) 1986 **19** (1), 113

The Control of Bank Exposure to Risk (Moore V, Consultant) 1979 **12** (5), 35

Corporate Planning and Control Systems in Williams & Glyn's Bank (Dugdale I, Williams & Glyn's Bank) 1978 **11** (5), 41

Corporate Planning and Modelling in a Large Bank (Degueldre J, Banque Bruxelles Lambert) 1980 **13** (4), 43

The Current Practice of Bank Long-Range Planning (Kudla R J, Coll of Business Administration) 1982 **15** (3), 132

Foreign Competition for the U.S. Banking World (Rabino S, Northeastern U) 1984 **17** (3), 115

The Future Ambitions of Japan's Financial Giants (Turner G) 1987 **20** (5), 11

Information Technology in Banking (Read C N, Postal HQ) 1983 **16** (4), 21

Long Range Planning in Large United States Banks (Wood D R, Virginia Commonwealth U) 1980 **13** (3), 91

The Long-Term Business Strategy of a Danish Savings Bank (Ringgard L, SDS Savings Bank) 1985 **18** (6), 25

A New Strategy at Barclays (Turner G) 1985 **18** (3), 12

Operations Research and Bank Planning (Blumberg L F, Cotter L, Consultants) 1975 **8** (5), 29

Personnel Policy and Manpower Planning in Banking (Lyons T P, Williams & Glyn's Bank) 1979 **12** (5), 2

Planning for Banking—The Indian Experience (Godse V T, Nat Inst of Bank Management, Bombay) 1986 **19** (1), 105

Planning for Giro (Singer A, Nat Giro) 1976 **9** (3), 38

Policy Making at Nederlandsche Middenstandsbank (NMB), Amsterdam (Scherpenhuifsem Rom, W E) 1980 **13** (5), 36

Rationalizing Branch Banking (Kitching D W C, Midland Bank) 1982 **15** (1), 53

Re-designing Bank Service Systems for Effective Marketing (Gupta Y P, Torkzadeh G) 1988 **21** (6), 38

Shaping the Future of Retail Banking (Morison I, Frazer P, Consultants) 1982 **15** (4), 105

Strategic Issues for the Trustee Savings Banks (Marshall I, TSB Group) 1985 **18** (4), 39

Strategic Planning in Banks — Does it Pay? (Gup B E, Whitehead D D) 1989 **22** (1), 124

Strategic Planning and Policy Making in Banks (Adolfse J, Vervoordelfonk F, Central Rabobank) 1979 **12** (3), 73

BIBLIOGRAPHY

A European Bibliography of Corporate Planning, 1972 (Kettlewell P J, Sandoz Products & Wander) 1974 **7** (1), 72

BICYCLE INDUSTRY

The Future of the Bicycle—Its Problems and Its Potentialities (Wilson D G, Massachusetts Inst of Technology) 1975 **8** (2), 81

BIO-TECHNOLOGY

Boning in on Biotechnology—Part II—Book Review Article (Cantley M F, Commission of European Communities) 1982 **15** (3), 181

Boning up on Biotechnology—Part I—Book Review Article (Cantley M F, Commission of European Communities) 1982 **15** (1), 110

Strategies of New Biotechnology Firms (Smith J G, Fleck V) 1988 **21** (3), 51

BOARD OF DIRECTORS

The Directors' Role in Planning: What Information Do They Need? (Aram J D, Cowen S S, Case Wstrn Reserve U Ohio) 1986 **19** (2), 117

Health and Safty Regulations—A Key Issue for the Board (Simeons C, Consultant) 1986 **19** (3), 86

The Role of the Board in Corporate Planning (Pinnell B) 1986 **19** (5) 27

What is the Board of Directors Good For? (Bavly D, Horwath Bavly Millner & Co., Tel Aviv) 1986 **19** (3), 20

BUDGETING

The World of Program Budgeting (Fisher G H, Rand) 1969 **2** (1), 50

see also **CAPITAL BUDGETING**

BUSINESS APPRAISAL

Appraising Companies for Acquisition (Cameron D, Consultant) 1977 **10** (4), 21

The Corporate Appraisal: Assessing Company Strengths and Weaknesses (Hussey D E, Elders & Fyffes) 1968 **1** (2), 19

BUSINESS CYCLES

Forecasting and the Business Cycle in an Uncertain Environment (Strigel W H, CIRET Centre) 1980 **13** (5), 21

Planning for the U.S. Political Cycle (Marcus A A, Mevorach B) 1988 **21** (4), 50

The Political Business Cycle—Have we Seen the End of it? (Peel D A, Liverpool U) 1982 **15** (1), 30

BUSINESS DEVELOPMENT

Corporate Development—Preferred Strategies in U.K. Companies (Littler D A, U of Manchester; Sweeting R C, UMIST) 1987 **20** (2), 125

BUSINESS ENVIRONMENT

Analyzing Industrial Trends—A Collaborative Approach (McCann J E, U of Florida) 1985 **18** (5), 116

Are Environmental Scanning Units Effective? (Stubbart C, Rochester Inst of Technology) 1982 **15** (3), 139

Assessing Your Competitor's People and Organization (Ball R, Cresap, McCormick & Paget) 1987 **20** (2), 32

The Business Environment in the 1980s (Dam A van, Consultant) 1977 **10** (4), 8

Corporate Environmental Analysis in Large U.S. Corporations (Diffenbach J, Boston U) 1983 **16** (3), 107

Data Bank on the Future Business Environment (Whaley R, Planning and Control Investment) 1984 **17** (4), 83

Dealing with Uncertainty in the Oil Industry (Taylor D T, Carmel A M, Gulf Oil) 1981 **14** (2), 12

Designing a Business Scanning System (Calori R) 1989 **22** (1), 69

Does Market Share Lead to Profitability? (Bourantas D, Athens Sch of Economics and Business Science; Mandes Y, Technical U of Athens) 1987 **20** (5), 102

Economic Trends (Forrest C, Consultant) 1982 **15** (5), 6

An Environmental Decision Model for Dynamic Planning (Kahalas H, Virginia Poly Inst and State U; Bjorklund R L, Worcester Poly) 1976 **9** (1), 81

Environmental Forecasting and Non-Profit Professional Organizations (Jain S C, Connecticut U; Singhvi S S, Armco Steel) 1977 **10** (3), 50

Environmental Pollution and Economic Growth: Implications for Corporate Planning With an Indian Case Study (Venu S, India Tobacco) 1974 **7** (3), 49

Environmental Pressures and Marketing in the 1970s (Healy D F, Delaware U) 1975 **8** (3), 41

Environmental Scanning and Forecasting in Strategic Planning—The State of the Art (Fahey L, King W R, Narayanan V K, Pittsburgh U) 1981 **14** (1), 32

An Environmental Scanning System for Business Planning (Narchal R M, Kittappa K, Bhattacharya P) 1987 **20** (6), 96

Environmental Scanning in U.S. Corporations (Jain S C, Connecticut U) 1984 **17** (2), 117

Environmental Scanning—Does it Help the Chief Executive? (Godiwalla Y M, Wisconsin U; Meinhart W A, Warde W D, Oklahoma State U) 1980 **13** (5), 87

Environmental Scanning—The State of the Art (Thomas P S, Indian Inst of Mgt) 1980 **13** (1), 20

Forecasting the Economic and Business Environment (Morrell J, Morrell Assoc) 1972 **5** (1), 52

Identifying Strategic Issues (Murphy J J) 1989 **22** (2), 101

The International Scene Towards 1980 (Millson P C, CBI) 1971 **4** (2), 36

Issues Management in an Uncertain Environment (Arrington C B, Sawaya R N, Atlantic Richfield) 1984 **17** (6), 17

Management in the 1980s—Key Issues and Priorities (Tolley L, British Inst of Mgt) 1981 **14** (1), 55

Management and Management for the 1980s. Much the Same, but More So!—Book Review Article (Fripp J, Ashridge Mgt Coll) 1981 **14** (1), 104

A Managerial Approach to Environmental Assessment (Neubauer F F, CEI; Solomon N, European Mgt Forum) 1977 **10** (2), 13

Managing in Uncertain Economic Times: The Case for Planning (La Londe B J, Zinser P H, Ohio State U) 1975 **8** (5), 18

Mapping the Environment: an Operational Environmental Analysis Model (Bates C S, Florida Atlantic U) 1985 **18** (5), 97

Marketing the Telephone in a De-regulated Environment (Kane N J A, British Telecom) 1986 **19** (4) 59

Mechanisms for Environmental Scanning (Terry P T, Chemistry & Allied Products Industry) 1977 **10** (3), 2

Opportunities and Pitfalls for Multinational Corporations in a Changed Political Environment (Sethi S P) 1987 **20** (6), 45

Planning for Restructured Competition (Anderson G G, SRI Intl) 1985 **18** (1), 21

Predicting the Political Environment of International Business (Smith C N, Consultant) 1971 **4** (1), 7

QUEST—Quest Environmental Scanning Technique (Nanus B, Sthn California U) 1982 **15** (2), 39

Response of Japanese Companies to Environmental Changes (Nagashima Y, Kanto Gakuin U) 1976 **9** (1), 20

Restructuring of Competition: The New Strategic Imperative (Wilson I) 1985 **18** (1), 19

Strategic Environmental Appraisal (Denning B W, Harbridge House Europe) 1973 **6** (1), 22

Strategic Planning for Multinationals—The Views of Government and Scientists (Gotcher J W, California State U) 1981 **14** (1), 23

Strategic Planning in a Rapidly Changing Environment—Book Review Article (Argenti J, Consultant) 1979 **12** (5), 110

Testing Plans Against Alternative Futures (Boshoff H) 1989 **22** (5), 69

A Tough Future for Australian Business (Laczniak E R, Pecotich A, Carroll B) 1989 **22** (1), 48

The TOWS Matrix—A Tool for Situational Analysis (Weihrich H, San Francisco U) 1982 **15** (2), 54

Whatever Happened to Environmental Analysis? (Engledow J L, Lenz R T, Indiana U) 1985 **18** (2), 93

Will 1990 Mark the End of the Will to Work—Or the Right to Manage? (Carter A, Foy N, STC) 1981 **14** (2), 42

The World's Changing Climate—Some Issues for Planners (Wilson L S, Harbridge House Europe) 1981 **14** (5), 83

BUSINESS FAILURES
Corporate Planning and Corporate Collapse (Argenti J, Consultant) 1976 **9** (6), 12

The Oracle that Failed (Stander A, Rickards T, Manchester Business Sch) 1975 **8** (5), 13

BUSINESS FORECASTING
Computerised Industrial Forecasting for Planning in Central Government (Wells J D, DTI) 1971 **4** (2), 41

Corporate Planning for an Uncertain Future (Beck P.W, Shell) 1982 **15** (4), 12

Forecasting the Future Business Environment: The State of the Art (Merritt T P, Stanford Research Inst) 1974 **7** (3), 54

Future Research—Working with Management Teams (Sims D, Eden C, Bath U) 1984 **17** (4), 51

How the Rip Van Winkle Approach Helps Oil Executives Plan (Finizza A J, Atlantic Richfield) 1985 **18** (1), 59

If we Cannot Forecast How Can we Plan? (Makridakis S, INSEAD) 1981 **14** (3), 10

The Three-Parameter Approach to Long Range Forecasting (Hendry I C, Stirling U) 1972 **5** (1), 40

BUSINESS GAMES
Can Business Learn from Wargames? (Ginter P M, Rucks A C, Alabama U) 1984 **17** (3), 123

BUSINESS MANAGEMENT
Managing in Uncertain Economic Times: The Case for Planning (La Londe B J, Zinser P H, Ohio State U) 1975 **8** (5), 18

BUSINESS PLANNING
An Environmental Scanning System for Business Planning (Narchal R M, Kittappa K, Bhattacharya P) 1987 **20** (6), 96

see also **CORPORATE PLANNING**

BUSINESS RESPONSIBILITY
Business and Government—A New Partnership? (Halal W E, George Washington U) 1987 **20** (1), 123

Growth in Activist Groups: How Can Business Cope? (Pattakos A N) 1989 **22** (3), 98

Managing Relations with Government and Society—The Business Perspective (Carroll D S A, Carroll Industries) 1983 **16** (2), 10

The Role of Business in Society (Kempner T, Hawkins K, MacMillan K, Bradford U) 1970 **2** (4), 2

BUSINESS STRATEGY *see* CORPORATE PLANNING

BUSINESS-GOVERNMENT RELATIONS
Airline Deregulation: Why the Supporters Lost Out (Marcus A A, U of Minnesota Sch of Mgt) 1987 **20** (1), 90

Big Business vs. Big Government—A New Social Contract (Halal W E, George Washington U) 1984 **17** (4), 30

Business and Government—A New Partnership (Halal W E, George Washington U) 1987 **20** (1), 123

Conflicts Between Public and Private Opinion (King S, MRB Intl) 1981 **14** (4), 90

Energy Policy: Government vs Industry (Jones P, Electricity Council) 1987 **20** (1), 12

Forecasting Environmental Protection Legislation Using Cross Impact Analysis (Beasley J E, Johnson R, Imperial Coll) 1984 **17** (6), 132

Forecasting Political Decisions and Their Impact on Business (Jonsson S, Petzall I, Federation of Swedish Industry) 1982 **15** (4), 98

The Future of U.S. Government-Corporate Relations (Fleming J E, Sthn California U) 1979 **12** (4), 20

Government Policies and Private Enterprise—Some Fundamental Trends (Rompuy V Van, Leuven U) 1975 **8** (4), 41

Managing Relations with Government and Society—The Business Perspective (Carroll D S A, Carroll Industries) 1983 **16** (2), 10

National Planning and the French Business Executive (Schollhammer H A, L.A. Grad Sch of Business Admin) 1971 **3** (3), 22

Opportunities and Pitfalls for Multinational Corporations in a Changed Political Environment (Sethi S P) 1987 **20** (6), 45

The Political Business Cycle—Have we Seen the End of it? (Peel D A, Liverpool U) 1982 **15** (1), 30

Politics, Government and Company Planning: The New Perspective (Liston D J, Central London Poly) 1980 **13** (5), 57

Public Planners and Business Investors—Why Can't They Collaborate? (Vichas R P, Contas K, Connecticut U) 1981 **14** (3), 77

Setting Investment Criteria for Government and Industry (Leemhuis J P; Shell Nederland) 1985 **18** (3), 33

Strategic Planning in Government-Dependent Businesses (Ramamurti R, Northeastern U, Boston, USA) 1986 **19** (3), 62

Waste Paper—Case for Government Action (Whiting P L, Thames Board Mills) 1975 **8** (5), 23

BUY-OUTS
The NFC Buy-Out—A New Form of Industrial Enterprise (Thompson Sir P, Nat Freight Consortium) 1985 **18** (5), 19

BUYING
Buying is Marketing Too—Japan's Influence on the Australian Coal Trade (Dowling G, U of New South Wales) 1987 **20** (1), 35

Forecasting and Research for Supply Markets-Commodity Buying Systems (Kingsman B G, Lancaster U and Commodity Systems) 1974 **7** (5), 24

see also **PURCHASING**

C

CANADA
Canadian Industrial Policy—Simulation and Analysis (Thompson W, Vertinsky I, Kane J, British Columbia U) 1973 **6** (4), 66

Corporate Planning in the Canadian National Railways (Maroti E, Canadian Nat Railways) 1970 **3** (1), 21

Corporate Planning in the Mineral Industry (Wright V C, Noranda Mines) 1976 **9** (2), 19

Optimising Railway Strategies (Detmold P, Canadian Transport Commission) 1969 **1** (3), 74

A Role for Transport in Canada (Gratwick J, Fahey W R, Schneiderman A, Canadian Nat Railways) 1976 **9** (1), 38

The State of Private Sector Strategic Planning in Canada (Frederick G D, Consultant) 1983 **16** (3), 40

Strategies for National Competitiveness (Rugman A M, Dalhousie U Nova Scotia) 1987 **20** (3), 92

Why Planning in State Enterprises Doesn't Work (Javidan M, Dastmalchian A) 1988 **21** (3), 98

CAPITAL BUDGETING

Capital Budgeting—The State of the Art (Mills R W) 1988 **21** (4), 76

The Cut-Off Rate for Investment Decisions in Growth Companies (Chandra G, Miami U) 1975 **8** (2), 95

Designing a Capital Budgeting System that Works (Camillus J C, Pittsburgh U) 1984 **17** (2), 103

CAPITAL EXPENDITURE

A Comparative Study of Capital Expenditure Evaluation (Porwal L S, Singhvi S S, Delhi and Armco Steel Corp, U S A) 1978 **11** (5), 25

Forecasting Expenditure on Capital Project (Keller A Z, Ashraft R A, Bradford U; Green N P, DHSS, Riyadhi U) 1984 **17** (4), 110

CAPITAL INVESTMENT

Changing Perspectives on the Capital Investment Process (Hall W K, Michigan U) 1979 **12** (1), 37

Classifying Capital Projects for Top Management Decision-Making (Piper J A, Loughborough U) 1980 **13** (3), 45

Computerized Analysis of Capital Projects by DCF Techniques (Palma F, FID. IMI) 1972 **5** (4), 53

How to Assess the Strategic Value of a Capital Investment (Wissema J G, Delft U of Technology) 1984 **17** (6), 25

Rate of Return on New Invested Capital—Its Relationship to Corporate Earnings Growth Rate and Equity Market Values (Moore C S, Ethyl Corp) 1972 **5** (4), 33

The Use of Life Cycle Costing in Acquiring Physical Assets (Taylor W B, Kent County Council) 1981 **14** (6), 32

see also **INVESTMENT**

CASE STUDIES

Betting The Bank on Technology—Strategic Planning at Bank of America (Raphael D E, Bank of America) 1986 **19** (2), 23

Brief Case: A Portfolio of Commentary and Opinion (Hussey D E) 1988 **21** (2), 104

Business Planning at Sperry Rand (Gedrich S F, Sperry Vickers) 1976 **9** (2), 38

Competing with AT & T (Reichert Smith K, GTE Sprint) 1985 **18** (1), 47

Competitive Superiority Through Data Base Marketing (Shaw B, Stone M) 1988 **21** (5), 24

Corporate Planning at Batchelors Foods Limited: A Case Study (Goodall A J, Batchelors Foods) 1974 **7** (5), 47

Corporate Planning at Dunlop (Rossiter P M, Dunlop) 1979 **12** (1), 17

Corporate Planning at Rolls-Royce Motors Limited (Young R, Rolls-Royce Motors; Hussey D E, Harbridge House Europe) 1977 **10** (2), 2

Corporate Planning and Control Systems in Williams & Glyn's Bank) 1978 **11** (5), 41

Corporate Planning in CPC Europe (Champion J R, CPC) 1970 **3** (2), 8

Corporate Planning in Domestic Airlines—An Indian Case Study (Subramaniam S, Sharma C K, Indian Inst of Mgt) 1975 **8** (4), 64

Corporate Planning in Indian Railways—A Case Study (Subramaniam S, Indian Inst of Mgt) 1979 **12** (3), 91

Corporate Planning in Local Government—A Case Study (Hawkins K, Tarr R J, Bradford Metropolitan District) 1980 **13** (2), 43

Corporate Planning for a Town—A Case History (Paine R E, Stockport Met Borough) 1975 **8** (5), 39

Corporate Planning for an Uncertain Future (Beck P W, Shell) 1982 **15** (4), 12

Corporate Planning Within the British Airports Authority (Turner D, British Airport Authority) 1986 **19** (3), 35

The Corporate Road-map—Planning at Babcock & Wilcox (Allio R J, Babcock & Wilcox) 1972 **5** (4), 9

Corporate Strategy at Admiram Manufacturing Company: An Iranian Case Study (Wright P, Florida Intl U) 1980 **13** (3), 115

Developing a Practical Planning System for a Steel Business (Rozman R, Slovenske Zelezarne) 1986 **19** (2), 90

Dynamic Planning for the Smaller Company—A Case History (House W C, Arkansas U) 1979 **12** (3), 38

Establishing Corporate Objectives at Solvay (Knoepfel R W, Solvay) 1970 **2** (4), 11

A Framework for Strategic Analysis (Ziemer D R, Mavcock P D, Texas Instruments Incorporated) 1973 **6** (2), 6

From Organization Development to Corporate Development at Trebor (Chapman A, Trebor) 1985 **18** (4), 50

Future Forecasting for Strategic Planning at General Electric (Wilson I H, Gen Electric) 1973 **6** (2), 39

GEC's Pragmatic Planners (Turner G) 1985 **18** (1), 12

Getting FIAT Back on the Road, (Galimberti F, Chief Economist, Fiat Group) 1986 **19** (1), 25

How Elf Aquitaine Provides Technological Assistance to Small Businesses (Turbil J-P, Elf Aquitaine) 1986 **19** (3), 59

How GKN Plans Now (Turner G, Consultant) 1984 **17** (4), 12

How the Japanese Came to Dominate the Machine Tool Business (Rendeiro J O, Science Policy Research Unit) 1985 **18** (3), 62

ICI Becomes Proactive (Turner G, Consultant) 1984 **17** (6), 12

ICL: Crisis and Swift Recovery (Marwood D C L) 1985 **18** (2), 10

Importance of Relative Market Share in Strategic Planning—A Case Study (Delombre J, Bruzelius B, SKF) 1977 **10** (4), 2

Inside Europe's Giant Companies: Cultural Revolution at Philips (Turner G) 1986 **19** (4), 12

Inside Europe's Giant Companies: Nestlé Finds a Better Formula (Turner G) 1986 **19** (3), 12

Inside Europe's Giant Companies: Olivetti Goes Bear-hunting (Turner G) 1986 **19** (2), 13

Inside Europe's Giant Companies—Daimler-Benz Goes Top of the Leauge (Turner G) 1986 **19** (5), 12

Installing a Computerized Planning System in Ghana (Babington E A, Peat Marwick McLintock) 1987 **20** (4), 110

Integrated Long Range Planning at Nestlé (Brey A, Gabsa G, Nestlé) 1972 **5** (2), 44

Integrating Regional and Functional Plans at Henkel (Grunewald H-G, Vellmann K, Thompson-Siegel) 1981 **14** (2), 19

Introducing Corporate Planning in a Medium-Size Company—A Case History (Finley P N, Loughborough U) 1982 **15** (2), 93

Introducing Corporate Planning—A Case History (Currill D L, Business Growth) 1977 **10** (4), 70

Investing in CAD: A Case of *ad hoc* Decision-making (Currie W L) 1989 **22** (6), 85

Japan's Drive for the European Car Market—Lessons from U.S. Experience (Wray M, Toftech; Norburn D, Imperial Coll, London) 1987 **20** (4), 60

Keeping it Simple: A Case Study in Corporate Planning (Sedgwick A, NCB) 1978 **11** (1), 10

Make or Buy—A Key Strategic Issue (Ford D, U of Bath; Farmer D, Henley—The Mgt Coll) 1986 **19** (5), 54

Managing a Global Electronics Company in Tomorrow's World (Dekker W, N.V. Philips Gloeilampenfabrieken) 1986 **19** (2), 31

Managing a Successful Turnaround (Zimmerman F M) 1989 **22** (3), 105

Market Planning at the National Coal Board (Edwards M J, The Nat Coal Board) 1986 **19** (3), 46

Massey-Ferguson's Diversification into Industrial and Construction Equipment (Houston J, Massey-Ferguson) 1970 **2** (3), 30

A New Strategy at Barclays (Turner G) 1985 **18** (3), 12

New Venture Development at Du Pont (Cohen A B, Du Pont de Nemours) 1970 **2** (4), 7

New Venture Management in a Electric Utility (Harrell G D, Michigan State U; Murray G O, Utility Technical Services Inc) 1986 **19** (2), 57

The Annual Planning Cycle (Wilson A C B, G.K.N) 1971 **3** (4), 62

Participation in Planning (Berschin H H, Brown Boveri and Cie) 1973 **6** (4), 25

Participative Planning at Swiss Reinsurance (Odermatt H K, Swiss Reinsurance) 1978 **11** (5), 11

Patterns of Success in German Business (Kruger W) 1989 **22** (2), 106

The Pechiney Ugine Kuhlmann Plan (Letourneur J S, Pechiney Ugine Kuhlmann) 1973 **6** (1), 9

Planning at Gulf—A Case Study (Holloway C, Gulf Oil; Jones G T, Durham U) 1975 **8** (2), 27

Planning Developments in British Nuclear Fuels Ltd (Roper D A, British Nuclear Fuels) 1978 **11** (5), 32

Planning for Executive Development at J.R. Geigy, SA (Niederhausern W von, J.R. Geigy) 1970 **3** (1), 63

Planning in the IBM Corporation (Katz A, IBM) 1978 **11** (3), 2

Planning for Ovaltine: Introducing Corporate Planning at A. Wander Ltd. (Hussey D E, A. Wander) 1971 **3** (3), 41

Planning for a Professional Association (Ayal I, Faculty of Mgt, Tel Aviv) 1986 **19** (3), 51

Portfolio Planning at Akzo (Tieleman T M, Akzo) 1981 **14** (6), 17

The Privatization of British Telecom—Its Impact on Management, (Morley W B, British Telecom) 1986 **19** (6), 124

Putting Modularity in Business Planning and Control (Morgan J I, Dow Chemical) 1971 **4** (1), 24

The Quest for Quality at Philips (van Ham K, Philips Intl; Williams R, Erasmus U Rotterdam) 1986 **19** (6), 25

The R.T.Z. Financial Modelling Programme (Archer W R Z, R.T.Z.) 1971 **3** (4), 32

Re-positioning a Leading Stockbroker (Dorwin K) 1988 **21** (6), 13

Reorganization for Export at Ideal Standard (Paterson R R, Ideal-Standard) 1970 **3** (2), 65

Scenarios, Past, Present, and Future (Zentner R D, Shell Oil) 1982 **15** (3), 12

The Scott Bader Commonwealth: Putting People First (Bader G, Scott Bader Co Ltd 1986 **19** (6), 66

Strategic Development as a Means of Organizational Change: Four Case Histories (Green J, Chemical and Allied Products; Jones T, Industry Training Board) 1981 **14** (3), 58

Strategic Issues for the Trustee Savings Banks (Marshall I, TSB Group) 1985 **18** (4), 39

Strategic Planning at the Copenhagen Telephone Company (Allesen-Holm J, Copenhagen Telephone Co) 1985 **18** (3), 68

Strategic Planning and Consensus Building for External Relations—Five Cases (Nielsen R P, Boston Coll) 1983 **16** (6), 74

Strategic Planning in IBM (Thoroman D G, IBM) 1971 **4** (1), 1

A Strategic Planning Process for Public and Non-profit Organizations (Bryson J M) 1988 **21** (1), 73

Strategic Planning in the Thomas Cook Group (Davies A H T, Thomas Cook Group) 1981 **14** (5), 27

Strategic Planning for Water—A Case History (Mohanty R P, Nat Inst of Training in Industrial Engineering) 1984 **17** (4), 79

Successful Strategies—The Story of Singapore Airlines (Singh K, Singapore Airlines) 1984 **17** (5), 17

Tetra Pak—A Model for Successful Innovation (Jones H G, Whyte and Mackay Distillers) 1982 **15** (6), 31

Tioxide: Computerization—The Key to the Future in Financial Planning (Benford P, Tioxide Group Headquarters) 1985 **18** (3), 102

The Turnaround at Italtel (Bellisario M, Italtel) 1985 **18** (6), 21

Turnaround at MFI—From a Troubled Mail-Order Firm to a Leading Furniture Retailer (Seabright J W, Henley Distance Learning) 1985 **18** (4), 27

Turnaround—A Painful Learning Process (Zimmerman F M) 1986 **19** (4), 104

Turning Plans into Action—A Case Study (Ahlquist C G, Simon Engineering) 1974 **7** (6), 59

The Use of a Model in Long Term Planning—A Case History (Mann C W, Harold Whitehead & Partners) 1978 **11** (5), 55

The Use of Scenarios in Corporate Planning—Eight Case Histories (Klein H E, Linneman R E, Temple U) 1981 **14** (5), 69

Xerox Charts a New Strategic Direction (Kennedy C) 1989 **22** (1), 10

CHAIRMEN

Corporate Planning—A Chairman's Guide (Hargreaves D P A, Consultants) 1969 **1** (3), 28

CHANGE

Careers for the 21st Century (Handy C) 1988 **21** (3), 90

Changement: Understanding and Managing Business Change—Book Review Article (Pinnell B, Pilkington) 1980 **13** (5), 112

Linking Organizational Effectiveness and Environmental Change (Shipper F, Arizona State U) 1983 **16** (3), 99

Managing Change (Worcester R M, Market & Opinion Research Intl) 1970 **3** (1), 31

CHANGE MANAGEMENT

BHP Reorganizes for Global Competition (Lewis G, Clark J, Moss B) 1988 **21** (3), 18

Change in Management and the Management of Change (Wilmot R W) 1987 **20** (6), 23

Five Stages of Growth in Small Business (Scott M, U of Cape Town; Bruce R, Graduate Sch of Business) 1987 **20** (3), 45

How NASA moved from R & D to Operations (Hunsucker J L, Brah S A, Santos D L) 1989 **22** (6), 38

Managing Strategic Change in a Mature Business (Whipp R, Rosenfield R, Pettigrew A) 1989 **22** (6), 92

Method Change at B.O.C. (Bayley W J, British Oxygen) 1972 **5** (2), 40

Strategies for Declining Businesses—Survival in the Fur Business (Siomkos G, Shrivastava P) 1987 **20** (6), 84

Strategy in Action—Techniques for Implementing Strategy (Reed R, Buckley M R) 1988 **21** (3), 67

Strategy as a System of Expedients (Hinterhuber H, Popp W) 1988 **21** (4), 107

The Transformation of AT & T (Kennedy C) 1989 **22** (3), 10

CHANNEL TUNNEL

The Effect of the Channel Tunnel on Europe (Bromhead P A, Bristol U) 1974 **7** (2), 65

CHEMICAL INDUSTRY

Business Planning at Union Carbide (Rush K, Union Carbide Corp) 1968 **1** (2), 10

Creating a Productive Culture at Shell Chemicals (Thornley I A) 1988 **21** (3), 34

ICI Becomes Proactive (Turner G, Consultant) 1984 **17** (6), 12

Planning for Emergencies—Lessons From the Chemical Industry (Kharbanda O P, Stallworthy E A) 1989 **22** (1), 83

Strategic Leadership through Corporate Planning at ICI (Pink A I H) 1988 **21** (1), 18

U.K. Chemicals—Strategic Planning or Industrial Strategy (Caudle P, Chemical Industries Assoc) 1977 **10** (6), 31

CHIEF EXECUTIVE OFFICERS

Corporate Planning and the Chief Executive (Godiwalla Y M, Wisconsin U; Meinhart W A, Warde W D, Oklahoma State U) 1979 **12** (2), 2

Environmental Scanning—Does it Help the Chief Executive? (Godiwalla Y M: Wisconsin U: Meinhart W A, Warde W D: Oklahoma State U) 1980 **13** (5), 87

How Leaders Use Goals (Molz R, Clarkson U) 1987 **20** (5), 91

How U.S. and Japanese CEO's Spend Their Time (Kudo H, Tachikawa T, Suzuki N) 1988 **21** (6), 79

Managing the Diversified Corporation: The Tensions Facing the Chief Executive (Goold M, Campbell A) 1988 **21** (4), 12

The New Class of Chief Executive Officer (Steiner G A, Consultant) 1981 **14** (4), 10

Planning and the Chief Executive—Book Review Article (Jones H, Consultant) 1978 **11** (3), 80

Strategic Leadership and the Chief Executive (Merwe A van der, Merwe S van der, U of Witwatersrand) 1985 **18** (1), 100

Strategic Planning and the Chief Executive (Forman R) 1988 **21** (4), 57

Strategic Planning—Myth or Reality?—A Chief Executive's View (Ford T M, Emhart Corporation) 1981 **14** (6), 9

Who Controls the Board? (Mills G) 1989 **22** (3), 125

CHINA

Japanese Business Strategy in China (Campbell N, Manchester Business Sch) 1987 **20** (5), 69

Planning for Business with China (Patten A J Van, Bronson, Bronson & McKinnon) 1974 **7** (4), 27

Regional Planning in China—A Systems Engineering Approach (Yuji W, Quanli C, Hunan Academy of Social Studies) 1987 **20** (1), 99

CHURCH MANAGEMENT

Corporate Planning for a Church (Hussey D E, Otis Elevator) 1974 **7** (2), 61

Corporate Strategy in Catholic Religious Orders (Goghlan D, Coll of Industrial Relations, Dublin) 1987 **20** (1), 44

Long Range Planning and the Church (Wasdell D, Urban Church Project) 1980 **13** (3), 99

Planning the Deployment of Clergy (King M, Loughborough U: Smith D K, Exeter U) 1982 **15** (2), 104

Strategies for Growth: Intervention in a Church (Kohl J P, Texas U) 1984 **17** (6), 76

CITIES

Milton Keynes: A Model for Regenerating our Cities? (Burrows B, Futures Information Assocs) 1987 **20** (1), 67

Wither or Whither London? An Application of Industry Structure Analysis (Burke T, Friends of the Earth; Wilson L, Harbridge House Europe) 1980 **13** (5), 79

CLIMATE

Developing a Climate for Planning (Nurmi R, Turku School of Economics) 1976 **9** (3), 48

CLOTHING INDUSTRY

Competitive Strategies in the Clothing Industry 1989 (McNamee P, McHugh M) 1989 **22** (4), 63

Mapping Competitive Groups in the Clothing Industry (McNamee P, McHugh M) 1989 **22** (5), 89

Why Textile and Clothing Industries are Shifting to the Third World (Fitzpatrick J, Consultant) 1983 **16** (6), 42

see also **TEXTILE INDUSTRY**

CO-OPERATIVES

Prospects for Industrial Co-operatives—An Alternative to Industrial Democracy? (Derrick P, Intl Co-operative Alliance) 1981 **14** (4), 106

COAL MINING INDUSTRY

Automation in Coal mining (Thring M W, Queen Mary Coll) 1983 **16** (4), 66

Buying is Marketing Too—Japan's Influence on the Australian Coal Trade (Dowling G, U of New South Wales) 1987 **20** (1), 35

Long Term Planning for Coal (Ezra D, N.C.B.) 1974 **7** (6), 21

Market Planning at the National Coal Board (Edwards M J, The Nat Coal Board) 1986 **19** (3), 46

COMECON

The Prospects to 1975 (Dudinsky I, Academy of Sci Research Inst of Economics of the World Socialist System) 1973 **6** (1), 69

COMMODITIES

Forecasting and Research for Supply Markets—Commodity Buying Systems (Kingsman B G, Lancaster U and Commodity Systems) 1974 **7** (5), 24

Strategic Planning for Commodities and Specialities (Unger L, Consultant) 1983 **16** (4), 12

COMMODITY MARKETS

The Future Prospects in Commodity Markets (Gare R J, Bean D G, Commodity Analysis) 1975 **8** (3), 2

COMMUNITY PLANNING

Decentralized Administration and Citizen Participation in Community Planning (Jackson R, Waterloo U) 1972 **5** (1), 16

Land Use Planning and the Community (Groves D L, McCart G D, Virginia Poly Inst and State U) 1976 **9** (2), 83

Local Politicians and Their Attitudes to Planning (Hill K O, Coomer J C, Houston U) 1977 **10** (6), 57

COMPANY FAILURES

Company Failure or Company Health? — Techniques for Measuring Company Health (Robertson J, Mills R W) 1988 **21** (2), 70

Company Rescue—An Example (Janzen L T, ASV) 1983 **16** (6), 88

COMPANY GROWTH

Bayer Reorganizes in Response to Growth (Vossberg H, Bayer) 1985 **18** (6), 13

A Complete Guide to Company Growth and Development (Danielsson C, Swedish Sch of Economics and Business Administration) 1982 **15** (6), 8

The Future for European Business—Strategies for Growth (Le Franc J D, Commissariat General du Plan) 1980 **13** (4), 18

How Large and Small Firms Can Grow Together (Wilson P, Gorb P, London Business Sch) 1983 **16** (2), 19

How Marriott Corporation Grew Five-fold in Ten Years (Kennedy C) 1988 **21** (2), 10

The Impact of Key Success Factors on Company Performance (Vasconcellos e Sá J) 1988 **21** (6), 56

'Minimum Level of Activity'—A Quick Method of Assessing Growth Potential in the Smaller Business (Marmuse C, I.A.E. Lille) 1983 **16** (1), 84

Planning for Growth (Armenakis A A, Burgh H B, Auburn Tech Assistance Cntr, Alabama) 1986 **19** (3), 93

Planning for Growth in a Japanese Business (Serizawa Y) 1989 **22** (2), 20

Planning for Growth in Leading U.S. Companies (Worcester R M, Market and Opinion Research Intl) 1970 **2** (3), 8

Strategies of New Biotechnology Firms (Smith J G, Fleck V) 1988 **21** (3), 51

What Growth Rate Can You Achieve? (Robinson S J Q, Shell Chemicals) 1979 **12** (4), 7

COMPANY PRESIDENTS

The Future from the Top: Presidential Perspectives on Planning— Part One (Rosen S, Marketing and Planning Group) 1974 **7** (2), 2

The Future from the Top: Presidential Perspectives on Planning— Part Three (Rosen S, Marketing and Planning Group Inc) 1974 **7** (4), 73

The Future from the Top: Presidential Perspectives on Planning— Part Two (Rosen S, Marketing and Planning Group) 1974 **7** (3), 34

COMPETITION

1992: The Implications for Management (Mitchell D) 1989 **22** (1), 32

Airline Deregulation: Why the Supporters Lost Out (Marcus A A, U of Minnesota Sch of Mgt) 1987 **20** (1), 90

Alliance: The New Strategic Focus (James B G, Ciba-Geigy) 1985 **18** (3), 76

Assessing Your Competitor's People and Organization (Ball R, Cresap, McCormick & Paget) 1987 **20** (2), 32

BHP Reorganizes for Global Competition (Lewis G, Clark J, Moss B) 1988 **21** (3), 18

Competing with Japan—The Rules of the Game (Stone M, Henley Mgt Coll) 1984 **17** (2), 33

Competing with the Japanese Approach to Technology (Prentice J, Consultant) 1984 **17** (2), 25

Competition in Retail Banking (Crawley F W, Lloyds Bank) 1982 **15** (3), 71

Competitive Analysis—Its Role in Purchasing (Farmer D, Henley Mgt and Advisory Service) 1984 **17** (3), 72

Competitive Information Systems (Rodriguez J I, King W R, Pittsburgh U) 1977 **10** (6), 45

Computer Integrated Management—The Next Competitive Breakthrough (Wilmot R) 1988 **21** (6), 65

Design and Competition in Engineering (Rothwell R, Gardiner P, Sussex U) 1984 **17** (3), 78

Foreign Competition for the U S Banking World (Rabino S, Northeastern U) 1984 **17** (3), 115

How is Competition Performing? (Kalff H, Consultant) 1979 **12** (3), 16

Integrated Circuits: The Coming Battle (Mackintosh I M, Mackintosh Consultants) 1979 **12** (3), 28

Managing in the Competitive Environment (Wilson L S, Harbridge House Europe) 1984 **17** (1), 59

Planning for Restructured Competition (Anderson G G, SRI Intl) 1985 **18** (1), 21

Projecting Consumptions of Competing Products (Hinomoto H, Illinois U) 1977 **10** (5), 46

Regaining Your Competitive Edge (Naylor M E, General Motors) 1985 **18** (1), 30

Regulating Private Monopolies and Promoting Competition (Carsberg B, Office of Telecommunications London) 1986 **19** (6), 75

Restructuring of Competition: The New Strategic Imperative (Wilson I) 1985 **18** (1), 19

Strategic Alliances—Guidelines for Success (Devlin G, Bleackley M) 1988 **21** (5), 18

Strategies for Global Competition (Lei D) 1989 **22** (1), 102

Successful Strategies—The Story of Singapore Airlines (Singh K, Singapore Airlines) 1984 **17** (4), 17

U.K. Competition Policy Evaluated (Pass C L, Sparkes J R, Bradford) 1983 **16** (4), 76

Using IT for Competitive Advantage at Thomson Holidays (Palmer C) 1988 **21** (6), 26

COMPUTER INDUSTRY

Strategies for Marketing New Computer Products (Stone M, Henley Mgt Coll) 1985 **18** (3), 41

COMPUTER MODELLING SYSTEMS

Decision Support System: A New Tool for Strategic Management (Yoo S, Bowling Green State U Ohio; Digman L A, U of Nebraska) 1987 **20** (2), 114

Developing Knowledge-based Systems for Strategic Corporate Planning (Mockler R J, Dologite D G) 1988 **21** (1), 97

see also **SIMULATION MODELS**

COMPUTER NETWORKS

Planning a Computer Network: The Octopus Experience (Fletcher J G, California U) 1975 **8** (3), 72

COMPUTER SYSTEMS

Creative Development of Computerized Information Systems (Seiler R E, Boockholdt J L, Houston U) 1983 **16** (5), 100

How to Computerize Your Personnel Planning (Ward S C, U of Southampton) 1987 **20** (4), 88

How Will Technology Impact Your Business? (Whaley R, Burrows B, Strategic Planning Society) 1987 **20** (5), 109

Installing a Computerized Planning System in Ghana (Babington E A, Peat Marwick McLintock) 1987 **20** (4), 110

Integration—The Key to Success with CAD/CAM (Schofield N A, PA Manufacturing Services) 1987 **20** (3), 84

Investing in CAD: A Case of *ad hoc* Decision-making (Currie W L) 1989 **22** (6), 85

The Software Life Cycle in Computer Applications (Lehner F) 1989 **22** (5), 38

The Strategic Dimension of Computer Systems Planning (Kriebel C H, Carnegie-Mellon U) 1968 **1** (1), 7

Towards the Library of the Future (Feigenbaum E A) 1989 **22** (1), 118

COMPUTERS

Computer Assisted Strategic Planning (Holloway C, Pearce J A, South Carolina U) 1982 **15** (4), 56

Computer Crime: Multi-Million Pound Problem (Hearnden K, Loughborough U) 1986 **19** (5), 18

Computer Integrated Management—The Next Competitive Breakthrough (Wilmot R) 1988 **21** (6), 65

Computer-aided Design and Manufacturing—A Managers Guide (Burrows B C, Futures Information Assocs) 1986 **19** (5), 76

Computerized Corporate Planning (Boulden J B, On-Line Decisions) 1971 **3** (4), 2

Computers and Financial Planning (Power P D, EPS Consultants) 1975 **8** (6), 53

Database Marketing for Competitive Advantage (Stone M, Taba Midas; Shaw R, Arthur Andersen) 1987 **20** (2), 12

Developing an Information Systems Strategy (Hayward R G, Massey U Palmerston North New Zealand) 1987 **20** (2), 100

Forecasting the Future Developments in Computers (Wilkes M W, Cambridge U) 1970 **2** (3), 15

The Future of Computers in Financial Institutions (Cleaver A B, IBM) 1980 **13** (3), 12

Future Trends in Computing (Firnberg D, National Computing Centre) 1978 **11** (6), 58

The Use of Computers in Town Planning (Wood P, Liverpool City Planning Dept) 1971 **3** (3), 59

CONFERENCES

Seventh World Planning Congress—A Report (Reid A, Consultant) 1979 **12** (2), 114

The Society for Long-Range Planning: Challenges in Corporate Planning—Third International Conference on Corporate Planning—Brussels September 1973 (Knowlson P, CBI) 1974 **7** (1), 69

CONFIDENTIALITY

PINCO: Personal Information and Confidentiality Controls (Wiedemann P, UNIDO) 1983 **16** (5), 107

CONSERVATION

Assessing Trunk Roads—The Conservationist Viewpoint (Tait I, Harman R, Conservation Society) 1979 **12** (1), 56

Solar Energy; Where Policy-makers and Conservationists Disagree (Shama A, Jacobs K, Solar Energy Research Inst) 1982 **15** (1), 63

CONSULTANTS

Planners and Bureaucrats—Developing the Consultant Client Relationship (Mushkat M, Hong Kong U) 1984 **17** (2), 111

Strategic Management in a Firm of Consulting Engineers (TenDam H, Consultant; Siffert C, Promon Engenharia) 1984 **17** (4), 21

Strategy Consulting—A Shooting Star? (Payne A, Lumsden C, Cranfield Sch of Mgt) 1987 **20** (3), 53

CONSUMER BEHAVIOUR

Competitive Strategies in Retailing (Walters D, Knee D) 1989 **22** (6), 74

The Consumer and Change (Erbe J P, Unilever) 1973 **6** (4), 13

CONSUMERISM

Forecasting Developments in Consumerism and Consumer Protection (Foxall G R, Newcastle upon Tyne U) 1980 **13** (1), 29

CONTINGENCY PLANNING

Contingency Planning (Clay M J, Consultant) 1971 **3** (3), 70

Corporate Crisis Management (Muller R, Corporate Planner) 1985 **18** (5), 38

Guidelines for Contingency Approach to Planning (Michael S R, Massachusetts U) 1979 **12** (6), 62

Planning for Disasters (Sillar W, Sthn General Hospital) 1975 **8** (5), 2

Preventive Planning for Disasters (O'Keefe P, Westgate K, Bradford U) 1977 **10** (3), 25

Strategic Planning—A Contingency Approach—Part 1. The Strategic Analysis (Ghosh B C, Nee A Y C, Singapore U) 1983 **16** (4), 93

Strategic Planning—A Contingency Approach—Part 2. The Plan (Ghosh B C, Nee A Y C, Nat U of Singapore) 1983 **16** (6), 46

CONTROL

Closing the Gap between Planning and Control (Machin J L J, Durham U; Wilson L S, Harbridge House Europe) 1979 **12** (2), 16

The Control Function in Major German Companies (Hand D, Institut fur Unternehmungsplanung) 1982 **15** (3), 21

Corporate Planning and Control in German Industry (Topfer A, Albert-Ludwigs U) 1978 **11** (1), 59

Designing an Effective Financial Planning and Control System (Cowen S S, Middaugh II J K) 1988 **21** (6), 83

The Incentive Effects of Ownership and Control in Management Buy-outs (Green S) 1988 **21** (1), 26

Management Information Systems for Corporate Planning Control (Kashyap R N, Consultant) 1972 **5** (2), 25

Managerial Attitudes Towards Computer Models for Planning and Control (Higgins J C, Finn R, Bradford U) 1976 **9** (6), 107

Managing Diversity: Strategy and Control in Diversified British Companies (Goold M, Campbell A, London Business Sch) 1987 **20** (5), 42

National or Global?—Control vs Flexibility (Fannin W R, U of Houston; Rodrigues A F, Francis Marion College Sth Carolina) 1986 **19** (5), 84

Strategic Control of Factory Automation (Meredith J R) 1987 **20** (6), 106

The Value of Accuracy in Information for Planning and Control (Higgins J C, Bradford U) 1974 **7** (4), 67

CORPORATE AUDIT

The Corporate Appraisal: Assessing Company Strengths and Weaknesses (Hussey D E, Elders & Fyffes) 1968 **1**, (2), 19

Corporate Self Renewal (Haggerty P E, Texas Instruments) 1969 **1** (3), 9

Strategic Planning for Information Systems at British Rail (Mainelli M R, Miller D R) 1988 **21** (4), 65

CORPORATE CULTURE

Corporate Planning: A Need to Examine Corporate Style (Emerson R V, Bank of America) 1985 **18** (6), 29

CORPORATE IMAGE

Assessing Your Competitor's People and Organization (Ball R, Cresap, McCormick & Paget) 1987 **20** (2), 32

Communicating Corporate Strategy — The Payoffs and the Risks (Higgins R B, Diffenbach J) 1989 **22** (3), 133

Corporate Self Renewal (Haggerty P E, Texas Instruments) 1969 **1** (3), 9

Dealing with a Corporate Identity Crisis (Stone W R, Stone, Howard, Nowill and Kouwenhoven; Heany D F, Strategic Planning Inst Massachusetts) 1984 **17** (1), 10

Strategic Issues for Charities and Philanthropies (Harvey J W, McCrohan K F) 1988 **21** (6), 44

CORPORATE LIFE CYCLE

The Theory of the Corporate Life Cycle (James B F, Syntex) 1974 **7** (2), 49

CORPORATE LIFESTYLE

Five Stages of Growth in Small Business (Scott M, U of Cape Town; Bruce R, Graduate Sch of Business) 1987 **20** (3), 45

CORPORATE MODELS

Computer Based Corporate Modelling—Book Review Article (Nutt W O, Estercrete) 1984 **17** (1), 114

Decision Support System: A New Tool for Strategic Management (Yoo S, Bowling Green State U Ohio; Digman L A, U of Nebraska) 1987 **20** (2), 114

Experience with Corporate Simulation Models—A Survey (Naylor T H, Duke U) 1976 **9** (2), 94

A Formal Model for Long Range Planning: 1. Relating the Company to the Economy (Hetrick J C, Arthur D Little) 1969 **1** (3), 16

A Formal Model for Long Range Planning: 2. The Assessment of Opportunity and Risk (Hetrick J C, Arthur D Little) 1969 **1** (4), 54

Managing the Diversified Corporation: The Tensions Facing the Chief Executive (Goold M, Campbell A) 1988 **21** (4), 12

Quantifying Level of Investment in Growth and Renewal (Ziemer D R, Texas Instruments) 1976 **9** (4), 2

Using Computer Models in Corporate Planning (Kumar R, Vrat P) 1989 **22** (2), 114

CORPORATE PLANNING

Airline Corporate Planning—A Conceptual Framework (Bouamrene M A, Flavel R, Imperial Coll of Science and Technology) 1980 **13** (1), 62

Analytical Techniques in Planning (Smalter D J, Intl Minerals and Chemical) 1968 **1** (1), 25

Approaches to Technological Forecasting as a Planning Tool (Lanford H W, Imundo L V, Wright State U) 1974 **7** (4), 49

Australian Industry: Sophisticated Planning and Weak R & D? (Christodoulou C) 1988 **21** (1), 82

Banking: Time to Unbundle the Services? (Pollock A J, Continental Illinois) 1985 **18** (1), 36

Behavioral Aspects of Corporate Planning (Baker C R, Columbia U) 1976 **9** (4), 72

Bringing Planning Systems to the Manager (Reilly D N, IBM) 1974 **7** (3), 45

Britain in the Year 2000: Some Issues for Planners (Bayliss D, Queensborough House) 1971 **3** (3), 65

Building Competitive Strength in International Markets (Hitt M A, Ireland R D, Texas A & M U; Mays W A, Baylor U Texas) 1987 **20** (1), 115

A Business Development Approach to Planning (Pearson B, Ashridge Mgt Coll) 1976 **9** (6), 54

Business Planning: The Gap Between Theory and Practice (Martin J, John Martin Publishing) 1979 **12** (6), 2

Business Planning at Sperry Rand (Gedrich S F, Sperry Vickers) 1976 **9** (2), 38

Business Planning at Union Carbide (Rush K, Union Carbide Corp) 1968 **1** (2), 10

Business Planning and Employee Democracy in Yugoslavia (Milisavljevic M, Belgrade U) 1983 **16** (4), 84

Business Planning in Europe (Kyle B S, European Planning Federation) 1981 **14** (5), 2

Business Planning in Tanzanian State Enterprises (El-Namaki M S S, Dares Salaam) 1977 **10** (5), 52

Business Policy and Management Development in Large American and European Concerns (Petroni G, Consultant), 1978 **11** (3), 26

Can Corporate Planning Invent the Future of the Third World? (Dam A van, Latin America CPC Intl) 1974 **7** (2), 8

Can we Plan for New Technology? (Fairtlough G, Celltech) 1984 **17** (3), 14

Changing the Corporate Culture of Rank Xerox (Chapman P) 1988 **21** (2), 23

Choosing a Diversification Project in a Regulated Economy (Das R, Mohanty B, Indian Inst of Mgt) 1981 **14** (2), 78

Closing the Gap between Planning and Control (Machin J L J, Durham U; Wilson L S, Harbridge House Europe) 1979 **12** (2), 16

Computerized Corporate Planning (Boulden J B, On-Line Decisions) 1971 **3** (4), 2

A Concept of Corporate Planning (Ackoff R, Pennsylvania U) 1970 **3** (1), 2

A Control Engineering Framework for Planning (Clowes G A, Marshall S A, Consultants) 1975 **8** (4), 70

Coordinating Business Strategy and Technical Planning (Frohman A L, Boston U; Biotondo D, Bendix Corporation) 1981 **14** (6), 58

Corporate Crisis Management (Muller R, Corporate Planner) 1985 **18** (5), 38

Corporate Development—Preferred Strategies in U.K. Companies (Littler D A, U of Manchester; Sweeting R C, UMIST) 1987 **20** (2), 125

The Corporate Energy Policy: A Management Planning Perspective (Lambert D M, Michigan State U; Stock J R, Notre Dame U) 1979 **12** (2), 45

Corporate Information Planning—Book Review Article (Nutt W O, Assoc Portland Cement Manufacturers) 1978 **11** (2), 77

Corporate Long Range Planning for Ocean Oriented Industries (Moore J J, Modern Mgt) 1971 **4** (2), 7

Corporate Management and Planning in Local Government (Williams D G, British Rail: Harris D J, Bath U) 1976 **9** (4), 46

Corporate Planning for the 1990s: The New Frontiers (Taylor B, Editor) 1986 **19** (6), 13

Corporate Planning: Its Impact on Management (Osmond C N, MSL) 1971 **3** (3), 34

Corporate Planning: The Keystone of the Management System (Simmons W W, Intl Business Machine Corp) 1968 **1** (2), 2

Corporate Planning: A Need to Examine Corporate Style (Emerson R V, Bank of America) 1985 **18** (6), 29

Corporate Planning for Asia, Latin America, and Africa (Dam A van, CPC International Inc) 1972 **5** (4), 2

Corporate Planning at Batchelors Foods Limited: A case Study (Goodall A J, Batchelors Foods) 1974 **7** (5), 47

Corporate Planning at Dunlop (Rossiter P M, Dunlop) 1979 **12** (1), 17

Corporate Planning at Rolls-Royce Motors (Young R, Rolls-Royce Motors; Hussey D E, Harbridge House, Europe) 1977 **10** (2), 2

Corporate Planning in the Canadian National Railways (Maroti E, Canadian Nat Railways) 1970 **3** (1), 21

Corporate Planning and the Chief Executive (Godiwalla Y M, Wisconsin U; Meinhart W A, Warde W D, Oklahoma State U) 1979 **12** (2), 2

Corporate Planning for a Church (Hussey D E, Otis Elevator) 1974 **7** (2), 61

Corporate Planning and Control in German Industry (Topfer A, Albert-Ludwigs-U) 1978 **11** (1), 59

Corporate Planning as a Control System in United Kingdom Nationalized Industries (Harris D J, Davies B C L, Bath U) 1981 **14** (1), 15

Corporate Planning and Control Systems in Williams & Glyn's Bank (Dugdale I, Williams & Glyn's Bank) 1978 **11** (5), 41

Corporate Planning and Corporate Collapse (Argenti J, Consultant) 1976 **9** (6), 12

Corporate Planning in CPC Europe (Champion J R, CPC) 1970 **3** (2), 8

Corporate Planning in Developing Economies (Carter R D, UNIDO; Hamilton J G, Williams P J, Consultants) 1973 **6** (2), 2

Corporate Planning in a Developing Economy: Indian Experience (Venu S, India Tobacco) 1972 **5** (3), 29

Corporate Planning in Domestic Airlines—An Indian Case Study (Subramaniam S, Sharma C K, Indian Inst of Mgt) 1975 **8** (4), 64

Corporate Planning in an Engineering Business (Booth H J, GEC, AEI Control Rectifiers) 1970 **3** (1), 67

Corporate Planning in Hungarian Companies (Csath M) 1989 **22** (4), 89

Corporate Planning In Nigeria (Bedford F A, U of Science & Technology, Nigeria) 1986 **19** (2), 125

Corporate Planning in Indian Railways—A Case Study (Subramaniam S, Indian Inst of Mgt) 1979 **12** (3), 91

Corporate Planning in an International Environment (Thomas F A, UAC Int) 1974 **7** (5), 13

The Corporate Planning Life Cycle—An International Business Point of View (Ringbakk K A, C.E.I.) 1972 **5** (3), 10

Corporate Planning in Local Government Implications for the Elected Member (Cartwright J, M.P.) 1975 **8** (2), 46

Corporate Planning in Local Government (Rugman C A, Kent County Council) 1973 **3** (3), 17

Corporate Planning in Local Government (Stewart J D, Birmingham U) 1973 **6** (2), 18

Corporate Planning in Local Government—A Case Study (Hawkins K, Tarr R J, Bradford Metropolitan District) 1980 **13** (2), 43

Corporate Planning and Management by Objectives (Haines W R, Consultant) 1977 **10** (4), 13

Corporate Planning and Management by Objectives (Humble J W, Urwick Orr and Partners) 1969 **1** (4), 36

Corporate Planning in Medium-sized Companies in the U.K. (Bhatty E F, Aston U) 1981 **14** (1), 60

Corporate Planning in the Mineral Industry (Wright V C, Noranda Mines Ltd) 1976 **9** (2), 19

Corporate Planning and Modelling in a Large Bank (Degueldre J, Banque Bruxelles Lambert) 1980 **13** (4), 43

Corporate Planning and Operations Research: Do They Go Together? (LaForge L, Clemson U; Wood D R, Virginia Commonwealth U) 1982 **15** (3), 152

Corporate Planning and Project Evaluation in Urban Transport (Tyson W J, Manchester U; Cochrane R L D, GMPTE) 1981 **14** (5), 62

Corporate Planning in Small Companies—A Survey (Shuman J G, Babson Coll) 1975 **8** (5), 81

Corporate Planning for Social Responsibility (Challen P, South London Industrial Mission) 1974 **7** (3), 38

Corporate Planning in South African Companies (Woodburn T L, Grey Mann Associates) 1984 **17** (1), 84

Corporate Planning Takes off in Singapore (Hou Wee C, Farley J U, Lee S K) 1989 **22** (2), 78

Corporate Planning in the U.S. Regional Airline Industry (Shuman J C, Babson Coll) 1973 **6** (4), 35

Corporate Planning for an Uncertain Future (Beck P W, Shell) 1982 **15** (4), 12

Corporate Planning within the British Airports Authority (Turner D, British Airports Authority) 1986 **19** (3), 35

Corporate Planning—A Chairman's Guide (Hargreaves D, P A Mgt Consultants) 1969 **1** (3), 28

Corporate Planning—A Conceptual Critique (Horwitz R, London Regional Management Centre) 1979 **12** (1), 62

Corporate Planning—A Functional Approach (Godiwalla Y M, Wisconsin U; Meinhart W A, Warde W D, Oklahoma U) 1978 **11** (5), 47

Corporate Planning—A Personal Viewpoint (Abernethy W L, Consultant) 1974 **7** (6), 49

Corporate Planning—A System View (Nadler G, Wisconsin U) 1978 **11** (6), 67

Corporate Product Planning: A Vector Analysis Approach (Mazze E M, Hamelman P W, Kucheman W H, Virginia Poly Inst and State U) 1973 **6** (2), 35

The Corporate Road-map—Planning at Babcock & Wilcox (Allio R J, Babcock & Wilcox) 1972 **5** (4), 9

Corporate Strategic Planning in Practice (Malmlow E G, B & S Corporate Development AG) 1972 **5** (3), 2

Corporate Strategy at Admiram Manufacturing Company: An Iranian Case Study (Wright P, Florida Intl U) 1980 **13** (3), 115

Creating a Climate Conducive to Planning (Higgins R B, Northeastern U) 1981 **14** (1), 49

Data and Effective Corporate Planning (Houlden B T, Warwick U) 1980 **13** (5), 106

Dealing with Uncertainty in the Oil Industry (Taylor D T, Carmel A M, Gulf Oil) 1981 **14** (2), 12

Defining the Role of the Board (Demb A, Chouet D, Lossius T, Neubauer F) 1989 **22** (1), 61

The Design of Computer-Based Planning and Modeling Systems (Naylor T H, Duke U; Mansfield M J, Social Systems) 1977 **10** (1), 16

Developing a Competitive Intelligence System for IT (Ewusi-Mensah K) 1989 **22** (5), 121

Developing a Corporate Planning Model for a Small Company (Kluyver C A de, Purdue U; McNally G M, Canterbury U) 1982 **15** (1), 97

Developing Corporate Policies for Innovation: a Program of Action (Norris W C, Control Data Corporation) 1981 **14** (4), 34

Developing a Data Base for Planning—A Shipping Industry Case, (Tomlinson D S, Panocean Anco), 1980 **13** (6), 42

Developing an Enterprise Culture at British Telecom (Brunnen D J) 1989 **22** (2), 27

Developing Knowledge-based Systems for Strategic Corporate Planning (Mockler R J, Dologite D G) 1988 **21** (1), 97

Developing Planning Models (Holloway C, Gulf Oil) 1974 **7** (1), 52

The Development of Long Term Corporate Planning at Pilkington (Pinnell L B, Pilkington Bros) 1969 **1** (4), 14

Does Futures Research Have a Corporate Role? (Holloway C, Consultant) 1978 **11** (5), 11

The Effects of the Future on Today's Decisions (Craver J K, Monsanto) 1973 **6** (2), 29

Elements of Effective Corporate Planning (Kudla R J, Pittsburgh U) 1976 **9** (4), 82

An Environmental Decision Model for Dynamic Planning (Kahalas H, Virginia Poly Inst and State U; Bjorklund R L, Worcester Poly) 1976 **9** (1), 77

Environmental Pollution and Economic Growth: Implications for Corporate Planning With an Indian Case Study (Venu S, Indian Tobacco) 1974 **7** (3), 49

Establishing Corporate Objectives at Solvay (Knoepfel R W, Solvay) 1970 **2** (4), 11

A European Bibliography of Corporate Planning, 1972 (Kettlewell P J, Sandoz Products & Wander) 1974 **7** (1), 72

Evaluating the Benefits of Formal Planning Systems (Camillus J C, Indian Inst of Mgt) 1975 **8** (3), 33

Financial Aspects of Company Planning (Welter P, Consultant) 1973 **6** (1), 36

Financial Evaluation of Corporate Plans (Merrett A J, Lehr M F, London Graduate Sch of Business) 1970 **2** (3), 37

Financial Forecasting for Corporate Planning (Kingshott A L, Ford Europe) 1968 **1** (2), 28

Financial Models in Corporate Planning—Book Review Article (Sutcliffe R, EPS Consultants) 1979 **12** (4), 91

Formal Planning in Major U.S. Corporations (Henry H W, Tennessee U) 1977 **10** (5), 40

Formulating Corporate Objectives and Strategies (Krijnen H G, Groningen U) 1977 **10** (4), 78

A Future for the Corporate Planner (Nutt W O, Associated Portland Cement) 1977 **10** (2), 90

The Future from the Top: Presidential Perspectives on Planning— Part One (Rosen S, Marketing and Planning Group) 1974 **7** (2), 2

Gap Analysis: Key to Super Growth (Kami M J, Corporate Planning Assocs) 1969 **1** (4), 44

Getting Management Commitment to Planning a New Approach (Humphrey A S, Business Planning & Devel) 1974 **7** (1), 45

Growth in Activist Groups: How Can Business Cope? (Pattakos A N) 1989 **22** (3), 98

How are Companies Planning Now?—A Survey (Boulton W R, Georgia U; Franklin S G, Emory U; Lindsay W M, Nthn Kentucky U; Fue L W, Georgia State U) 1982 **15** (1), 82

How Companies Keep Abreast of Technological Change (Quinn J J, Tech Change Centre) 1985 **18** (2), 69

How Corporate Planning Responds to Uncertainty (Harrison F L, Henley Mgt Centre) 1976 **9** (2), 88

How Danish Companies Plan (Ackelsberg R, Harris W C) 1989 **22** (6), 111

How French Industry Plans (Montebello M, Buigues P, Institut d'Administration des Enterprises) 1982 **15** (3), 116

How GKN Plans Now (Turner G, Consultant) 1984 **17** (4), 12

How Information Technology is Transforming Corporate Planning (Hohn S, Volkswagen AG) 1986 **19** (4), 18

How Managers Plan—The Analysis of Managers' Activities (Snyder N, Glueck W F, Georgia U) 1980 **13** (1), 70

How Planning Works in Practice—A Survey of 48 U.K. Companies (Al-Bazzaz S, Grinyer P M, St. Andrews U) 1980 **13** (4), 30

How the Rip Van Winkle Approach Helps Oil Executives Plan (Finizza A J, Atlantic Richfield) 1985 **18** (1), 59

Human and Organization Problems in Corporate Planning (Wilson A C B, GKN) 1972 **5** (1), 67

The Impact of Supply Markets on Corporate Planning (Farmer D, Consultant) 1972 **5** (1), 10

Implementing Corporate Strategy: Using Management Education and Training (Hussey D E, Harbridge Consulting) 1985 **18** (5), 28

Implications of Qualitative Growth for a Business (Perutz P, Battelle Inst) 1976 **9** (5), 42

Incomes, Productivity and Planning (Blakeman L T, Ford Motor Co) 1969 **1** (4), 10

Information Systems for Planning (Ewusi-Mensah K, Hawaii U) 1984 **17** (4), 111

Integrating Models into the Planning Process (Naylor T H, Duke U, SSI) 1977 **10** (6), 11

Integrating Planning and Management Development (Dill W R, New York U) 1975 **8** (5), 8

Integrating Planning with Management (Miesing P, New York State U) 1984 **17** (4), 118

Integrating Regional and Functional Plans at Henkel (Grunewald H-G, Vellmann K, Thompson-Siegel) 1981 **14** (2), 19

Integration—The Key to Success with CAD/CAM (Schofield N A, PA Manufacturing Services) 1987 **20** (3), 84

Introducing Corporate Planning in a Medium-Size Company—A Case History (Finley P N, Loughborough U) 1982 **15** (2), 93

Introducing Corporate Planning—A Case History (Currill D L, Business Growth) 1977 **10** (4), 70

Introducing Management Information Systems for Corporate Planning and Control (Kashyap R N, R N Kashyap Assocs) 1973 **6** (1), 28

Keeping Corporate Planning Relevant—A Key Task for the Planning Department (Pinnell B) 1986 **19** (1), 45

Keeping it Simple: A Case Study in Corporate Planning (Sedgwick A, NCB) 1978 **11** (1), 10

A Look at Major Planning Methods: Development, Implementation Strengths and Limitations (Kahalas H, New York State U) 1978 **11** (4), 84

Making Corporate Planning Work in Developing Countries (Haines W R) 1988 **21** (2), 91

Making Quality a Fundamental Part of Strategy (Ross J E, Florida Atlantic U; Shetty Y K, Utah State U) 1985 **18** (1), 53

Management Buy-outs in Britain—A Monograph (Wright M, Coyne J, Robbie K, Centre for Mgt Buy-out Research, Nottingham) 1987 **20** (4), 38

Management Control for Effective Corporate Planning (Rhodes D, Wright M, Jarrett M, Nottingham U) 1984 **17** (4), 115

Management Information Systems for Corporate Planning Control (Kashyap R N, Consultant) 1972 **5** (2), 25

Management Information Systems (Green J F, Urwick Dynamics) 1970 **2** (4), 74

Management Information Systems in Planning (Sethi N K, St John's U) 1978 **11** (3), 75

Managerial Attitudes Towards Computer Models for Planning and Control (Higgins J C, Finn R, Bradford U) 1976 **9** (6), 107

Managing the Process of Corporate Development (Taylor B, Staff Coll, Henley) 1976 **9** (3), 81

Managing in Uncertain Economic Times: The Case for Planning (La Londe B J, Zinser P H, Ohio State U) 1975 **8** (5), 18

Manpower in Corporate Planning (Bell D J, United Dominions Trust) 1976 **9** (2), 31

Market Concentration—Challenge to Corporate Planning (Blois K J, Loughborough U) 1980 **13** (4), 56

Marketing and Airline Corporate Planning (Shuman J C, Babson Coll) 1974 **7** (6), 68

Marketing Planning and Corporate Planning (Leyshon A M, Littlewoods Ltd) 1976 **9** (1), 29

Modelling for Corporate Planning—Book Review Article (Power P D, Macgregor J M, EPS) 1980 **13** (3), 125

Multinational Corporate Planning: Is it Really Different?—Book Review Article (Hussey D E, Harbridge House Europe) 1980 **13** (2), 105

Multinational Planning Systems (Boulden J B, On-Line Decisions) 1972 **5** (3), 25

A New Approach to Corporate Planning (Naor J, Maine U) 1978 **11** (2), 55

New Dimensions in Corporate Planning (Taylor B, Administrative Staff Coll, Henley) 1976 **9** (6), 80

The Annual Planning Cycle (Wilson A C B, G.K.N.) 1971 **3** (4), 62

The Organisation and Practice of Corporate Planning in the U.K. (Higgins J C, Finn R, Bradford U) 1977 **10** (4), 88

Organised Planning in Major U.S. Companies (Ringbakk K A, C.E.I.) 1969 **2** (2), 46

Organization for Corporate Development (Kraushar P M, Consultant) 1976 **9** (3), 43

Organization of the Planning Department in a Divisionalized Concern (Friedrich A, Land A van't, Dortmund) 1974 **7** (2), 27

Organized Planning in Major U.K. Companies (Taylor B, Irving P, Bradford U) 1971 **3** (4), 10

Organizing the Corporate Planning Function (Denning B W, London Grad Sch of Business Studies) 1969 **1** (4), 67

The Theory of the Corporate Life Cycle (James B G, Syntex) 1973 **6** (2), 689

The Theory of the Corporate Life Cycle (James B G, Syntex Europe) 1974 **7** (2), 49

Paralysis by Analysis: Is Your Planning System Becoming Too Rational? (Lenz R T, Indiana U; Lyles M A, U of Illinois) 1985 **18** (4), 64

Participation in Planning (Berschin H H, Brown Boveri) 1973 **6** (4), 25

Participation in Planning—A Study of Two Organizations in The Netherlands (Dyson R G, Warwick U) 1978 **11** (4), 61

The Pechiney Ugine Kuhlmann Plan (Letourneur J S, Pechiney Ugine Kuhlmann) 1973 **6** (1), 9

Performance Review: Key to Effective Planning (Berry S J, Carleton Board of Education) 1979 **12** (6), 17

Piggybacking for Business and Nonprofits: A Strategy for Hard Times (Neilsen R P, Boston Coll) 1984 **17** (2), 96

The Planner's Dual Role—A Survey for U.S. Companies (Lorange P, IMEDE Lausanne) 1973 **6** (1), 13

Planning at Gulf—A Case Study (Holloway C, Gulf Oil; Jones G T, Durham U) 1975 **8** (2), 27

Planning for Changes in Stages of Corporate Development (Leontiades M, Rutgers U) 1979 **12** (6), 70

Planning and the Chief Executive—Book Review Article (Jones H, Consultant) 1978 **11** (3), 80

Planning for Corporate Social Programs—Problems and Guidelines (Gray E R, Louisiana State U) 1981 **14** (2), 49

Planning for Flexibility (Mascarenhas B, California U) 1981 **14** (5), 78

Planning in a German Engineering Business (Heckman N, Consultant) 1971 **3** (4), 54

Planning for Growth in Leading U.S. Companies (Worcester R M, Market and Opinion Research Intl) 1970 **2** (3), 8

Planning for Heavy Industry in South Africa (Kieser P J, African Explosives & Chemical Industries) 1972 **5** (1), 78

Planning in the IBM Corporation (Katz A, IBM) 1978 **11** (3), 2

Planning and Management by Objectives (Migliore R H, Tulsa U) 1976 **9** (4), 58

Planning in a Nationalised Industry (Kingshott A L, BSC) 1975 **8** (5), 58

Planning for Ovaltine: Introducing Corporate Planning at A. Wander Ltd (Hussey D E, A. Wander) 1971 **3** (3), 41

Planning Procedures in German Companies—Findings and Consequences (Scholz C, Regensburg U) 1984 **17** (6), 94

Planning for a Rapidly Changing Environment in SAS (Stiwenius O, Consultant) 1985 **18** (2), 22

Planning for Restructured Competition (Anderson G G, SRI Intl) 1985 **18** (1), 21

Planning in the Smaller Company (Foster D, Planning for Growth) 1971 **4** (1), 71

Planning in a State of Turbulence (Edwards J P, Harris D J, Bath University) 1977 **10** (3), 43

Planning for Technological Innovation: Part II—Investment in Technological Change in Three Major Industries (Cox J G, Essex U) 1978 **11** (4), 70

Planning for Technology as a Corporate Resource (van Gunsteren L A, Erasmus U Rotterdam, Rotterdam Consulting Group) 1987 **20** (2), 51

Planning—Satisfaction and Productivity (Groves D L, Kahalas H, Lamb F, Virginia Poly Inst and State U) 1976 **9** (4), 52

Plans—Their Preparation and Implementation (Chandler W J, Reed International) 1978 **11** (6), 14

Policy Experiments with a Paper Industry Model (Price D H R, Thillainathan V, Bradford U) 1981 **14** (1), 73

Policy Making at Nederlandsche Middenstandsbank (NMB), Amsterdam (Scherpenjuijsen Rom W E, NMB) 1980 **13** (5), 36

Politics, Government and Company Planning: The New Perspective (Liston D J, Central London Poly) 1980 **13** (5), 57

The Politics of Planning: Man in the Decision Process (Knoepfel R W, Solvay American Corp) 1973 **6** (1), 17

Portfolio Theory—A Planning Tool (Gup B E, Tulsa U) 1977 **10** (3), 10

Practical Planning (Simmons W W, Consultant) 1972 **5** (2), 32

Psychological Aspects of Planning (Taylor R N, U of British Columbia) 1976 **9** (2), 66

The Public Affairs Function in American Corporations: Development and Relations with Corporate Planning (Post J E, Murray E A, Dickie R, Mahon J F, Boston U) 1982 **15** (2), 12

Public Participation in Corporate Planning—Strategic Management in a Kibitzer's World (Dill W R, New York U) 1975 **8** (1), 57

Putting Modularity in Business Planning and Control (Morgan J I, Dow Chemical) 1971 **4** (1), 24

R & D and Corporate Planning in Government (Peretz D, Inter-Bank Research Organisation) 1972 **5** (4), 67

Rational and Non-Rational Planning (Smith J de, Rade N L, Delft Graduate Sch of Mgt) 1980 **13** (2), 87

Resource Planning for Technology-Oriented Companies (Gansler J S, Consultant) 1973 **6** (4), 17

Response of Japanese Companies to Environmental Changes (Nagashima Y, Kanto Gakuin U) 1976 **9** (1), 20

Reunite Management and Planning (Higgins R B, Northeastern U) 1976 **9** (4), 40

Risk Management in Corporate Planning (Haner F T, Business Environment Risk) 1981 **14** (6), 12

Risk Return Approach to Product Portfolio Strategy (Cardozo R N, U of Minnesota; Wind J, U of Pennsylvania) 1985 **18** (2), 77

The Role of the Board in Corporate Planning (Pinnell B) 1986 **19** (5), 27

Setting Corporate Goals and Measuring Organizational Effectiveness—A Practical Approach (Mendelow A L, Pittsburgh U) 1983 **16** (1), 70

Setting Corporate Objectives as a Basis for Action (Pearson G J, Clay Cross) 1979 **12** (4), 13

Setting Corporate Objectives (Redwood H, Fisons) 1977 **10** (6), 2

Setting up Corporate Planning (Allmen E von, Safeguard Industries) 1969 **2** (1), 2

A Simulation System for Corporate Planning (Craig G D, Waikato U) 1980 **13** (5), 43

Social Forecasting: An Integral Part of Corporate Planning? (Higgins J C, Romano D, Bradford U) 1980 **13** (2), 82

Social Forecasting for Company Planning—Book Review Article (MacNulty C A R, Consultant) 1983 **16** (2), 118

Strategic Leadership through Corporate Planning at ICI (Pink A I H) 1988 **21** (1), 18

Strategies for Diversification (Hake B, Consultant) 1972 **5** (2), 65

Strategies in Managing Turnaround (Melin L, Linkoping U) 1985 **18** (1), 80

Strategy and Flexibility in the Smaller Business (MacMillan I C, South Africa U) 1975 **8** (3), 62

Strategy—The Key to Planning in the Public Corporation (Smith J G, City U) 1981 **14** (6), 24

Successful Strategies—The Story of Singapore Airlines (Singh K, Singapore Airlines) 1984 **17** (5), 17

Survival of the Corporate Planner (Houlden B T, U of Warwick) 1985 **18** (5), 49

Systematic Planning and Re-organization (Janzen L T, Nordisk Aluminium Industry) 1971 **4** (2), 58

A Systems Approach to Corporate Development (Wilemon D L, Porter L H, Syracuse U) 1972 **5** (1), 46

Tailor-made Planning: Making Planning Fit for the Firm (Michael S R, Massachusetts U) 1980 **13** (6), 74

Technological Forecasting in Corporate Planning (Jantsch E, Consultant) 1968 **1** (1), 40

Technological Forecasting as a Guide for Managerial Planning (Jeckovich S, PPG Industries) 1971 **4** (1), 29

Ten Years of Business Planners (Blass W P, AT & T) 1983 **16** (3), 21

Top Management's Role in Planning (Steiner G A, U of California) 1969 **1** (4), 2

Translating Planning into Action (Cornfield K, STC plc) 1984 **17** (4), 23

Turning Plans into Action—A Case Study (Ahlquist C G, Simon Engineering) 1974 **7** (6), 59

The Use of Multiple Scenarios by U.S. Industrial Companies (Linneman R E, Klein H E, Philadelphia U) 1979 **12** (1), 83

The Use of Scenarios in Corporate Planning—Eight Case Histories (Klein H E, Linneman R E, Temple U) 1981 **14** (5), 69

The Uses and Abuses of Experience Curves (Sallenave J-P, U of Sherbrooke) 1985 **18** (1), 64

Using Computer Models in Corporate Planning (Kumar R, Vrat P) 1989 **22** (2), 114

Using Scenarios to Develop Strategies (Leemhuis J P, Shell Nederland) 1985 **18** (2), 30

The Value of Accuracy in Information for Planning and Control (Higgins J C, Bradford U) 1974 **7** (4), 67

What Kind of Corporate Planner Do You Need? (Leontiades M, New Jersey State U) 1977 **10** (2), 56

Where Planning Fails—An Executive Survey (Javidan M, U of Alberta) 1985 **18** (5), 89

Who Says Planners Don't (Hussey D E, Harbridge House Europe) 1977 **10** (5), 83

Why Has Planning Failed? (Pennington M W, Golightly Intl) 1972 **5** (1), 2

Will Hong Kong's Entrepreneurs Move to Planning? (Warrington M B, Napier Coll) 1982 **15** (3), 157

Xerox Charts a New Strategic Direction (Kennedy C) 1989 **22** (1), 10

CORPORATE STRATEGY

Alternatives to Merger—Joint Ventures and Other Strategies (Harrison J S) 1987 **20** (6), 78

Assessing Company Strength Using Added Value (Bryant J) 1989 **22** (3), 34

Building a Competitive Advantage Through Information Technology (Jackson C) 1989 **22** (4), 29

The Choice of Corporate Objectives (Cantley M F, Lancaster U) 1970 **3** (1), 36

Communicating Corporate Strategy — The Payoffs and the Risks (Higgins R B, Diffenbach J) **22** (3), 133

Competitive Strategies in the Clothing Industry (McNamee P, McHugh M) 1989 **22** (4), 63

Conflict of Values—The Central Strategy Problem (Taylor B, Administrative Staff College) 1975 **8** (6), 20

Corporate Strategies for Political Action (Gram H A, Crawford R L, Concordia U) 1979 **12** (5), 62

Corporate Strategy in Catholic Religious Orders (Goghlan D, Coll of Industrial Relations, Dublin) 1987 **20** (1), 44

Corporate Strategy in the Eighties (Cornelissen J A, Van Melle Nederlan BV, VSB) 1977 **10** (5), 2

Corporate Strategy and Entrepreneurial Vision (Shirley S) 1989 **22** (6), 107

Corporate Strategy and Public Policy in Saudi Arabia (Luqmani M, Yavas U, Quraeshi Z A) 1989 **22** (4), 79

Creating Value to Keep the Raiders at Bay (Reimann B C) 1989 **22** (3), 18

Developing Competitive Advantage in Small and Medium-size Firms (Bamberger I) 1989 **22** (5), 80

Developing Corporate Strategy Through Planning, Programming and Budgeting (Dougharty L A, Rand Corp) 1970 **2** (3), 24

Developing a Product Market Strategy (Foster D W, Planning for Growth) 1970 **2** (3), 70

Developing Strategies: A Practical Approach (Weir G A, Weir Group) 1974 **7** (5), 7

The External Corporate Venture Capital Fund—A Valuable Vehicle for Growth (Bleicher K, Paul H) 1987 **20** (6), 64

The Future for European Business—Strategies for Growth (Le Franc J-D, Commissariat General Du Plan) 1980 **13** (4), 18

GE's High-tech Strategy (Koerner E) 1989 **22** (4), 11

International Business Through Barter and Countertrade (Aggarwal R) 1989 **22** (3), 75

The Long-Term Business Strategy of a Danish Savings Bank (Ringgard L, SDS Savings Bank) 1985 **18** (6), 25

Massey-Ferguson's Diversification into Industrial and Construction Equipment (Houston J, Massey-Ferguson) 1970 **2** (3), 30

Pricing Policies and Corporate Strategy (May R, British Printing Corp) 1970 **2** (4), 49

Strategic Credibility — The Basis of a Strong Share Price (Higgins R B, Diffenbach J) 1989 **22** (6), 10

Strategies for a Pan European Market (Vandermerwe S) 1989 **22** (3), 45

Strategies of the United States Airlines (Huffmire D W, Connecticut U) 1975 **8** (2), 72

Strategy and the Business Portfolio (Hedley B D, Boston Consulting) 1977 **10** (1), 9

Understanding Corporate Strategy (Stopford J M, London Business Sch) 1982 **15** (6), 104

see also **CORPORATE PLANNING**

COST REDUCTION

Energy Cost Saving Starts on the Shop Floor (Beatfield D, 3M U.K.) 1984 **17** (1), 73

CRIME
Some Law Enforcement Operations Implications of Crime
Seasonality (McPheters I R, Strong W B, Atlantic U) 1974 **7** (2), 57
CRIMINAL LAW
The Long Range Planning of Criminal Justice Systems (Clifford W,
Australian Inst of Criminology) 1979 **12** (4), 42
CROSS IMPACT ANALYSIS
Industrial Applications of Cross-Impact Analysis (Fontela E, Geneva
U) 1976 **9** (4), 29
CURRENCY
Currency Problems in Multinational Long Range Planning (Bruns J,
Deutsche Edelstahlwerke) 1970 **3** (2), 71
The Medium-Term Currency Outlook (Kern D, Nat Westminster
Bank) 1980 **13** (2), 2
Reducing Exposure to Exchange Rate Risk: A Case Study (Boothe
R, Memphis State U; Madura J, U of Central Florida) 1985 **18** (3),
98

D

DATA BASES
Building a Strategic Data Base (Szewczak E J) 1988 **21** (2), 97
Competitive Superiority Through Data Base Marketing (Shaw B,
Stone M) 1988 **21** (5), 24
Data Bank on the Future Business Environment (Whaley R, Planning
and Control Investment) 1984 **17** (4), 83
Database Marketing for Competitive Advantage (Stone M, Taba
Midas; Shaw R, Arthur Andersen) 1987 **20** (2), 12
Database—A Neglected Corporate Resource? (Hitschheim R A,
London Sch of Economics) 1983 **16** (5), 79
Developing a Competitive Intelligence System for IT (Ewusi-Mensah
K) 1989 **22** (5), 121
Developing a Data Base for Planning—A Shipping Industry Case
(Tomlinson D S, Panocean-Anco) 1980 **13** (6), 42
How to Computerize Your Personnel Planning (Ward S C, U of
Southampton) 1987 **20** (4), 88
The Impact of Key Success Factors on Company Performance
(Vasconcellos e Sá J) 1988 **21** (6), 56
Strategic Management of Consumer Services (Allen M) 1988 **21** (6),
20
DATA PROCESSING
Database Marketing for Competitive Advantage (Stone M, Taba
Midas; Shaw R, Arthur Andersen) 1987 **20** (2), 12
Key Issues in Managing Information (Sizer R, BCS) 1983 **16** (5), 10
A Management Strategy for Information Processing. 1—The Segas
Case (Collins A C, South Eastern Gas) 1983 **16** (5), 29
A Management Strategy for Information Processing (Collins A C,
South Eastern Gas) 1983 **16** (6), 21
DECISION ANALYSIS
Analysing Complex Decisions for Electric Utilities (Chao H P, Electric
Power Research Inst; Judd B R, Morris P A, Applied Decision
Analysis; Peck S C, Electric Power Research Inst) 1985 **18** (2), 46
Decision Analysis and Strategic Policy Formulation (Bunn D, Thomas
H, London Business Sch & Australian Graduate Sch of Mgt) 1977
10 (6), 23
Decision Analysis for Top Management (Sneddon L M, Sunridge
Park Mgt Centre) 1970 **3** (1), 50
Force Field Analysis—A Framework for Strategic Thinking (Ajimal K
S, Consultant) 1985 **18** (5), 55
Making Corporate Planning Work in Developing Countries (Haines W
R) 1988 **21** (2), 91
DECISION MAKING
Classifying Capital Projects for Top Management Decision-Making
(Piper J A, Loughborough U) 1980 **13** (3), 45
The Cut-Off Rate for Investment Decisions in Growth Companies
(Chandra G, Miami U) 1975 **8** (2), 95
Decision making in the Public Sector—A Logical Model (Kahalas H,
Virginia Poly Inst State U) 1976 **9** (3), 75
Decision Support System: A New Tool for Strategic Management
(Yoo S, Bowling Green State U Ohio; Digman, L A, U of Nebraska)
1987 **20** (2), 114
The Decision-Making Process for Strategic Adaptation (Ronchi L,
Rome U) 1980 **13** (1), 48

Decisions, Judgement and Style (Loveridge D J, Pilkingtons) 1979
12 (1), 22
Designing Information Systems for Strategic Decisions (Hayes R L,
Radosevich R, Vanderbilt U) 1974 **7** (4), 45
Effect of Economic Planning on Business Decisions (Jain S C,
Connecticut U) 1977 **10** (4), 42
A Framework of Decision Making for Technological Change (Cox J
G, Essex U) 1978 **11** (1), 53
How Managers Decide to Use Planning Models (Blanning R W,
Pennsylvania U) 1980 **13** (2), 32
How Strategic Decisions are Made (Mazzolini R, Columbia U) 1981
14 (3), 85
How U.S. and Japanese CEO's Spend Their Time (Kudo H,
Tachikawa T, Suzuki N) 1988 **21** (6), 79
Improving Government Expenditure Decisions through Programme
Analysis and Review (East R J, Consultant) 1973 **6** (1), 2
Investing in CAD: A Case of *ad hoc* Decision-making (Currie W L)
1989 **22** (6), 85
Management Illusions and Biases: Their Impact on Strategic
Decisions (Schwenk C R, U of Illinois) 1985 **18** (5), 74
Planning Participation in Public Decision Making (Davies J,
Newcastle Upon Tyne U) 1970 **2** (4), 23
Who Influences Strategic Decisions? (Hegarty W H, Indiana U;
Hoffman R C, Coll of William and Mary, Virginia) 1987 **20** (2), 61
DECISION MODELS
An Environmental Decision Model for Dynamic Planning (Kahalas H,
Virginia Poly Inst State U; Bjorklund R L, Worcester Poly) 1976 **9**
(1), 81
DECISION SUPPORT SYSTEMS
Building a Strategic Data Base (Szewczak E J) 1988 **21** (2), 97
Designing Communication Support Systems for Strategic Planning
(Charalambides L C) 1988 **21** (6), 93
Designing an Effective Financial Planning and Control System
(Cowen S S, Middaugh II J K) 1988 **21** (6), 83
Developing Knowledge-based Systems for Strategic Corporate
Planning (Mockler R J, Dologite D G) 1988 **21** (1), 97
Developing Strategies for Management Information Systems (Tozer
E E, Consultant) 1986 **19** (4), 31
Planning for Strategic Decision Support Systems (King W R,
Pittsburgh U) 1983 **16** (5), 73
DEFENCE
Civil Spin-off from Defence Research: A Fresh Approach (Herdan B
L, Defence Technology Enterprises) 1987 **20** (1), 84
Defence Planning: The Uncertainty Factor (Moulton J L, Consultant)
1971 **3** (4), 50
Long Range Defence Planning in the U.K. (Cooper F, MOD) 1970 **3**
(2), 18
Long Range Planning in the Defence Equipment Business (Bowman
D O, Autonetics) 1970 **2** (3), 66
An Organizational Study Approach to Planning Problems in an
Industrial-Military Activity (Weston F C, Colorado State U) 1973 **6**
(4), 58
Risk-Decision Analysis in Weapons Systems Acquisitions (Cuff J D,
Consultant) 1973 **6** (1), 49
Strategic Planning for the Armed Forces (Russell Colonel W N,
Canadian National Defence HQ) 1986 **19** (4), 41
DEFENCE INDUSTRIES
French '*Savoir-Faire*' in Selling Arms: A New Way of Doing
Business? (Anastassopoulos J-P, Dussauge P, Hautes Etudes
Commerciales) 1985 **18** (5), 13
DELPHI TECHNIQUE
The Delphi Method and Urbanization (Marley-Clarke B, Environment
Canada) 1974 **7** (6), 81
Energy and the Environment—A Delphi Forecast (Smil V, Manitoba
U) 1972 **5** (4), 27
Long Range Planning for Public Libraries—A Delphi Study
(Kennington D, Information) 1977 **10** (2), 73
Medicines in the 1990's: Experience with a Delphi Forecast
(Teeling-Smith G, Office of Health Economics) 1971 **3** (4), 69
New Uses of Delphi in Strategy Formulation (Wedley W C, Simon
Fraser U) 1977 **10** (6), 70
The Oracle that Failed (Stander A, Rickards T, Manchester Business
Sch) 1975 **8** (5), 13

Personnel Administration in 1980: A Delphi Study (Lachmann O, Danish Inst of Graduate Engineers) 1972 **5** (2), 21

Realistic Planning for Transportation — A Flexible Approach (Khan A M) 1989 **22** (5), 128

Technological Forecasting and the Delphi Technique—A Reply (Rowlands D G, Unilever Research Laboratory) 1969 **2** (2), 78

Technological Forecasting for Power Generation—A Study Using the Delphi Technique (Garde V D, Patel R R, Bharat Heavy Electricals) 1985 **18** (4), 73

Technological Forecasting—a Criticism of the Delphi Technique (Overbury R E, Min of Tech) 1969 **1** (4), 76

A Unique Event and Delphi Technique (Wilson L S, Durham U) 1977 **10** (1), 79

DEMOGRAPHY

Demographic and Social Trends 1970—1980 (Sadler P, Barham K, Ashridge Mgt Coll) 1982 **15** (5), 52

Demography and Planning (Moore P G, London Grad Sch of Business) 1969 **2** (2), 18

Middle Class Decline in Post-industrial Society (Simmie J, Brady R) 1989 **22** (4), 52

DENMARK

How Danish Companies Plan (Ackelsberg R, Harris W C) 1989 **22** (6), 111

DESIGN MANAGEMENT

Computer-aided Design and Manufacturing—A Manager's Guide (Burrows B C, Futures Information Assocs) 1986 **19** (5), 76

Design and Competition in Engineering (Rothwell R, Gardiner P, Sussex U) 1984 **17** (3), 78

The Function of Design in Long Range Planning (Black M, Design Research Unit) 1972 **5** (2), 9

Integration—The Key to Success with CAD/CAM (Schofield N A, PA Manufacturing Services) 1987 **20** (3), 84

The Strategic Design of Buildings (Nutt B) 1988 **21** (4), 130

DEVELOPING COUNTRIES

Are We Taking the World Development Problems Seriously?—An Overview of Recent Reports and Publications—Book Review Article (Lloyd B, Bank of Credit and Commerce Intl SA) 1979 **12** (3), 9

Corporate Planning in Developing Economies (Carter R D, UNIDO; Hamilton J G, Williams P J, Consultants) 1973 **6** (2), 2

Corporate Planning in a Developing Economy: Indian Experience (Venu S, India Tobacco) 1972 **5** (3), 29

The Developing World to 1990: Trends and Implications for Multinational Business (Wright P, Townsend D, Kinard J, Iverstine J, SE & NW Louisiana U) 1982 **15** (4), 116

Encouraging Entrepreneurs in Developing Countries (El-Namaki M S S) 1988 **21** (4), 98

Force Field Analysis—A Framework for Strategic Thinking (Ajimal K S, Consultant) 1985 **18** (5), 55

Future Demand Patterns in the Emerging World (Dam A van, CPC International Inc) 1974 **7** (4), 34

A Health Strategy for Nigeria (Adeyami K S, Petu A O) 1989 **22** (6), 55

Housing the Deprived and Underprivileged: India's Experience (Rao B B, Inst of Management India) 1979 **12** (1), 75

India: Can We Eliminate Poverty? (Bhargava P K, Banara Hindu U) 1987 **20** (2), 21

Installing a Computerized Planning System in Ghana (Babington E A, Peat Marwick McLintock) 1987 **20** (4), 110

Making Corporate Planning Work in Developing Countries (Haines W R) 1988 **21** (2), 91

Managing Toxic Wastes—After Bhopal and Sandoz (Mahon J F, Kelley P C, Boston U Sch of Mgt) 1987 **20** (4), 50

Marketing in Developing Countries: The New Frontier (Varadarajan P R, Texas U) 1984 **17** (6), 118

The New Industrializing Countries of Asia—Perspectives and Opportunities (Lasserre P, INSEAD) 1981 **14** (3), 36

Planned Divestment—A Five-step Approach (Clarke C J, Gall F, Wallace Smith Trust) 1987 **20** (1), 17

Planning Development Projects: Lessons from Developing Countries (Rondinelli D A, Syracuse U) 1979 **12** (3), 48

Planning for Industrial Development in Newly Independent Countries—An Operational Approach (Verhulst M, Montreal U) 1975 **8** (3), 79

Private Investment in Developing Countries (Porter R S, ODA) 1971 **4** (1), 58

The Second Decade—The Economic Outlook for a Developing Nation (Shelley R, Hume Industries) 1976 **9** (4), 66

Strategic Planning for Corporate Growth in Developing Countries (Dam A van, Corn Products Latin America) 1969 **2** (1), 9

Training: Key to Technological Transfer (Lasserre P, INSEAD) 1982 **15** (3), 51

Transferring Technology to Developing Countries — Critical Factors for Success (Madu C N) 1989 **22** (4), 115

Vaulting Trade Barriers: The Japanese Approach (Varadarajan P R, Texas A & M U) 1985 **18** (1), 73

DEVELOPMENT

Are We Taking the World Development Problems Seriously?—An Overview of Recent Reports and Publications—Book Review Article (Lloyd B, Bank of Credit and Commerce Intl SA) 1979 **12** (3), 97

Assessing the Performance of a Development Bank (Jain P K) 1989 **22** (6), 100

Corporate Development—Preferred Strategies in U.K. Companies (Littler D A, U of Manchester; Sweeting R C, UMIST) 1987 **20** (2), 125

Development Planning—An Adaptive Approach (Sachdeva P S, Indian Institute of Management) 1984 **17** (4), 96

DISASTERS

Planning for Disasters (Sillar W, Sthn General Hospital) 1975 **8** (5), 2

Planning for Emergencies-Lessons From the Chemical Industry (Kharbanda O P, Stallworthy E A) 1989 **22** (1), 83

Preventive Planning for Disasters (O'Keefe P, Westgate K, Bradford U) 1977 **10** (3), 25

DISCOUNTED CASH FLOW

Computerized Analysis of Capital Projects by DCF Techniques (Palma F, FID.IMI) 1972 **5** (4), 53

The Strategic Discount—Protecting New Business Projects Against DCF (Pearson G, Manchester Business School) 1986 **19** (1), 18

Using Finance for Competitive Advantage (Clarke C J) 1988 **21** (2), 63

Why Different Divisions Require Different Hurdle Rates (Andrews G S, Firer C, U of the Witwatersrand) 1987 **20** (5), 62

DISPOSABLES

Throwing Away Millions—Long Range Planning for Disposables (Lockett A G, Armstrong K, Manchester Business Sch) 1971 **4** (1), 15

DISTRIBUTION

Avoiding Dependence on Suppliers and Distributors (Bourantas D) 1989 **22** (3), 140

The Changing Pattern of Distribution (Slater A C, Manchester Poly) 1977 **10** (4), 29

An Effective Tool for the Optimization of Distribution Systems (Matt H, Berger Lenz Consultants) 1972 **5** (4), 48

Integrated Distribution Management—The American Perspective (La Londe B J, Ohio State U) 1969 **2** (2), 61

Logistics Systems Engineering—Solving the Distribution Planning Problem (Christopher M, Cranfield Inst of Technology) 1974 **7** (6), 72

Physical Distribution: A Suitable Case for Treatment (Ball R, Consultants) 1980 **13** (1), 2

Planning for Better Channel Management (Hardy K G, Magrath A J) 1988 **21** (6), 30

Planning for Physical Distribution (Weeks J, Hoover) 1977 **10** (3), 64

Reorganisation for Physical Distribution (Lancioni R A, Temple U) 1975 **8** (4), 46

Strategic Planning for Distribution (La Londe B J, Ohio State U) 1971 **4** (2), 23

DIVERSIFICATION

Assessing Opportunities for Diversification—An Analytical Approach (Younger M, Arthur D Little) 1984 **17** (4), 10

Building Competitive Strength in International Markets (Hitt M A, Ireland R D, Texas A & M U; Mays W A, Baylor U Texas) 1987 **20** (1), 115

Choosing a Diversification Project in a Regulated Economy (Das R, Mohanty B, Indian Inst of Mgt) 1981 **14** (2), 78

Diversification as a Factor in U.K. Industrial Strategy (Constable J, British Inst of Mgt) 1986 **19** (1), 52

Diversification in the Swiss Chemical Industry (Eugster C, J.R. Geigy) 1969 **2** (1), 42

Diversification—the Key Factors for Success (Detrie J-P, Ramanantsoa B) 1986 **19** (1), 31

How Successful Companies Manage Diverse Businesses (Calori R, CESMA) 1988 **21** (3), 80

Massey-Ferguson's Diversification into Industrial and Construction Equipment (Houston J, Massey Ferguson) 1970 **2** (3), 30

Risk Analysis and the Formulation of Acquisition/Diversification Strategies (Thomas H, Illinois U) 1983 **16** (2), 28

Strategies for Diversification (Hake B, Consultant) 1972 **5** (2), 65

A Systematic Approach to Diversification (Malmlow E G, B & S Corporate Devel) 1973 **6** (4), 2

DIVESTMENT

Management Buy-outs in Britain—A Monograph (Wright M, Coyne J, Robbie K, Centre for Mgt Buy-out Research, Nottingham) 1987 **20** (4), 38

Planned Divestment—A Five-step Approach (Clarke C J, Gall F, Wallace Smith Trust) 1987 **20** (1), 17

The Strategic Divestment Decision (Davis J B, Vanderbilt U) 1974 **7** (1), 15

DIVISIONALIZED COMPANIES

Business Synergy Does Not Always Pay Off (Mahajan V, Wind Y) 1988 **21** (1), 59

Financial Planning in a Divisionalized Firm (Singhvi S S, Armco Steel Corp and Miami U) 1972 **5** (4), 15

Organization of the Planning Department in a Divisionalized Concern (Friedrich A, Land A van't, Consultants) 1974 **7** (2), 27

DOCKS *see* **PORTS**

DYNAMIC MODELS

A Dynamic Programming Model for Long Range Educational Planning (Bailey D, Schotta C, Virginia Poly Inst and State U) 1971 **4** (1), 45

E

EARNINGS

Acquiring Firms With Higher PE Ratios (Roy A) 1988 **21** (5), 96

Quality of Earnings: A Key Factor in Financial Planning (Siegel J G, Shim J K, New York City U) 1981 **14** (6), 68

Rate of Return on New Invested Capital—Its Relationship to Corporate Earnings Growth Rate and Equity Market Values (Moore C S, Ethyl Corp) 1972 **5** (4), 33

Setting Corporate Objectives Using Market Required Earnings (Walsh C, Irish Mgt Inst; Mock E, FIN-ECON) 1979 **12** (5), 54

The V-Matrix—A New Tool for Plotting Earnings (McNamee P B, Ulster U) 1984 **17** (1), 19

ECOLOGY

Ecology, Pollution and Business: A Proposed Planning solution (Kahalas H, Groves D L, New York U) 1978 **11** (6), 62

Economic Development and Ecological Equilibrium—A Target Conflict in Modern Industrial Enterprises (Hohn S, Volkswagenwerk) 1982 **15** (4), 22

ECONOMETRIC MODELS

An Economic Model of World Energy 1900–2020 (Rothkopf M H, Shell Int) 1973 **6** (2), 43

ECONOMIC ANALYSIS

Economic Analysis of Public Water Supply in the Piscataqua River Watershed (Forste R H, Christensen R L, Water Resources Research Centre) 1971 **3** (4), 75

ECONOMIC CONDITIONS

Economic Trends (Forrest C, Consultant) 1982 **15** (5), 6

ECONOMIC DEVELOPMENT

The Management of Development—The Next Decade (Declerck R P, Ottawa U) 1977 **10** (3), 59

Promoting Small Business in Northern Ireland (Birley S, Cranfield Sch of Mgt; Bridge S, Local Enterprise Development Unit, Belfast) 1987 **20** (6), 71

Turnaround Strategies for Economic Development (Allen D N, Plosila W H) 1988 **21** (3), 59

ECONOMIC FORECASTING

Economic Forecasting for a Television Company (Bennett B C, Trident Management) 1978 **11** (5), 63

Forecasting the Economic and Business Environment (Morrell J, Morrell Assocs) 1972 **5** (1), 52

ECONOMIC GROWTH

Economic Development and Ecological Equilibrium—A Target Conflict in Modern Industrial Enterprises (Hohn S, Volkswagenwerk) 1982 **15** (4), 22

Economic and Industrial Development—A New Ingredient (Karger D W, Renssedaer Poly Inst) 1976 **9** (5), 90

Energy Resources and World Economic Growth (Brookes L G, U.K. Atomic Energy) 1973 **6** (3), 39

Innovation as the Source of Long Term Economic Growth (Ray G F, Nat Inst of Economic and Social Research) 1980 **13** (2), 9

ECONOMIC INDICATORS

Economic Impact Reports—Management Controls for the 1980's (Shorrock J, Dobson S, Honeywell) 1979 **12** (6), 26

ECONOMIC PLANNING

The Dangers of Centralized Economic Planning (Duncombe H L, General Motors Corp) 1976 **9** (3), 16

Economic Planning in India: Failure or Success? (Bhargava P K, Benares Hindu U) 1982 **15** (1), 87

Effect of Economic Planning on Business Decisions (Jain S C, Connecticut U) 1977 **10** (4), 42

National Policy Making in a Global Economy: The Case for U.S. Economic Planning (Bolling R, Boston Coll; Krauthoff L C, U.S. Government) 1983 **16** (3), 25

New Methods of Economic Management must be Developed (Bray J, Min of Tech) 1968 **1** (1), 51

Planning and Economics (Semister L, Bradford U) 1971 **4** (2), 63

Planning for Industrial Development in Newly Independent Countries—An Operational Approach (Verhulst M, Montreal U) 1975 **8** (3), 79

The Relationship between Land Use and Economic Planning in the United Kingdom (Sharp E, Consultant) 1970 **3** (1), 16

ECONOMY

Energy and the Economy—A Reply to Smil and Kuz (Brookes L G, UKAEA) 1977 **10** (1), 54

EDUCATION

Assessing the Environment for an Educational Institution (Huff A S, Ranney J M, Consultant) 1981 **14** (3), 107

A Dynamic Programming Model for Long Range Educational Planning (Bailey D, Schotta C, Virginia Poly Inst and State U) 1971 **4** (1), 45

see also **HIGHER EDUCATION**

EFFECTIVENESS

How Effective is Your Information Systems Planning? (King W R) 1988 **21** (5), 103

Making Planning More Effective (Dyson R G, Warwick U; Foster M J, Kingston Poly) 1983 **16** (6), 68

ELECTRICITY SUPPLY INDUSTRY

Analysing Complex Decisions for Electric Utilities (Chao H P, Electric Power Research Inst; Judd B R, Morris P A, Decision Analysis Inc; Peck S C, Electric Power Research Inst) 1985 **18** (2), 46

Building Scenarios for an Electric Utility (Goldfarb D L, Huss W R) 1988 **21** (2), 78

A Computer-Based Modelling System for Electric Utility Planning (Ben-Yaacov G Z, Electricity Supply Commission) 1978 **11** (6), 30

Energy Scenarios—The Sizewell Experience (Hankinson G A, Kingston Poly) 1986 **19** (5), 94

Marketing Electricity—A Military Approach (Faruqui A, Battelle Columbus, Palo Alto) 1987 **20** (4), 67

New Venture Management in a Electric Utility (Harrell G D, Michigan State U; Murray G O, Utility Technical Services Inc) 1986 **19** (2), 57

Planning for Electricity Generation in India (Patel R R, Bharat Heavy Electrical) 1983 **16** (4), 61

ELECTRONIC DATA PROCESSING

Managing the Growth of Electronic Office Information Systems (Hirschheim R A, LSE) 1983 **16** (6), 59

ELECTRONICS INDUSTRY

Business Strategies in Small High-technology Companies (Smith J G, Fleck V, Cambridge U) 1987 **20** (2), 61

Exploratory Planning in an Electronics Industry (Geradin L A, Look Out Studies) 1973 **6** (3), 72

Integrated Circuits: The Coming Battle (Mackintosh I M, Mackintosh Consultants) 1979 **12** (3), 28

Japanese Manufacturing: Strategy and Practice (Bolwijn P T, Brinkman S, Philips Intl BV) 1987 **20** (1), 25

Managing a Global Electronics Company in Tomorrow's World (Dekker W, N.V. Philips Gloeilampenfabrieken) 1986 **19** (2), 31

Planning Research and Development at Hitachi (Kuwahara Y, Okada O, Horikoshi H) 1989 **22** (3), 54

EMPLOYEE PARTICIPATION

Business Planning and Employee Democracy in Yugoslavia (Milisavljevic M, Belgrade U) 1983 **16** (4), 84

Winning Customers Through Employee Involvement (Bailey J, Bristol Mgt Centre) 1984 **17** (4), 79

ENERGY

Advanced Concepts for Bulk Power Systems Studies (Masud E, US Energy Research and Devel Administration) 1977 **10** (5), 25

Alternative Technologies and the Rising cost of Energy (Clarke F J P, Harwell Laboratory) 1981 **14** (4), 51

The Corporate Energy Policy: A Management Planning Perspective (Lambert D M, Michigan State U: Stock J R, Notre Dame U) 1979 **12** (2), 45

Energy: Long Term Prospects, On Some Recent Significant Energy Publications—Book Review Article (Ray G F, Nat Inst of Economic and Social Research) 1978 **11** (2), 71

Energy Choices for the Future (Jones P M S, Atomic Energy Authority) 1980 **13** (6), 18

Energy and the Economy—A Global and National Analysis (Smil V, U of Manitoba; Kuz T, U of Winnipeg) 1976 **9** (3), 65

Energy and the Economy—a Reply to Smil and Kuz (Brookes L G, UKAEA) 1977 **10** (1), 54

Energy and the Environment—A Delphi Forecast (Smil V, Manitoba U) 1972 **5** (4), 27

The Energy Manager and His Corporate Role (Bowonder B, Coll of India) 1984 **17** (4), 74

The Energy Market and Energy Planning (Robinson C, Surrey U) 1976 **9** (6), 30

Energy Modeling as a Tool for Planning (Kopelman J B, Weaver N L, SRI Energy Center) 1978 **11** (1), 25

Energy Options to 2030 (Fells I, Newcastle upon Tyne U) 1982 **15** (4), 76

Energy Planning in India (Venu S, Inst of Financial Mgt and Research) 1982 **15** (3), 146

Energy Policy: Government vs Industry (Jones P, Electricity Council) 1987 **20** (1), 12

Energy and Primary Materials (Ray G, Consultant) 1982 **15** (5), 95

Energy Resources and the Impact of New Technologies (Ibrahim S M A, Al-Azhar U) 1980 **13** (4), 63

Energy Resources and World Economic Growth (Brookes L G, U.K. Atomic Energy), 1973 **6** (3), 39

Energy Scenarios—The Sizewell Experience (Hankinson G A, Kingston Poly) 1986 **19** (5), 94

Energy and U.K. Agriculture (Wilson P N, Brigstocke T, BOCM Silcock) 1977 **10** (5), 64

New Jobs in Energy Research and Development—A Survey (Davis D L, Houston U) 1977 **10** (4), 51

Resources and Demand in This Century and Beyond (Ray G F, Nat Inst of Economic and Social Research) 1973 **6** (1), 56

Three Energy Scenarios for the United Kingdom (Chapman P F, Open U) 1976 **9** (2), 2

World Energy Resources and the Limitations of Computer Modelling (Chesshire J H, Surrey A J, Sussex U) 1975 **8** (3), 54

ENERGY SAVING

Energy Cost Saving Starts on the Shop Floor (Boatfield D, 3M U.K.) 1984 **17** (1), 73

ENGINEERING

The Strategic Design of Buildings (Nutt B) 1988 **21** (4), 130

ENGINEERING INDUSTRY

Corporate Planning in an Engineering Business (Booth H J, GEC AEI Control Rectifiers) 1970 **3** (1), 67

The Corporate Road-map—Planning at Babcock & Wilcox (Allio R J, Babcock & Wilcox) 1972 **5** (4), 9

Design and Competition in Engineering (Rothwell R, Gardiner P, Sussex U) 1984 **17** (3), 78

Materials Developments and Planning—Future Implications in the Engineering and Chemical Industries (Locke B, Nat Research Devel Corp) 1969 **2** (1), 66

Planning in a German Engineering Business (Heckman N, Consultant) 1971 **3** (4), 54

Product Planning at Perkins Engines Group (Kraushar C A A, Perkins Engines Group) 1968 **1** (2), 15

ENTERPRISE

Lessons of Privatization (Lord King) 1987 **20** (6), 18

ENTREPRENEURSHIP

Corporate Strategy and Entrepreneurial Vision (Shirley S) 1989 **22** (6), 107

The Delusion of Intrapreneurship (Morse C W, California State U) 1986 **19** (6), 92

Encouraging Entrepreneurs in Developing Countries (El-Namaki M S S) 1988 **21** (4), 98

Getting a Quicker Pay-off From R & D (van den Kroonenberg H H) 1989 **22** (5), 51

How Entrepreneurs Manage Growth (O'Neill H M, Connecticut U) 1983 **16** (1), 116

Promoting Entrepreneurship in Large Companies (Pearson G J) 1989 **22** (3), 87

Strategy as a System of Expedients (Hinterhuber H, Popp W) 1988 **21** (4), 107

ENVIRONMENT

Energy and the Environment—A Delphi Forecast (Smil V, Manitoba U) 1972 **5** (4), 27

Entering the 21st Century: The Global 2000 Report to the President—Book Review Article (Nutt W O, Estercrete) 1983 **16** (3), 120

Enviromental Impact Assessments—Their Development and Application (Kelcey J G, Consultant Ecologist) 1986 **19** (1), 67

Linking Organizational Effectiveness and Environmental Change (Shipper F, Arizona State U) 1983 **16** (3), 99

Road Transport and the Environment (Cottee B, Nat Freight Corporation) 1978 **11** (2), 39

ENVIRONMENT MANAGEMENT

Policy Planning for Environmental Management (Marley-Clarke B W G, Environment Canada) 1976 **9** (5), 2

ENVIRONMENTAL PROTECTION

Strategic Planning for the World Wildlife Fund (Medley G J) 1988 **21** (1), 46

The Thames Tidal Flood Prevention Scheme (Horner R W, GLC) 1976 **9** (5), 78

EUROPE

Business Planning in Europe (Kyle B S, European Planning Federation) 1981 **14** (5), 2

The European Automobile Industry—Three Possible Scenarios (Hohn S, Volkswagenwerk) 1980 **13** (4), 12

A European Bibliography of Corporate Planning, 1972 (Kettlewell P J, Sandoz Products & Wander) 1974 **7** (1), 72

The European Cultural Foundation's Plan Europe 2000 (Chabert J, European Cultural Foundation) 1975 **8** (4), 23

Formation of European Society 1968 **1** (2), 37

The Future for European Business—Strategies for Growth (Le Franc J-D, Commissariat General du Plan) 1980 **13** (4), 18

Japan's Drive for the European Car Market—Lessons from U.S. Experience (Wray M, Toftech; Norburn D, Imperial Coll, London) 1987 **20** (4), 60

Key Social Issues for European Business (Taylor B, Henley Mgt Coll; Ferro L, Turin Centre for Mgt Devel) 1983 **16** (1), 42

Long-Term Planning and Forecasting in Europe (Sombart N, Council of Europe) 1972 **5** (2), 47

The New Environment of European Corporations (Lefebvre M, Dor P, Germay J, Verraver J, SCES) 1978 **11** (1), 15

Predicting Plant Closures in European Industry (Baden-Fuller C, Longley R) 1988 **21** (1), 90

Strategic Decision Making in Large European Firms (Guoy M, French Embassy) 1978 **11** (3), 41

Strategic Planning in European Multinationals (Gotcher J W, California State U) 1977 **10** (5), 7

Strategic Planning for Internationalization—The European Dilemma and some Possible Solutions (Franko L G, CEI) 1973 **6** (2), 58

Technological Innovation in European Industry: The Need for a World Perspective (Pavitt K, OECD) 1969 **2** (2), 8

Towards 1992: A Strategy for Training (Day D) 1989 **22** (6), 48

EUROPEAN ECONOMIC COMMUNITY

1992: A European Market for Cars? (Perrin-Pelletier F) 1988 **21** (3), 27

Trucks and Road Transport Towards 1992 (Garuzo G) 1988 **21** (4), 45

Why Europeans are Weak in Asia—An Organizational Perspective (Lasserre P) 1988 **21** (4), 25

Working Women in the European Community—The Future Prospect (Davidson M J, Cooper G L, Manchester U) 1983 **16** (4), 49

see also **SINGLE EUROPEAN MARKET**

EUROPEANS

Why Europeans are Weak in Asia—An Organizational Perspective (Lasserre P) 1988 **21** (4), 25

EVALUATION

How to Evaluate a Long-Range Plan (Noya L E De, US Govt Printing Office) 1978 **11** (3), 36

UK Competition Policy Evaluated (Pass C L, Sparkes J R, Bradford) 1983 **16** (4), 76

EXPERIENCE CURVES

The Experience Curve and History of the Cellophane Business (Cowley P R, Cranfield Sch of Mgt) 1985 **18** (6), 84

The Uses and Abuses of Experience Curves (Sallenave J-P, U of Sherbrooke) 1985 **18** (1), 64

EXPORTING

Federated Marketing—A Practical Approach to Export for the Smaller Company or Division (Claxton C, Europa Industrial Projects) 1979 **12** (6), 43

Reorganization for Export at Ideal Standard (Paterson R R, Ideal-Standard) 1970 **3** (2), 65

F

FASHIONS

Long Range Planning in a Fast Changing Fashion Market (Stait N H, Urwick, Orr & Partners) 1970 **3** (2), 55

FEDERAL REPUBLIC OF GERMANY

The Control Function in Major German Companies (Hand D, Institut fur Unternehmungsplanung) 1982 **15** (3), 21

Corporate Planning and Control in German Industry (Topfer A, Albert-Ludwigs-U) 1978 **11** (1), 59

Key Strategic Issues for German Companies (Hohn S, Volkswagen AG) 1986 **19** (6), 38

Organization for Long Range Planning—A Survey of German Companies (Keppler W, Bamberger I, Gabele E, Rutgerswerke AG; Inst de Gestion de Rennes) 1979 **12** (5), 69

Patterns of Success in German Business (Kruger W) 1989 **22** (2), 106

Planning in a German Engineering Business (Hackman N, Consultant) 1971 **3** (4), 54

Planning in a German Steel Company (Friedrich A, Hoesch AG) 1972 **5** (4), 78

Planning Procedures in German Companies—Findings and Consequences (Scholz C, Regensburg U) 1984 **17** (6), 94

Planning in West German Industry (Strigel W H, IFO-Inst for Econ Research) 1970 **3** (1), 9

FINANCIAL ANALYSIS

Acquiring Firms With Higher PE Ratios (Roy A) 1988 **21** (5), 96

Company Failure or Company Health?—Techniques for Measuring Company Health (Robertson J, Mills R W) 1988 **21** (2), 70

Financial Evaluation of Corporate Plans (Merrett A J, Lehr M F, London Graduate Sch of Business) 1970 **2** (3), 37

FINANCIAL CENTRES

The Future of London as an International Financial Centre (Kendrick D W, Lloyd's Bank) 1980 **13** (1), 42

FINANCIAL FORECASTING

Financial Forecasting for Corporate Planning (Kingshott A L, Ford Europe) 1968 **1** (2), 28

Financial Trends (Kern D, Economic Analysis) 1982 **15** (5), 18

Forecasting Expenditure on Capital Project (Keller A Z, Ashraft R A, Bradford U; Green N P, DHSS, Riyadh U) 1984 **17** (4), 110

The V-Matrix—A New Tool for Plotting Earnings (McNamee P B, Ulster U) 1984 **17** (1), 19

FINANCIAL INSTITUTIONS

Appraising Financial Performance for Financial Institutions (Brown K, W Greenwell) 1980 **13** (1), 82

The Future of Computers in Financial Institutions (Cleaver A B, IBM) 1980 **13** (3), 12

The Impact of Retailers on Financial Services (Bliss M) 1988 **21** (1), 55

The Revolution in Building Societies (Wells G E) 1989 **22** (5), 30

The Stock Exchange After the Big Bang (Valentine S) 1988 **21** (2), 35

FINANCIAL MODELS

Acquiring Firms With Higher PE Ratios (Roy A) 1988 **21** (5), 96

Financial Modelling for Planning in the U.K. (Grinyer P H, St Andrews U) 1983 **16** (5), 58

Financial Modelling for Planning—Book Review Article (Sutcliffe R, EPS Consultants) 1979 **12** (4), 91

Financial Modelling—A Tool for Raising Management Performance (Beerel A C) 1986 **19** (4), 47

Financial Models in Corporate Planning—Book Review Article (Sutcliffe R, EPS Consultants) 1979 **12** (4), 91

The R.T.Z. Financial Modelling Programme (Archer W R Z, R.T.Z.) 1971 **3** (4), 32

Re-positioning a Leading Stockbroker (Dorwin K) 1988 **21** (6), 13

The Use of Financial Models in Long Range Planning (Dohrn P J, P-E Consulting Group; Salkin G R, Imperial Coll) 1969 **2** (2), 27

FINANCIAL PERFORMANCE

Appraising Financial Performance for Financial Institutions (Brown K, W Greenwell) 1980 **13** (1), 82

Measuring Performance in Capital Project Management (Snowdon M, Cleveland Project Services) 1980 **13** (4), 51

FINANCIAL PLANNING

Calculating the Cost of Capital (Dimson E, March P, London Business Sch) 1982 **15** (2), 112

Classes of Financial Planning Package—A Management Perspective (Finlay P N, Loughborough U) 1985 **18** (6), 94

Computers and Financial Planning (Power P D, EPS Consultants) 1975 **8** (6), 53

Designing an Effective Financial Planning and Control System (Cowen S S, Middaugh II J K) 1988 **21** (6), 83

Establishing a Financial Objective—A Practical Approach (Allen D, Cadbury Schweppes) 1979 **12** (6), 11

Financial Aspects of Company Planning (Welter P, Consultant) 1973 **6** (1), 36

Financial Issues in Strategic Planning (Zettergren L, Consultant) 1975 **8** (3), 23

Financial Planning in a Divisionalized Firm (Singhvi S S, Armco Steel Corp) 1972 **5** (4), 15

Financial Planning for New Products Part 1—Basis for Model Formulation (Albala A, Technion) 1977 **10** (4), 61

Financial Planning, Using Goal Programming (Batson R G) 1989 **22** (5), 112

How to Design a Financial Planning Model (Hayen R L, Nebraska U) 1983 **16** (5), 111

Quality of Earnings: A Key Factor in Financial Planning (Siegel J G, Shim J K, New York City U) 1981 **14** (6), 68

Strategies of New Biotechnology Firms (Smith J G, Fleck V) 1988 **21** (3), 51

Tioxide: Computerization—The Key to the Future in Financial Planning (Benford P, Tioxide Group) 1985 **18** (3), 102

Using Finance for Competitive Advantage (Clarke C J) 1988 **21** (2), 63

FINANCIAL POLICY

Critical Decision Areas in Corporate Financial Policy (Hartley W C F, Bradford U) 1970 **2** (4), 54

Managing Diversity: Strategy and Control in Diversified British Companies (Goold M, Campbell A, London Business Sch) 1987 **20** (5), 42

FINANCIAL REPORTING

The Projection of Financial Results (Packer J P L, Cunard Steam Ship) 1971 **3** (3), 49

FINANCIAL SERVICES

Re-designing Bank Service Systems for Effective Marketing (Gupta Y P, Torkzadeh G) 1988 **21** (6), 38

Re-positioning a Leading Stockbroker (Dorwin K) 1988 **21** (6), 13

The Revolution in Building Societies (Wells G E) 1989 **22** (5), 30

FINANCING

Financing the Smaller Company (Dimson E, London Business Sch) 1978 **11** (6), 9

Industrial Investment and Financial Requirements (Mast H J, Credit Suisse) 1978 **11** (6), 42

Investing and Financing in a New Era (Coussement A M, Kredietbank SA) 1978 **11** (5), 2

FISHING INDUSTRY

A Future for Fishing (Eddie G C, Consultant) 1975 **8** (5), 76

The Management of Offshore Resources—Some Implications of the 200-Mile Limit (Puccini D S, Fisheries & Oceans; Marley-Clarke B W G, Corporate Services) 1979 **12** (5), 8

FOOD

The World Food Prospect (Brown L R, Worldwatch Inst) 1977 **10** (1), 26

FOOD AND DRINKS INDUSTRY

Food Manufacturing: The Future Prospect (Darling P, Boehampton Inst of Higher Education) 1983 **16** (1), 26

Food Retailing in the Eighties—Technological Opportunities and Social Constraints (MacLaurin I, Tesco Stores) 1982 **15** (1), 40

The Future of the British Breakfast Cereals Industry (Wheale P R, St. John's Coll) 1978 **11** (2), 60

The Impact of the EEC on the U.K. Food, Drink and Tobacco Processing Industry (Nicholls J R, Bath U) 1979 **12** (3), 82

The Influence of Retailing Trends on the Food Industry (Tanburn J, Booler McConnell) 1975 **8** (3), 10

FORECASTING

Can Recessions be Predicted? (Majani B, Aussedat-Rey; Makridakis S, INSEAD) 1977 **10** (2), 31

Creating Confidence about the Future: The Forecasting Business-Book Review Article (Brech R, Bradford U) 1978 **11** (5), 89

Environmental Scanning and Forecasting in Strategic Planning—The State of the Art (Fahey L, King W R, Narayanan V K, Pittsburgh U) 1981 **14** (1), 32

Forecasting and the Business Cycle in an Uncertain Environment (Strigel W H, CIRET Centre) 1980 **13** (5), 21

Forecasting in Conditions of Uncertainty (Fildes R, Jalland M, Wood D, Manchester Business Sch) 1978 **11** (4), 29

Forecasting Demand for Food in Libya—Using Confidence Limits (Malik M A K, Ahmad I, Nat Academy for Scientific Research) 1981 **14** (5), 90

Forecasting Environmental Protection Legislation Using Cross Impact Analysis (Beasley J E, Johnson R, Imperial Coll) 1984 **17** (6), 132

Forecasting the Impact of Public Policies (Renfro W L, Policy Analysis) 1980 **13** (4), 80

Forecasting the Impact of Social change (Morris G K, Matrix Consultants) 1975 **8** (3), 64

Forecasting Mexico's Oil Potential (Uri N D, US Govt) 1982 **15** (4), 86

Forecasting Organizational Changes (Elbing A O, IMEDE Mgt Devel Inst) 1974 **7** (6), 43

Forecasting Political Decisions and Their Impact on Business (Jonsson S, Petzall I, Federation of Swedish Industry) 1982 **15** (4), 98

Foresight Activities in the U.S.A.: Time for a Re-Assesment (Lederman L L, National Science Foundation) 1984 **17** (3), 41

The Futility of Forecasting (Moyer R, California U) 1984 **15** (4), 91

Future Forecasting with LEAP (Preble J F, New York State U) 1982 **15** (4), 64

How Scenarios Trigger Strategic Thinking (Millett S M) 1988 **21** (5), 61

How to Develop and Use Scenarios (Schnaars S P, City U of New York) 1987 **20** (1), 105

If we Cannot Forecast How Can we Plan? (Makridakis S, INSEAD) 1981 **14** (3), 10

Integrating Forecasting and Planning (Makridakis S, INSEAD; Wheelwright S, Harvard U) 1973 **6** (3), 53

Long-Term Planning and Forecasting in Europe (Sombart N, Council of Europe) 1972 **5** (2), 47

Management in the 21st Century (Makridakis S) 1989 **22** (2), 37

Managing Public Policy Issues (Barrows D S, Morris S) 1989 **22** (6), 66

Medicines in the 1990's: Experience with a Delphi Forecast (Teeling-Smith G, Office of Health Economics) 1971 **3** (4), 69

The Modern Prophets—How Can They Help Us? (Wissema J G, Consultant) 1982 **15** (4), 126

A Note on Forecasting the Market Demand for Waste Paper (Livesey F, Consultant) 1978 **11** (1), 87

Planning for the U.S. Political Cycle (Marcus A A, Mevorach B) 1988 **21** (4), 50

Planning for a University, Using Interactive Forecasting (Moore L F, Charach L, British Columbia U) 1980 **13** (3), 109

Predicting Plant Closures in European Industry (Baden-Fuller C, Longley R) 1988 **21** (1), 90

Product Forecasting: The BAC 3–11 Airliner (Thomas C H, BAC) 1970 **2** (4), 36

Projecting Consumptions of Competing Products (Hinomoto H, Illinois U) 1977 **10** (5), 46

Realistic Planning for Transportation — A Flexible Approach (Khan A M) 1989 **22** (5), 128

Scenario Planning—What Style Should You Use? (Huss W R, Xenergy; Honton E J, Battelle Columbus) 1987 **20** (4), 21

Strategy as a System of Expedients (Hinterhuber H, Popp W) 1988 **21** (4), 107

Tourism—Key Issues for the 1980s (Burkart A J, Surrey U) 1982 **15** (4), 91

Values in Forecasting and Planning (Redmond W H, Houston U) 1978 **11** (3), 22

FOREIGN EXCHANGE

Foreign Exchange Risk Management (Donaldson J A, ICI) 1979 **12** (3), 22

The Medium-Term Currency Outlook (Kern D, Nat Westminster Bank) 1980 **13** (2), 2

FOREIGN INVESTMENT

Assessing Country Risk for Foreign Investment Decisions (Leavy B, Nat Inst for Higher Education Dublin) 1984 **17** (3), 141

Private Investment in Developing Countries (Porter R S, ODA) 1971 **4** (1), 58

Selecting a Foreign Partner for Technology Transfer (Lasserre P, INSEAD) 1984 **17** (6), 43

Strategic Alliances with Japanese Firms (Kobayashi N) 1988 **21** (2), 29

FORESTRY INDUSTRY

Forest Policy—Formulation and Implementation (Johnston D R, Forestry Commission) 1975 **8** (6), 30

Forestry and Long Range Planning (Convery F J, Duke U Sch of Forestry) 1973 **6** (2), 27

FRANCE

French '*Savoir-Faire*' in Selling Arms: A New Way of Doing Business? (Anastassopoulos J-P, Dussauge P, Hautes Etudes Commerciales) 1985 **18** (5), 13

How French Industry Plans (Montebello M, Buigues P, Institut d'Administration des Enterprises) 1982 **15** (3), 116

Long Range Planning and Regional Policy. 2. France and Italy—Latecomers to the Industrial Urban Scene (Despicht N, Sussex U) 1970 **3** (1), 75

National Planning and the French Business Executive (Schollhammer H, UCLA Grad Sch of Business Admin) 1971 **3** (3), 22

The Pechiney Ugine Kuhlmann Plan (Letourneur J S, Pechiney Ugine Kuhlmann) 1973 **6** (1), 9

Successful Strategies in French High Technology Companies (Calori R, Noel R, Group Ecole Superieure de Commerce de Lyon) 1986 **19** (6), 54

Techniques and Methodology of the French Fifth Plan (Kidel A, Intl Monetary Fund) 1969 **1** (3), 60

FREE TRADE

North Atlantic Free Trade Area—the Implications for British Industry (Cowie H, Maxwell Stamp Assocs) 1969 **2** (2), 2

FREIGHT TRANSPORT

The Motor Freight Industry—A Case against Planning (Kallman E A, Shapiro H J, New York U) 1978 **11** (1), 81

FUEL

Alternative Fuels for Automobiles—the Medium-Term Realities (Williamson E I, Longley R C M, Chem Systems Intl) 1982 **15** (2), 32

FUTURE

Careers for the 21st Century (Handy C) 1988 **21** (3), 90

Creating Confidence about the Future: The Forecasting Business—Book Review Article (Brech R, Bradford U) 1978 **11** (5), 89

The Effects of the Future on Today's Decisions (Craver J K, Monsanto) 1973 **6** (2), 29

The Future of Leisure (Culligan K, Murphy J) 1989 **22** (6), 127

A Method for Exploring the Future (Chapman P F, Open U) 1976 **9** (1), 2

FUTURE STUDIES

2000 or Bust!—Book Review Article (Shanks M, National Consumer Council) 1979 **12** (1), 97

Branch Banking in the Year 2000 (Rosenberg R, Wells Fargo Bank) 1980 **13** (5), 65

Britain in the Year 2000: Some Issues for Planners (Bayliss D, Queensborough House) 1971 **3** (3), 65

Does Future Research Have a Corporate Role? (Holloway C, Consultant) 1978 **11** (5), 17

An Economic Model of World Energy 1900—2020 (Rothkopf M H, Shell Int) 1973 **6** (2), 43

Energy Options to 2030 (Fells I, Newcastle upon Tyne U) 1982 **15** (4), 76

The European Cultural Foundation's Plan Europe 2000 (Chabert J, European Cultural Foundation) 1975 **8** (4), 23

Future Forecasting with LEAP (Preble J F, New York State U) 1982 **15** (4), 64

Future Forecasting for Strategic Planning at General Electric (Wilson I H, Gen Electric) 1973 **6** (2), 39

Future Research—Working with Management Teams (Sims D, Eden C, Bath U) 1984 **17** (4), 51

Future Trends in Computing (Firnberg D, National Computing Centre) 1978 **11** (6), 58

Future Trends in World Trade (A Review of the Lima Target) (Aczel J, Morris G, European Manpower Advisory Services) 1978 **11** (2), 19

Futures Research: New Directions—Book Review Article (Holroyd P, Pilkington) 1980 **13** (1), 90

Futures Research—Is it Used? (Eppink D J, Free U) 1981 **14** (2), 33

Futures Research—Is it Useful? (Wissema J G, Bakkenist, Spits & Co) 1981 **14** (2), 29

The Modern Prophets—How Can They Help Us? (Wissema J G, Consultant) 1982 **15** (4), 126

Psychological Perspectives on the Future (Kay H, Exeter U) 1975 **8** (2), 51

Resources and Demand in This Century and Beyond (Ray G F, Nat Inst of Economic and Social Research) 1973 **6** (1), 56

Testing Plans Against Alternative Futures (Boshoff H) 1989 **22** (5), 69

The Use of Futures Research in Product Planning (Morris G K, Matrix Corporate Affairs Consultants) 1982 **15** (6), 67

Values and Future's Research (Croft W, NASA) 1977 **10** (6), 51

G

GAME THEORY

Game Theory Technique in Investment Planning (Singhvi S S, Armco Steel Corp & Miami U) 1974 **7** (4), 59

GAS INDUSTRY

A Management Strategy for Information Processing. 1—The Segas Case (Collins A C, South Eastern Gas) 1983 **16** (5), 29

Planning an Information System at Netherlands Gas (Adriaans W, Hoogakker J T) 1989 **22** (3), 64

Third World Oil and Gas—Underexplored and Underdeveloped (Odell P R, Economic Geography Inst) 1981 **14** (1), 10

GATT

What the New GATT Trade Agreement Means for Plastics (Christopher W F, Consultant) 1980 **13** (1), 77

GHANA

Installing a Computerized Planning System in Ghana (Babington E A, Peat Marwick McLintock) 1987 **20** (4), 110

GLASS INDUSTRY

The Development of Long Term Corporate Planning at Pilkington (Pinnell L B, Pilkington Bros.) 1969 **1** (4), 14

GOAL SETTING

Formal Approaches to Setting Long Range Goals (Dobbie J W, Pacific Lutheran U) 1974 **7** (3), 75

Goal Setting and Efficiency in Social Service Agencies (Keating B P, Notre Dame U; Keating M O, St. Mary's Coll) 1981 **14** (1), 40

How Leaders Use Goals (Molz R, Clarkson U) 1987 **20** (5), 91

Setting Goals in a Professional Service Firm (Keeney R L, Intl Inst for Applied Systems Analysis; Nair K, Wood-Clyde Consultants) 1976 **9** (3), 54

Setting Operational Goals for Corporate Social Responsibility (Carroll A B, Georgia U) 1978 **11** (2), 35

Strategy in Action—Techniques for Implementing Strategy (Reed R, Buckley M R) 1988 **21** (3), 67

GOALS

Conflict of Values—The Central Strategy Problem (Taylor B, Administrative Staff Coll) 1975 **8** (6), 20

Defining Goals—A Systems Approach (Morasky R L, Montana State U) 1977 **10** (2), 85

Establishing Goals (Tibbits G E, Wollongong U) 1979 **12** (2), 97

Setting Corporate Goals and Measuring Organizational Effectiveness—A Practical Approach (Mendelow A L, Pittsburgh U) 1983 **16** (1), 70

GOVERNMENT

Comparison of Strategic Planning in Large Corporations and Government (East R J, H.M. Treasury) 1972 **5** (2), 2

Computerised Industrial Forecasting for Planning in Central Government (Wells J D, DTI) 1971 **4** (2), 41

Corporate Planning as a Control System in United Kingdom Nationalized Industries (Harris D J, Davies B C L, Bath U) 1981 **14** (1), 15

The Dangers of Centralized Economic Planning (Duncombe H L, General Motors) 1976 **9** (3), 16

The Federal Government as a Source of Strategic Planning Information (Noya L E De, US Govt Printing Office) 1980 **13** (5), 100

The Frontiers of Government (Williams S, M.P.) 1972 **5** (3), 21

Manpower Planning at National and Company Level (Cox J, DTI) 1971 **3** (4), 27

R & D and Corporate Planning in Government (Peretz D, Inter-Bank Research Organisation) 1972 **5** (4), 67

Regulating Private Monopolies and Promoting Competition (Carsberg B, Office of Telecommunications London) 1986 **19** (6), 75

The Role of government in Industrial Innovation (Knight K E, Baca H R, Texas U) 1978 **11** (6), 79

Sector Policy in government (Marshall R, DOE) 1974 **7** (4), 2

A System of Government for the Seventies (Holt S C, Sheffield U) 1969 **2** (1), 61

Techniques and Methodology of the French Fifth Plan (Kidel A, Intl Monetary Fund) 1969 **1** (3), 60

The Thatcher Revolution — Radical Policies in a Changing Society (Worcester R M) 1989 **22** (4), 72

GOVERNMENT DEPARTMENTS

Can Bureaucracies Become More Flexible and Responsive (Longford M D, Dept of Health and Social Security) 1986 **19** (1), 99

Installing a Computerized Planning System in Ghana (Babington E A, Peat Marwick McLintock) 1987 **20** (4), 110

A Planning System for the British Prison Department (Garrett J, AIC Management Consultants; Home N, Home Office) 1972 **5** (3), 36

Strategic Management in a Government Agency (TenDam H, Mgt Consultant) 1986 **19** (4), 7

Systems Analysis and Planning for the Criminal Justice System (Blumstein A, Carnegie-Mellon U) 1972 **5** (4), 61

GOVERNMENT EXPENDITURE

Improving Government Expenditure Decisions through Programme Analysis and Review (East R J; Consultant) 1973 **6** (1), 2

GOVERNMENT-BUSINESS RELATIONS see **BUSINESS-GOVERNMENT RELATIONS**

GREECE

Planning for Esso Greece — The Impact of Nationalization (Labroukos N S, Lioukas S) 1989 **22** (4), 98

Strategies for Declining Businesses—Survival in the Fur Business (Siomkos G, Shrivastava P) 1987 **20** (6), 84

GROWTH

Balancing Total System Growth with Special Interests Protections-Book Review Article (Nielsen R P, Boston Coll) 1984 **17** (3), 153

The Cut-Off Rate for Investment Decisions in Growth Companies (Chandra G, Miami U) 1975 **8** (2), 95

The External Corporate Venture Capital Fund—A Valuable Vehicle for Growth (Bleicher K, Paul H) 1987 **20** (6), 64

Five Stages of Growth in Small Business (Scott M, U of Cape Town; Bruce R, Graduate Sch of Business) 1987 **20** (3), 45

Growth by Acquisition (Buckley A, Redland) 1975 **8** (4), 53

How Entrepreneurs Manage Growth (O'Neill H M, Connecticut U) 1983 **16** (1), 116

The Internationalization of Dutch Insurance Companies (Eppink D J, Van Rhijn B M) 1988 **21** (5), 54

Managing the Growth of Electronic Office Information Systems (Hirschhein R A, LSE) 1983 **16** (6), 59

see also **COMPANY GROWTH**

H

HEALTH

The Future for Pharmaceuticals in a Health Care Crisis (Redwood H) 1989 **22** (1), 18

A Health Strategy for Nigeria (Adeyami K S, Petu A O) 1989 **22** (6), 55

Improving Health Care Planning—Some Lessons from Immunization (Fottler M D, Alabama U) 1984 **17** (4), 88

Multiple Objective Planning for Regional Blood Centers (Kendall K E, Nebraska U) 1980 **13** (4), 98

Planning for Innovation in Health Care: A Breakthrough in Blood Banking (Kendall K E, Nebraska U) 1984 **17** (6), 127

Planning for the Physically Handicapped (Kenny B, Richards G, Clarke-Hill C) 1989 **22** (2), 91

HEALTH SERVICE

Planning and Health Care—The Approach in a Reorganized NHS (Donald B L, Manchester U) 1974 **7** (6), 33

Planning for Hospitals: No Focus, No Strategy (Thakur M, U of Texas) 1985 **18** (6), 77

Strategic Planning for Hospitals—A Health-needs Approach (Champagne F, Contandriopoulos A-P, Larouche D, Clemenhagen C, Barbir C, U of Montreal) 1987 **20** (3), 77

Strategic Planning in the Scottish Health Service—A Mixed-Scanning Approach (Wiseman C, Scottish Inst for Operational Research) 1979 **12** (2), 103

Systemic Health Planning (Sepulveda C R, UN Asia and Pacific Devel Inst) 1979 **12** (3), 62

What Should we Spend on Health Care? (Hardie M C, King's Fund Centre) 1974 **7** (1), 2

HIGH TECHNOLOGY

Computer Integrated Management—The Next Competitive Breakthrough (Wilmot R) 1988 **21** (6), 65

Designing Communication Support Systems for Strategic Planning (Charalambides L C) 1988 **21** (6), 93

GE's High-tech Strategy (Koerner E) 1989 **22** (4), 11

Strategic Management in Major Japanese Hightech Companies (Nakamura G-I, Asia U Tokyo) 1986 **19** (6), 82

HIGH TECHNOLOGY COMPANIES

Business Strategies in Small High-technology Companies (Smith J G, Fleck V, Cambridge U) 1987 **20** (2), 61

HIGHER EDUCATION

A Model for Long Range Planning in Higher Education (McKay C W, Cutting G D, Houston U) 1974 **7** (5), 58

HONG KONG

Will Hong Kong's Entrepreneurs Move to Planning? (Warrington M B, Napier Coll) 1982 **15** (3), 157

HOSPITAL MANAGEMENT

Integrated Planning for Health Care Organizations Especially Hospitals (Karger D W, West Florida U; Vora J A, St Cloud State Coll) 1979 **12** (1), 91

Shared Services—A Recipe for Cost-cutting in Hospitals (Griffin A, Adams S, Texas U) 1981 **14** (6), 76

Strategic Planning for Hospitals—A Health-needs Approach (Champagne F, Contandriopoulos A-P, Larouche D, Clemenhagen C, Barbir C, U of Montreal) 1987 **20** (3), 77

HOTEL AND CATERING INDUSTRY

How Marriott Corporation Grew Five-fold in Ten Years (Kennedy C) 1988 **21** (2), 10

Prospects for the British Hotel Industry (Bosman J, Consultant) 1976 **9** (6), 47

HOUSING

Home Ownership in the U.K. in the 1980s (Melville-Ross T, Nationwide Building Society) 1981 **14** (4), 43

Housing the Deprived and Underprivileged: India's Experience (Rao B B, Indian Inst of Mgt) 1979 **12** (1), 75

HUMAN RELATIONS

Marital Breakdown and the Future of Marriage (Dominian J, Marriage Research Centre) 1984 **17** (2), 77

HUMAN RESOURCE ACCOUNTING

Human Asset Accounting (Robinson D F, Spicer and Pegler) 1974 **7** (1), 58

HUNGARY

Corporate Planning in Hungarian Companies (Csath M) 1989 **22** (4), 89

Long-Term Planning in Hungarian Industry (Roman S, Hungarian Academy of Science) 1970 **3** (2), 23

Mathematical Models in National Planning (Vandorffy J, Min for Metallurgy and Mechanical Engineering) 1973 **6** (1), 42

Selection of Mission Oriented Programmes (Szakasits G D, State Office Technical Devel, Hungary) 1972 **5** (3), 58

Strategic Planning—A New Arrival in Hungarian Industry (Csath M, National Mgt Devel Centre) 1983 **16** (2), 85

I

INCOMES

Incomes, Productivity and Planning (Blakeman L T, Ford Motor Co) 1969 **1** (4), 10

INDIA

Assessing the Performance of a Development Bank (Jain P K) 1989 **22** (6), 100

Choosing a Diversification Project in a Regulated Economy (Das R, Mohanty B, Indian Inst of Mgt) 1981 **14** (2), 78

Corporate Planning in a Developing Economy: Indian Experience (Venu S, India Tobacco) 1972 **5** (3), 29

Corporate Planning in Domestic Airlines—An Indian Case Study (Subramaniam S, Sharma C K, Indian Inst of Mgt) 1975 **8** (4), 64

Corporate Planning in Indian Railways—A Case Study (Subramaniam S, Indian Inst of Mgt) 1979 **12** (3), 91

Cost-Benefit Analysis of Training—An Appraisal (Reddy Y R K, Administrative Staff Coll of India) 1979 **12** (6), 50

Development Planning—An Adaptive Approach (Sachdeva P S, Indian Inst of Mgt) 1984 **17** (4), 96

Economic Planning in India: Failure or Success? (Bhargava P K, Benares Hindu U) 1982 **15** (1), 87

Energy Planning in India (Venu S, Inst of Financial Mgt and Research) 1982 **15** (3), 146

Environmental Pollution and Economic Growth: Implications for Corporate Planning With an Indian Case Study (Venu S, India Tobacco) 1974 **7** (3), 49

Evaluating the Benefits of Formal Planning Systems (Camillus J C, Indian Inst of Mgt) 1975 **8** (3), 33

Housing the Deprived and Underprivileged: India's Experience (Rao B B, Indian Inst of Mgt) 1979 **12** (1), 75

India: Can We Eliminate Poverty? (Bhargava P K, Banara Hindu U) 1987 **20** (2), 21

India—The Plan for Steel (Rao R, Iron Ore Board) 1978 **11** (4), 22

Key Strategic Issues for Public Corporations (Subramaniam S, Balasubramaniam R, Admin Staff Coll of India) 1974 **7** (5), 39

Long-Term Planning for Indian Shipping (Kumar S P, Indian Inst of Mgt) 1976 **9** (6), 63

Marketing Planning in India—A Survey (Kapoor M C, Singh J D, Delhi U) 1981 **14** (3), 97

Planning for Banking—The Indian Experience (Godse V T, Nat Inst of Bank Management, Bombay) 1986 **19** (1), 105

Planning for Electricity Generation in India (Patel R R, Bharat Heavy Electrical) 1983 **16** (4), 61

Planning Problems of State Road Transport—India (Subramaniam S, Indian Inst of Mgt) 1976 **9** (1), 77

Scenarios for the Indian Iron and Steel Industry (Rao T R, Mineral Development Board) 1984 **17** (4), 91

Strategic Planning for Power Equipment Manufacture (Shah R K D) 1989 **22** (5), 98

Technology Management in Indian Companies (Desai A V, National Council for Applied Economic Research) 1972 **5** (4), 70

Turnaround of a Cable Company (Gopal R) 1989 **22** (1), 98

Urban Planning in India. A Case Study (Subramaniam S, Balasubramaniam R, Admin Staff Coll of India) 1974 **7** (2), 39

INDIVIDUAL BEHAVIOUR

Careers for the 21st Century (Handy C) 1988 **21** (3), 90

Manpower Planning and Individual Goals (Gohl J, Oppelland H J, Researchers) 1979 **12** (6), 29

INDUSTRIAL DEMOCRACY

Prospects for Industrial Co-operatives—An Alternative to Industrial Democracy? (Derrick P, Intl Co-operative Alliance) 1981 **14** (4), 106

INDUSTRIAL DEVELOPMENT

Economic and Industrial Development—A Key Ingredient (Karger D W, Rensselaer Poly Inst) 1976 **9** (5), 90

Planning for Industrial Development in Newly Independent Countries—An Operational Approach (Verhulst M, Montreal U) 1975 **8** (3), 79

Strategic Alliances with Japanese Firms (Kobayashi N) 1988 **21** (2), 29

U.S. Industry: Decline and Fall? (Richetto J P) 1988 **21** (1), 35

INDUSTRIAL ENTERPRISES

The Use of Multiple Scenarios by U.S. Industrial Companies: A Comparison Study, 1977–1981 (Linneman R E, Klein H E, Temple U) 1983 **16** (6), 94

INDUSTRIAL EVOLUTION

The Experience Curve and History of the Cellophane Business (Cowley P R, Cranfield Sch of Mgt) 1985 **18** (6), 84

INDUSTRIAL MARKETING

Competitive Industrial Marketing Strategies (Mathur S S, London Business Sch) 1984 **17** (4), 102

Planning for Better Channel Management (Hardy K G, Magrath A J) 1988 **21** (6), 30

INDUSTRIAL PERFORMANCE

Industrial Performance Analysis—Book Review Article (Wood E G, Sheffield City Poly) 1978 **11** (4), 91

INDUSTRIAL PLANT

Long Range Planning of Industrial Facilities (Muther R, Richard Muther & Assocs) 1969 **2** (2), 58

Predicting Plant Closures in European Industry (Baden-Fuller C, Longley R) 1988 **21** (1), 90

Risk Analysis in Plant Design (Cameron D A, Beecham Research Labs) 1973 **6** (3), 30

Three Simple Steps to Determine Optimum Plant Capacity (Cameron D, Burmah Oil) 1974 **7** (1), 40

INDUSTRIAL POLICY

Air Pollution: its Implications for Industrial Planning (Scorer R S, Imperial Coll) 1970 **3** (2), 46

Balancing Total System Growth with Special Interests Protections— Book Review Article (Nielson R P, Boston Coll) 1984 **17** (3), 153

Canadian Industrial Policy—Simulation and Analysis (Thompson W, Vertinsky I, Kane J, British Columbia U) 1973 **6** (4), 66

Government Policy and its Impact on the Motor Industry (Berg M, Society of Motors Manufacturers and Traders) 1985 **18** (6), 40

India—The Plan for Steel (Rao R, Iron Ore Board) 1978 **11** (4), 22

Industrial Policy: The Case for National Strategies for World Markets (Nielsen R P, Boston Sch of Mgt) 1984 **11** (4), 22

Long Range Planning and Regional Policy. 2. France and Italy— Latecomers to the Industrial Urban Scene (Despicht N, Sussex U) 1970 **3** (1), 75

Long-Term Planning in Hungarian Industry (Roman Z, Hungarian Academy of Science) 1970 **3** (2), 23

National Planning in the United States (Michael S R, Carlisle A E, U of Massachusetts) 1976 **9** (3), 21

A New Industrial Strategy for the United Kingdom (Edwardes M, Chloride Group) 1977 **10** (3), 14

Sector Policy in Government (Marshall R, DOE) 1974 **7** (4), 2

Swedish Industrial Policy Planning—A Workshop Report, Stockholm, 6–7 March 1980 (Finlay A W, Society for Long Range Planning) 1980 **13** (6), 55

Techniques and Methodology of the French Fifth Plan (Kidel A, Intl Monetary Fund) 1969 **1** (3), 60

Towards a New Industrial Policy (Douma S, Groningen U) 1984 **17** (4), 16

U.K. Chemicals-Strategic Planning or Industrial Strategy (Caudle P, Chemical Industries Assoc) 1977 **10** (6), 31

INDUSTRIAL RELATIONS

The Next Decade in Industrial Relations (Neal L, Commission on Industrial Relations) 1974 **7** (4), 7

Scenarios for Industrial Relations: Sweden Evolves a New Consensus (Jones H G, U of Strathclyde) 1987 **20** (3), 65

Towards More Productive Industrial Relations (Wilson B, Cranfield) 1983 **16**, (6), 35

INDUSTRIAL REORGANISATION CORPORATION

The Industrial Reorganisation Corporation—A Positive Approach to the Structure of Industry (Pass C, Bradford U) 1971 **4** (1), 63

INDUSTRIAL SOCIETIES

The Fading of an Ideology (Brown C C, Columbia U) 1968 **1** (1), 34

Formation of European Society 1968 **1** (2), 37

The Programmable Society and the Individual as a Unit of Data (Butler D, Cox G, Diebold Group) 1974 **7** (5), 43

INDUSTRIAL STRUCTURE

The Future of the British Breakfast Cereals Industry (Wheale P R, St. John's Coll) 1978 **11** (2), 60

The Industrial Reorganisation Corporation–A Positive Approach to the Structure of Industry (Pass C, Bradford U) 1971 **4** (1), 63

Industrial Structure (Channon D, Manchester Business Sch) 1982 **15** (5), 78

International Comparison of Industrial Structures Using Input-Output Analysis (Borovits I, Carol A, Tel Aviv U) 1973 **6** (1), 63

Japan's New Industrial Era—I. Restructuring Traditional Industries (Yamamoto S, Industrial Bank of Japan, Ltd) 1986 **19** (1), 61

Japan's New Industrial Era—II. The New Information and Services Industries (Yamamoto S, Ind Bank of Japan Ltd) 1986 **19** (2), 65

The Prospect for Petrochemicals—Merger and Rationalization? (Walley K H, Shell Chemicals) 1982 **15** (1), 47

Why Ownership Matters (Chappell P) 1986 **19** (6), 130

INDUSTRIAL TRAINING BOARDS

Developing a Strategy for an Industrial Training Board—a Participative Approach (Beavan P R, Green G J L and Russell J G R, Industry Training Board) 1979 **12** (1), 41

INDUSTRIES

1992: A European Market for Cars? (Perrin-Pelletier F) 1988 **21** (3), 27

Air Pollution: its Implications for Industrial Planning (Scorer R S, Imperial Coll) 1970 **3** (2), 46

Developing a Manpower Strategy for an Industry (Moss A, Consultant) 1980 **13** (3), 69

The Industrial Reorganisation Corporation–A Positive Approach to the Structure of Industry (Pass C, Bradford U)) 1971 **4** (1), 63

Japan's New Industrial Era—I. Restructuring Traditional Industries (Yamamoto S, Industrial Bank of Japan, Ltd) 1986 **19** (1), 61

Manpower Studies for Industrial Sectors (Venning M, EITB) 1974 **7** (3), 27

Planning in West German Industry (Strigel W H, IFO-Inst for Econ Research) 1970 **3** (1), 9

Strategic Planning—A New Arrival in Hungarian Industry (Csath M, National Mgt Devel Centre) 1983 **16** (2), 85

Strategy Alternatives for Vehicle Component Manufacturers (Carr C) 1988 **21** (4), 86

Trucks and Road Transport Towards 1992 (Garuzo G) 1988 **21** (4), 45

The Use of Multiple Scenarios by U.S. Industrial Companies: A Comparison Study, 1977—1981 (Linneman R E, Klein H E, Temple U) 1983 **16** (6), 94

INDUSTRY

Market Planning at the National Coal Board (Edwards M J, The Nat Coal Board) 1986 **19** (3), 46

The Strategic Design of Buildings (Nutt B) 1988 **21** (4), 130

INFLATION

Developing Inflation Scenarios (Lanzenauer C H von, Western Ontario U; Sprung M R, Confederation Life Insurance) 1982 **15** (4), 37

The Social and Psychological Causes of Inflation (Daniel W W, PEP) 1977 **10** (3), 37

Strategic Planning and Inflation (Hussey D E, Harbridge House Europe) 1976 **9** (2), 24

INFORMATION

Diagnosing Long-Term Information Problems (White M, Ashridge Mgt Coll; Leigh A, London Borough of Hammersmith) 1974 **7** (1), 27

INFORMATION INDUSTRY

Japan's New Undustrial Era—II. The New Information and Services Industries (Yamamoto S, Ind Bank of Japan Ltd) 1986 **19** (2), 65

Long Range Planning for Information Services (Lientz B P, Chen M, California U) 1980 **13** (1), 55

INFORMATION PROCESSING *see* **DATA PROCESSING**

INFORMATION SYSTEMS

Assessing the Impact of New Technology in Information Systems (Lientz B P, Graduate Sch of Mgt; Chen M, Atlantic Richfield) 1981 **14** (6), 44

Building a Strategic Data Base (Szewczak E J) 1988 **21** (2), 97

Competitive Information Systems (Rodriguez J I, King W R, Pittsburgh U) 1977 **10** (6), 45

Competitive Strategies for Service Businesses (Wilson I) 1988 **21** (6), 10

Computer Integrated Management—The Next Competitive Breakthrough (Wilmot R) 1988 **21** (6), 65

Corporate Information Planning—Book Review Article (Nutt W O, Assoc Portland Cement Manufacturers) 1978 **11** (2), 77

Corporate Planning Using Government Information Systems (Hinomoto H, Reddy J M, Illinois U & Swift Agricultural Chemical) 1977 **10** (6), 79

Creative Development of Computerized Information Systems (Seiler R E, Boockholdt J L, Houston U) 1983 **16** (5), 100

Data and Effective Corporate Planning (Houlden B T, Warwick U) 1980 **13** (5), 106

Designing Communication Support Systems for Strategic Planning (Charalambides L C) 1988 **21** (6), 93

Designing Information Systems for Strategic Decisions (Hayes R L, Radosevich R, Vanderbilt U) 1974 **7** (4), 45

Developing an Information Systems Strategy (Hayward R G, Massey U Palmerston North New Zealand) 1987 **20** (2), 100

Developing Plans for Information Systems (Tozer E E, Consultant) 1986 **19** (5), 63

The Federal Government as a Source of Strategic Planning Information (Noya L E De, US Govt Printing Office) 1980 **13** (5), 100

How Belgian Businesses Make Strategic Planning Work (Caeldries F, van Dierdonck R) 1988 **21** (2), 41

How Information Technology is Transforming Corporate Planning (Hohn S, Volkswagen AG) 1986 **19** (4), 18

Information for More Effective Strategic Planning (King W R, Cleland D I, Pittsburgh U) 1977 **10** (1), 59

An Information System for Just-In-Time (Yoo S) 1989 **22** (6), 117

Information Systems for Planning (Ewusi-Mensah K, Hawaii U) 1984 **17** (4), 111

Information Technology in Banking (Read C N, Postal HQ) 1983 **16** (4), 21

Information Technology—Its Impact on Property (Burrows B C, Futures Information Associates) 1984 **17** (4), 60

Integrating Information Systems into Business Strategies (Ward J M, Cranfield Sch of Mgt) 1987 **20** (3), 79

A Management Strategy for Information Processing 3—Management Information Requirements (Collins A C, South Eastern Gas) 1984 **17** (1), 33

Managing the Growth of Electronic Office Information Systems (Hirschhein R A, LSE) 1983 **16** (6), 59

Personnel Planning and Information Systems (Domsch M, Wirtschaft U) 1971 **4** (2), 12

PINCO: Personal Information and Confidentiality Controls (Wiedemann P, UNIDO) 1983 **16** (5), 107

Planning an Information System at Netherlands Gas (Adriaans W, Hoogakker J T) 1989 **22** (3), 64

Planning Information Technology and the Post-Industrial Society (Burrows B C, Futures Information Assocs) 1986 **19** (2), 79

Strategic Planning for Information Systems at British Rail (Mainelli M R, Miller D R) 1988 **21** (4), 65

Using IT for Competitive Advantage at Thomson Holidays (Palmer C) 1988 **21** (6), 26

The Value of Accuracy in Information for Planning and Control (Higgins J C, Bradford U) 1974 **7** (4), 67

see also **MANAGEMENT INFORMATION SYSTEMS**

INFORMATION SYSTEMS PLANNING

How Effective is Your Information Systems Planning? (King W R) 1988 **21** (5), 103

INFORMATION TECHNOLOGY

Building a Competitive Advantage Through Information Technology (Jackson C) 1989 **22** (4), 29

Developing a Competitive Intelligence System for IT (Ewusi-Mensah K) 1989 **22** (5), 121

An Information System for Just-In-Time (Yoo S) 1989 **22** (6), 117

INNOVATION

Accelerating Innovation Through Real-time Workshops (Rhodes J D, Thame S) 1988 **21** (5), 41

Adaptors and Innovators—Why New Initiatives Get Blocked (Kirron M J, Hatfield Poly) 1984 **17** (2), 137

Breakthrough: The Development of the Canon Personal Copier (Yamanouchi T) 1989 **22** (5), 11

Change in Management and the Management of Change (Wilmot R W) 1987 **20** (6), 23

Computer Integrated Management—The Next Competitive Breakthrough (Wilmot R) 1988 **21** (6), 65

Creating a Climate for Innovation (Humble J, Jones G) **22** (4), 46

Designing Innovating Systems (Radosevich R, New Mexico U) 1977 **10** (2), 79

Developing Corporate Policies for Innovation: A Program of Action (Norris W C, Control Data Corporation) 1981 **14** (4), 34

Developing an Enterprise Culture at British Telecom (Brunnen D J) 1989 **22** (2), 27

Focusing Innovative Effort Through a Convergent Dialogue (Ward E P, NPM Planning and Research) 1980 **13** (6), 32

Innovation: The Multinational Corporation: Some Implications for National Science Policy (Cordell A J, Science Council Canada) 1973 **6** (3), 22

Innovation: The Way Out of the Recession? (Smith F M, Ciba-Geigy) 1982 **15** (1), 19

Innovation by Design (Locke H B, NRDC) 1976 **9** (4), 34

Innovation in Organizations (Sawyer G C, Consultant) 1978 **11** (6), 53

Innovation as the Source of Long Term Economic Growth (Ray G F, Nat Inst of Economic and Social Research) 1980 **13** (2), 9

The Innovative Firm (Ansoff H I, Vanderbilt U) 1968 **1** (2), 26

Planning for Innovation in Health Care: A Breakthrough in Blood Banking (Kendall K E, Nebraska U) 1984 **17** (6), 127

Planning Innovation (Locke B H, Cadogan Consultants) 1978 **11** (6), 21

Planning for Innovation (Locke H B, Wilson A, Grossfield K, NRDC) 1974 **7** (2), 19

Promoting Entrepreneurship in Large Companies (Pearson G J) 1989 **22** (3), 87

The Role of Government in Industrial Innovation (Knight K E, Baca H R, Texas U) 1978 **11** (6), 79

Selection of Mission Oriented Technical Programmes (Szakasits G D, State Office Technical Devel) 1972 **5** (3), 58

Social Innovation—Management's New Dimension (Drucker P F) 1987 **20** (6), 29

Technological Innovation and Long Range Planning (Zvegintzov M, Nat Res and Devel Corp) 1968 **1** (2), 46

Tetra Pak—A Model for Successful Innovation (Jones H G, Whyte and Mackay Distillers) 1982 **15** (6), 31

INPUT–OUTPUT ANALYSIS

An Input-Output Model of the Irish Economy (Henry E W, Economic and Social Research Inst) 1973 **6** (3), 64

International Comparison of Industrial Structures Using Input-Output Analysis (Borovits I, Carol A, Tel Aviv U) 1973 **6** (1), 63

The Planning Function and Input-Output Analysis (Mathieson R F, Scudder, Steven & Clarke) 1972 **5** (4), 73

INSURANCE COMPANIES

Competitive Strategies in the Dutch Insurance Industry (Eppink J, Free U Amsterdam) 1987 **20** (4), 30

Controlling Overseas Insurance Subsidiaries (Petroni G) 1989 **22** (4), 106

Creating a Successful Marketing Strategy for UNI Insurance (Overland T) 1989 **22** (4), 25

International Strategies of Dutch Insurance Companies (Eppink D J, van Rhijn B M) 1989 **22** (1), 41

The Internationalization of Dutch Insurance Companies (Eppink D J, Van Rhijn B M) 1988 **21** (5), 54

Strategic Thinking in Insurance (Howard E F) 1989 **22** (5), 76

INTERNATIONAL BUSINESS

Corporate Planning in an International Environment (Thomas F A, UAC Int) 1974 **7** (5), 13

The Corporate Planning Life Cycle—An International Business Point of View (Ringbakk K-A, C.E.I.) 1972 **5** (3), 10

Developing a Strategy for International Business (Fannin W R, U of Houston-Clear Lake; Gilmore C B, U of Maine at Orono) 1986 **19** (3), 81

The Developing World to 1990: Trends and Implications for Multinational Business (Wright P, Townsend D, Kinard J, Iverstine J, SE & NW Louisiana U) 1982 **15** (4), 116

Going Global—Global Strategies vs National Strategies, (Leontiades J, Manchester Business School) 1986 **19** (6), 96

How Marriott Corporation Grew Five-fold in Ten Years (Kennedy C) 1988 **21** (2), 10

The Identification and Assessment of Political Risk in the International Environment (Lloyd B, Commonwealth Devel) 1974 **7** (6), 24

International Comparison of Industrial Structures Using Input-Output Analysis (Borovits I, Carol A, Tel Aviv U) 1973 **6** (1), 63

The International Scene Towards 1980 (Millson P C, CBI) 1971 **4** (2), 36

International Security and the World Economy (Schmid G, Inst for the Future) 1981 **14** (3), 21

International Strategies of Dutch Insurance Companies (Eppink D J, van Rhijn B M) 1989 **22** (1), 41

The Internationalization of Dutch Insurance Companies (Eppink D J, Van Rhijn B M) 1988 **21** (5), 54

Long Range Planning—Japan—USA—A Comparative Study (Kono T, Gakushuin U) 1976 **9** (5), 61

Planning Major International Projects (Claxton C, Europa Industrial Projects) 1978 **11** (2), 25

Planning Strategy for World Markets (Leontiades J, Pennsylvania U) 1970 **3** (2), 40

Plant Location—The International Perspective (Leontiades J C, EIASM) 1974 **7** (1), 10

Predicting the Political Environment of International Business (Smith C N, Consultant) 1971 **4** (1), 7

Selecting a Foreign Partner for Technology Transfer (Lasserre P, INSEAD) 1984 **17** (6), 43

Strategic Alliances with Japanese Firms (Kobayashi N) 1988 **21** (2), 29

Strategic Alternatives for Australian Iron-Ore Producers (Frost F, Australian Inst of Technology) 1986 **19** (1), 89

Strategic Planning for International Business (Hussey D E, Wander) 1972 **5** (2), 16

Strategic Planning for Internationalization—The European Dilemma and some Possible Solutions (Franko L G, CEI) 1973 **6** (2), 58

Strategic Planning in a Turbulent International Environment (Ringbakk K-A, Amon Tuck Sch, Dartmouth Coll) 1976 **9** (3), 2

Strategies for National Competitiveness (Rugman A M, Dalhousie U Nova Scotia) 1987 **20** (3), 92

Stratetgies for International Growth in the Automobile Industry (Moulins J-L, U d'Aix-Marseille) 1978 **11** (1), 34

The U.K. and its OECD competitors (Norse D, DOE) 1982 **15** (5), 131

see also **MULTINATIONAL COMPANIES**

INTERNATIONAL FINANCE

The Future Ambitions of Japan's Financial Giants (Turner G) 1987 **20** (5), 11

Investing and Financing in a New Era (Coussement A M, Kredierbank) 1978 **11** (5), 2

INTERNATIONAL MARKETING

Blunders in International Marketing: Fact or Fiction (Ricks D A, South Carolina U; Mahajan V, Southern Methodist U) 1984 **17** (1), 78

Building Competitive Strength in International Markets (Hitt M A, Ireland R D, Texas A & M U; Mays W A, Baylor U Texas) 1987 **20** (1), 115

Product Regrouping can Aid MNE Planning (Kirpalani V H, Concordia U) 1978 **11** (3), 16

Vaulting Trade Barriers: The Japanese Approach (Varadarajan P R, Texas A & M U) 1985 **18** (1), 73

INTERNATIONAL TRADE

Competing Against Low Cost Cutlery Imports (Grant R M) 1989 **22** (5), 59

Future Demand Patterns in the Emerging World (Dam A van, CPC International Inc) 1974 **7** (4), 34

Future Trends in World Trade (A Review of the Lima Target) (Aczel J, Morris G, European Manpower Advisory Services) 1978 **11** (2), 19

International Business Through Barter and Countertrade (Aggarwal R) 1989 **22** (3), 75

Japanese Business Strategy in China (Campbell N, Manchester Business Sch) 1987 **20** (5), 69

New Opportunities in Global Services (Trondsen E, SRI Intl; Edfelt R, San Jose State U) 1987 **20** (5), 53

What the New GATT Trade Agreement Means for Plastics (Christopher W F, Consultant) 1980 **13** (1), 77

INVESTMENT

The Cut-Off Rate for Investment Decisions in Growth Companies (Chandra G, Miami U) 1975 **8** (2), 95

The External Corporate Venture Capital Fund—A Valuable Vehicle for Growth (Bleicher K, Paul H) 1987 **20** (6), 64

Industrial Investment and Financial Requirements (Mast H J, Credit Suisse) 1978 **11** (6), 42

Investing and Financing in a New Era (Coussement A M, Kredietbank SA) 1978 **11** (5), 2

see also **CAPITAL INVESTMENT**

INVESTMENT APPRAISAL

Acquiring Companies in the U.S.A. (Adler H S, Peat Marwick Group New York; Sneath C G, Peat Marwick London) 1987 **20** (2), 42

Risk Analysis and Investment Appraisal in Marketing (Cameron D A, Beecham Research Laboratories) 1972 **5** (4), 43

The Strategic Discount—Protecting New Business Projects Against DCF (Pearson G, Manchester Business School) 1986 **19** (1), 18

Why Different Divisions Require Different Hurdle Rates (Andrews G S, Firer C, U of the Witwatersrand) 1987 **20** (5), 62

INVESTMENT PLANNING

Game Theory Technique in Investment Planning (Singhvi S S, Armco Steel Corp & Miami U) 1974 **7** (4), 59

Investment Strategies for Pension Funds (in an Age of Inflation) (Skelton J D, Bradford U) 1973 **6** (4), 47

Pre-Investment Planning (Derkinderen F, Netherlands Sch of Business) 1977 **10** (1), 2

Setting Investment Criteria for Government and Industry (Leemhuis J P, Shell Nederland) 1985 **18** (3), 33

Why Different Divisions Require Different Hurdle Rates (Andrews G S, Firer C, U of the Witwatersrand) 1987 **20** (5), 62

IRAN

Corporate Strategy at Admiram Manufacturing Company: An Iranian Case Study (Wright P, Florida Intl U) 1980 **13** (3), 115

IRISH REPUBLIC

An Input-Output Model of the Irish Economy (Hentry E W, Economic and Social Research Inst) 1973 **6** (3), 64

Planning in Ireland (FitzGerald G, Eire PM) 1971 **4** (2), 30

ITALY

Long Range Planning and Regional Policy. 2. France and Italy— Latecomers to the Industrial Urban Scene (Despicht N, Sussex U) 1970 **3** (1), 75

J

JAPAN

Achieving Japanese Productivity and Quality Levels at a U.S. Plant (Ishikure K) 1988 **21** (5), 10

Breakthrough: The Development of the Canon Personal Copier (Yamanouchi T) 1989 **22** (5), 11

Buying is Marketing Too—Japan's Influence on the Australian Coal Trade (Dowling G, U of New South Wales) 1987 **20** (1), 35

Competing with Japan—The Rules of the Game (Stone M, Henley Mgt Coll) 1984 **17** (2), 33

Competing with the Japanese Approach to Technology (Prentice J, Consultant) 1984 **17** (2), 25

The Future Ambitions of Japan's Financial Giants (Turner G) 1987 **20** (5), 11

How the Japanese Came to Dominate the Machine Tool Business (Rendeiro J O, Sussex U) 1985 **18** (3), 62

How U.S. and Japanese CEO's Spend Their Time (Kudo H, Tachikawa T, Suzuki N) 1988 **21** (6), 79

Japanese Business Strategy in China (Campbell N, Manchester Business Sch) 1987 **20** (5), 69

Japanese Management Philosophy: Can it be Exported? (Kono T, Gakushuin U) 1982 **15** (3), 90

Japanese Manufacturing: Strategy and Practice (Bolwijn P T, Brinkman S, Philips Intl BV) 1987 **20** (1), 25

Japanese Marketing Strategies in the United Kingdom (Wong V, Saunders J, Doyle P) 1987 **20** (6), 54

The Japanese Multinational (Yoshihara H, Kobe U) 1977 **10** (2), 41

Japan's Drive for the European Car Market—Lessons from U.S. Experience (Wray M, Toftech; Norburn D, Imperial Coll, London) 1987 **20** (4), 60

Japan's New Industrial Era—I. Restructuring Traditional Industries (Yamamoto S, Industrial Bank of Japan, Ltd) 1986 **19** (1), 61

Japan's New Industrial Era—II. The New Information and Services Industries (Yamamoto S, Ind Bank of Japan Ltd) 1986 **19** (2), 65

Long Range Planning of U.K. and Japanese Corporations—A Comparative Study (Kono T, Gakushuin U) 1984 **17** (2), 58

Long Range Planning—Japan—USA—A Comparative Study (Kono T, Gakushuin U) 1976 **9** (5), 61

New Product Planning at Hitachi (Nishikawa T) 1989 **22** (4), 20

Planning for Growth in a Japanese Business (Serizawa Y) 1989 **22** (2), 20

Productivity: Lessons from Japan (Keegan W J, New York U) 1975 **8** (2), 61

Quality Control—Learning From the Japanese (Trevor M, Policy Studies Inst) 1986 **19** (5), 46

Recent Changes in Long Range Corporate Planning in Japan (Murakami T, Nomura Research Inst.) 1978 **11** (2), 2

Response of Japanese Companies to Environmental Changes (Nagashima Y, Kanto Gakuin U) 1976 **9** (1), 20

Strategic Alliances with Japanese Firms (Kobayashi N) 1988 **21** (2), 29

Strategic Management in Major Japanese Hightech Companies (Nakamura G-I, Asia U Tokyo) 1986 **19** (6), 82

Success Through Culture Change in a Japanese Brewery (Nakajo T, Kono T) 1989 **22** (6), 29

Vaulting Trade Barriers: The Japanese Approach (Varadarajan P R, Texas A & M U) 1985 **18** (1), 73

JOB CREATION

Careers for the 21st Century (Handy C) 1988 **21** (3), 90

New Jobs in Energy Research and Development—A Survey (Davis D L, Houston U) 1977 **10** (4), 51

Planning for Job Creation (Falk N, Urban and Economic Devel) 1980 **13** (2), 20

Planning for Job Creation (May G, Green H, Leeds Poly) 1984 **17** (1), 100

JOURNALS *see* **PERIODICALS**

K

KOREA

Can Hyundai Go It Alone? (Hyun Y, Lee J) 1989 **22** (2), 63

L

LABOUR SUPPLY

Manpower and Unemployment in the U.K. (Lawrence J, ICI) 1979 **12** (5), 16

LABOUR TURNOVER

Productivity Improvement Through Reduced Labour turnover (Rothwell S, Henley Centre) 1982 **15** (2), 67

LAND USE

Land Use Planning and the Community (Groves D L, McCart G D, Virginia Poly Inst and State U) 1976 **9** (2), 83

Land-Use Planning in a World of Shrinking Resources (Coleman A, London U) 1978 **11** (1), 47

The Relationship between Land Use and Economic Planning in the United Kingdom (Sharp E, Consultant) 1970 **3** (1), 16

LARGE BUSINESSES

Business Policy and Management Development in Large American and European Concerns (Petroni G, Consultant) 1978 **11** (3), 26

The Control Function in Major German Companies (Hand D, Institut fur Unternehmungsplanung) 1982 **15** (3), 21

Corporate Environmental Analysis in Large U.S. Corporations (Diffenbach J, Boston U) 1983 **16** (3), 107

Formal Planning in Major U.S. Corporations (Henry H W, Tennessee U) 1977 **10** (5), 40

GE's High-tech Strategy (Koerner E) 1989 **22** (4), 11

How Large and Small Firms Can Grow Together (Wilson P, Goth P, London Business Sch) 1983 **16** (2), 19

Long Range Planning in Large United States Corporations—A Survey (Ang J S, Chua J H, Oklahoma State U) 1979 **12** (2), 99

Managing Diversity: Strategy and Control in Diversified British Companies (Goold M, Campbell A, London Business Sch) 1987 **20** (5), 42

Promoting Entrepreneurship in Large Companies (Pearson G J) 1989 **22** (3), 87

Strategic Decision Making in Large European Firms (Guoy M, French Embassy) 1978 **11** (3), 41

LATIN AMERICA

Corporate Planning for Asia, Latin America and Africa (Dam A van, CPC International Inc) 1972 **5** (4), 2

LAW

Some Law Enforcement Operations Implications of Crime Seasonality (McPheters I.R, Strong W B, Atlantic U) 1974 **7** (2), 57

LEADERSHIP

The NASA Approach (Beggs J M, NASA) 1984 **17** (2), 12

Strategic Leadership and the Chief Executive (Merwe A van der, Merwe S van der, U of Witwatersrand) 1985 **18** (1), 100

Who Controls the Board? (Mills G) 1989 **22** (3), 125

LEARNING CURVES

Adding Life Cycles to Learning Curves (Yelle L E, Lowell U) 1983 **16** (6), 82

LEISURE INDUSTRY

Alcohol: Is it Time to Say 'When'? (Steele D W, Action on Alcohol Abuse) 1987 **20** (5), 86

The Future of Leisure (Culligan K, Murphy J) 1989 **22** (6), 127

Leisure 1980 and Beyond (Martin W H, Mason S, Leisure Consultants) 1976 **9** (2), 58

Planning for Leisure in Sweden (Tobe E I, Consultant) 1971 **4** (1), 50

Planning for Leisure (Turnbull P, Exeter County Hall) 1975 **8** (5), 55

Using IT for Competitive Advantage at Thomson Holidays (Palmer C) 1988 **21** (6), 26

LESS DEVELOPED COUNTRIES

The Management of Development—The Next Decade (Declerck R P, Ottawa U) 1977 **10** (3), 59

Opportunities and Pitfalls for Multinational Corporations in a Changed Political Environment (Sethi S P) 1987 **20** (6), 45

Transferring Technology to Developing Countries — Critical Factors for Success (Madu C N) 1989 **22** (4), 115

LIBRARIES

Assessing Performance in Libraries (Karunaratne N D, Queensland U) 1978 **11** (2), 66

Comprehensive Planning for Libraries (Bell J A, Keusch R B, East Carolina U) 1976 **9** (5), 48

The Corporate Library as a Source of New Technology (McKinnon L M B, Sanders) 1980 **13** (2), 102

Long Range Planning for Public Libraries—A Delphi Study (Kennington D, Information) 1977 **10** (2), 73

Towards the Library of the Future (Feigenbaum E A) 1989 **22** (1), 118

LIBYA

Forecasting Demand for Food in Libya—Using Confidence Limits (Malik M A K, Ahmad I, Nat Academy for Scientific Research) 1981 **14** (5), 90

LIFE CYCLE COSTS

Life Cycle Costing for Construction Projects (Wubbenhorst K L, Bertalsmann AG) 1986 **19** (4), 87

The Use of Life Cycle Costing in Acquiring Physical Assets (Taylor W B, Kent County Council) 1981 **14** (6), 32

LIFE CYCLES

Adding Life Cycles to Learning Curves (Yelle L E, Lowell U) 1983 **16** (6), 82

The Software Life Cycle in Computer Applications (Lehner F) 1989 **22** (5), 38

LINEAR PROGRAMMING

Linear Programming Techniques in R & D Project Planning (Allen D H, Nottingham U) 1974 **7** (1), 61

LOCAL GOVERNMENT

Assessing Performance in Local Government (Jackson W U, Civil Servant) 1984 **17** (3), 24

Corporate Management and Planning in Local Government (Williams D G, British Rail; Harris D J, Bath U) 1976 **9** (4), 46

Corporate Planning in Local Government (Rugman C A, Kent County Council) 1973 **3** (3), 17

Corporate Planning in Local Government (Stewart J D, Birmingham U) 1973 **6** (2), 18

Corporate Planning in Local Government—A Case Study (Hawkins K, Tarr R J, Bradford Metropolitan District) 1980 **13** (2), 43

Corporate Planning in Local Government—Implications for the Elected Member (Cartwright J, M.P.) 1975 **8** (2), 46

Ethics and Social Responsibility in Local Government (Amos F J C, Birmingham U) 1982 **15** (2), 121

Local Politicians and Their Attitudes to Planning (Hill K Q, Coomer J C, Houston U) 1977 **10** (6), 57

Making Strategic Planning Work in Local Government (Rider R W, Hawaii Government) 1983 **16** (3), 73

A Modelling System for Local Government Resource Planning (Howard K, Wagle B V, Bradford U) 1978 **11** (4), 77

Planning for Local Government—A Grass-Roots Approach (Kemp R L, City Administrator of Placentia) 1985 **18** (6), 91

Planning for Strategic Performance in Local Government (McGill R) 1988 **21** (5), 77

The Use of Games in Planning (Armstrong R H R, Hobson M, Birmingham U) 1972 **5** (1), 62

LOGISTICS

Logistics Systems Engineering—Solving the Distribution Planning Problem (Christopher M, Cranfield Inst of Technology) 1974 **7** (6), 72

LONG RANGE PLANNING

Anatomy of a Long Range Plan (Smalter D J, Intl Minerals and Chemical Corp) 1969 **1** (3), 2

Corporate Long-Range Planning Groups—Some Different Approaches (Litschert R J, Virginia Poly Inst and State U; Nicholson E A, Wright State U) 1974 **7** (4), 62

Creative Strategic Planning Using Imagery (Maddox N, Stetson U; Anthony W P, Florida State U; Wheatley Jr W, U of West Florida) 1987 **20** (5), 118

Currency Problems in Multinational Long Range Planning (Bruns J, Deutsche Edelstahlwerke) 1970 **3** (2), 71

The Current Practice of Bank Long-Range Planning (Kudla R J, Arizona State U) 1982 **15** (3), 132

The Cut-Off Rate for Investment Decisions in Growth Companies (Chandra G, Miami U) 1975 **8** (2), 95

Designing an ADP Planning Process (Sporn D L, Food & Drug Administration) 1978 **11** (1), 43

Designing a Long Range Marketing Strategy for Services (Gronroos C, Swedish Sch of Economics and Business Administration) 1980 **13** (2), 36

Develop Your Technology Strategy (Ford D) 1988 **21** (5), 85

Developing a Climate for Planning (Nurmi R, Turku Sch of Economics) 1976 **9** (3), 48

An Environmental Scanning System for Business Planning (Narchal R M, Kittappa K, Bhattacharya P) 1987 **20** (6), 96

Forestry and Long Range Planning (Convery F J, Duke U Sch of Forestry) 1973 **6** (2), 27

Formal Approaches to Setting Long-Range Goals (Dobbie J W, Pacific Lutheran U) 1974 **7** (3), 75

A Formal Model for Long Range Planning: 1. Relating the Company to the Economy (Hetrick J C, Arthur D Little) 1969 **2** (1), 12

A Formal Model for Long Range Planning: 3. Allocating and Appraising Capital Investment (Hetrick J C, Arthur D Little) 1969 **1** (3), 16

The Function of Design in Long Range Planning (Black M, Design Research Unit) 1972 **5** (2), 9

GEC's Pragmatic Planners (Turner G) 1985 **18** (1), 12

How Scenarios Trigger Strategic Thinking (Millett S M) 1988 **21** (5), 61

How to Evaluate a Long-Range Plan (Noya L E De, US Govt Printing Office) 1978 **11** (3), 36

Integrated Formal Long Range Planning and How to Do it (Karger D W, Rensselaer Poly Inst) 1973 **6** (4), 31

Integrated Long Range Planning at Nestlé (Brey A, Gabsa G, Nestlé) 1972 **5** (2), 44

Is Your Information System Mature Enough for Computerized Planning? (Brightman H J, Harris S E, Georgia State U) 1985 **18** (5), 68

Long Range Defence Planning in the U.K. (Cooper F, MOD) 1970 **3** (2), 18

Long Range Planning: The Concept and the Need (Perrin R, P.A. Consultants) 1968 **1** (1), 3

Long Range Planning and Advertising (Doyle P, Bradford U) 1977 **10** (6), 16

Long Range Planning at Continental Oil (Cecil J B, Continental Oil) 1971 **4** (1), 54

Long Range Planning in Bell Canada (Day L H, Consultant) 1973 **6** (3), 44

Long Range Planning and the Church (Wasdell D, Urban Church Project) 1980 **13** (3), 99

The Long Range Planning of Criminal Justice Systems (Clifford W, Australian Inst of Criminology) 1979 **12** (4), 42

Long Range Planning in the Defense Equipment Business (Bowman D O, Autonetics) 1970 **3** (2), 55

Long Range Planning in a Fast Changing Fashion Market (Stait N H, Urwick, Orr & Partners) 1970 **3** (2), 55

Long Range Planning of Industrial Facilities (Muther R, Richard Muther & Assocs) 1969 **2** (2), 58

Long Range Planning for Information Services (Lientz B P, Chen M, California U) 1980 **13** (1), 55

Long Range Planning in Large United States Banks (Wood D R, Virginia Commonwealth U) 1980 **13** (3), 91

Long Range Planning in Large United States Corporations—A Survey (Ang J S, Chua J H, Oklahoma State U) 1979 **12** (2), 99

Long Range Planning for London Transport (Ellen E R, London Transport) 1973 **3** (3), 10

Long Range Planning and Organizational Performance (Karger D W, Malik Z A, Rensselaer Poly Inst) 1975 **8** (6), 60

Long Range Planning of Paper and Board Supplies (Vincent J D, Reed) 1980 **13** (2), 60

Long Range Planning in a Politicized Environment (Windsor D, Greanias G, Texas Sch of Administration) 1983 **16** (3), 82

Long Range Planning for Production (Corke D K, P-E Consulting Group) 1970 **3** (2), 27

Long Range Planning for Public Libraries—A Delphi Study (Kennington D, Information) 1977 **10** (2), 73

Long Range Planning and Regional Policy 1. Britain—A European Pioneer (Despicht N, Sussex U) 1970 **2** (4), 28

Long Range Planning and Regional Policy 2. France and Italy—Latecomers to the Industrial Urban Scene (Despicht N, Sussex U) 1970 **3** (1), 75

Long Range Planning for the Small Firm (Forbes A M, Natal U) 1974 **7** (2), 43

Long Range Planning for Transport (Stuart C, British Transport Staff Coll) 1968 **1** (2), 38

Long Range Planning of U.K. and Japanese Corporations—A Comparative Study (Kono T, Gakushuin U) 1984 **17** (2), 58

Long Range Planning in the U.S.A.—N.I.C.B. Survey (Brown J K, Sands S S and Thompson G C, Nat Industrial Conference Board) 1969 **1** (3), 44

Long Range Planning in Under-developed Countries—A Case History (Stanbridge P J, Sabi-Limpopo Authority) 1969 **2** (2), 38

Long Range Planning for Universities (Doyle P, Lynch J E, Bradford U) 1976 **9** (6), 39

Long Range Planning—An Open Systems View (Kahalas H, New York State U) 1977 **10** (5), 78

Long Range Planning—Japan—USA—A Comparative Study (Kono T, Gakushuin U) 1976 **9** (5), 61

Long-Term Planning for Coal (Ezra D, N.C.B.) 1974 **7** (6), 21

Long-Term Planning and Forecasting in Europe (Sombart N, Council of Europe) 1972 **5** (2), 47

Long-Term Planning for Indian Shipping (Kumar S P, Indian Inst of Mgt) 1976 **9** (6), 63

Management Training Film on Long Range Planning (Perrin H F R, PA Mgt Consultants) 1971 **4** (2), 67

A Method for Planning Long Term Strategy in Basic Industries (Bernard G, Interconsult) 1977 **10** (2), 46

Monitoring Long-Range Plans (Holmberg S R, Maryland U) 1974 **7** (3), 63

Organization for Long Range Planning—A Survey of German Companies (Keppler W, Bamberger I, Gabele E, Rutgerswerk AG; Inst de Gestion de Rennes) 1979 **12** (5), 69

Pitfalls in Multi-National Long-Range Planning (Steiner G A, Schollhammer H, California U) 1975 **8** (2), 2

Privatization — A Cure for all Ills? (Hammer R M, Hinterhuber H H, Lorentz J) 1989 **22** (6), 19

Recent Changes in Long Range Corporate Planning in Japan (Murakami T, Nomura Research Inst) 1978 **11** (2), 2

Recent Trends in Long Range Forecasting for Technology-Based Organizations—Book Review Article (Twiss B C, Bradford U) 1979 **12** (2), 120

Scenario Planning—What Style Should You Use? (Huss W R, Xenergy; Honton E J, Battelle Columbus) 1987 **20** (4), 21

Selling Long Range Planning to Management (Berteaux R, Solvay) 1969 **2** (2), 32

Shirt-sleeved Approach to Long Range Planning for the Smaller Growing Corporation—Book Review Article (Teager R H, Consultant) 1980 **13** (6), 83

The Society for Long-Range Planning: Challenges in Corporate Planning—Third International Conference on Corporate Planning—Brussels September 1973 (Knowlson P, CBI) 1974 **7** (1), 69

Staffing Long Range Planning Groups (Litschert R J, Nicholson E A, Virginia Poly Inst and State U) 1972 **5** (1), 37

Strategic Alliances—Guidelines for Success (Devlin G, Bleackley M) 1988 **21** (5), 18

Strategic Leadership through Corporate Planning at ICI (Pink A I H) 1988 **21** (1), 18

Strategic Planning in Tanzania (Mrema E L, Tanzania Wood Industry Corp) 1987 **20** (3), 105

Strategies for Global Competition (Lei D) 1989 **22** (1), 102

Technological Innovation and Long Range Planning (Zvegintzov M, Nat Res and Devel Corp) 1968 **1** (2), 46

Testing Plans Against Alternative Futures (Boshoff H) 1989 **22** (5), 69

The Three-Parameter Approach to Long Range Forecasting (Hendry I C, Stirling U) 1972 **5** (1), 40

Throwing Away Millions—Long Range Planning for Disposables (Lockett A G, Armstrong K, Manchester Business Sch) 1971 **4** (1), 15

'Titanic Planning' in an Uncertain Environment (Trowbridge A V) 1988 **21** (2), 86

Tools and Techniques of Long-Range Planners (Rue L W, Indiana U) 1974 **7** (5), 61

The Use of Financial Models in Long Range Planning (Dohrn P J, P-E Consulting Group; Salkin G R, Imperial Coll) 1969 **2** (2), 27

The Use of a Model in Long Term Planning—A Case History (Mann C W, Harold Whitehead & Partners) 1978 **11** (5), 55

The World's Changing Climate-Some Issues for Planners (Wilson L S, Harbridge House Europe) 1981 **14** (5), 83

Xerox Charts a New Strategic Direction (Kennedy C) 1989 **22** (1), 10

LUBRICATION SYSTEMS

Competitive Superiority Through Data Base Marketing (Shaw B, Stone M) 1988 **21** (5), 24

M

MACHINE TOOL INDUSTRY

How the Japanese Came to Dominate the Machine Tool Business (Rendeiro J O, Sussex U) 1985 **18** (3), 62

MANAGEMENT

1992: The Implications for Management (Mitchell D) 1989 **22** (1), 32

Change in Management and the Management of Change (Wilmot R W) 1987 **20** (6), 23

Computer Integrated Management—The Next Competitive Breakthrough (Wilmot R) 1988 **21** (6), 65

Corporate Strategies for Political Action (Gram H A, Crawford R L, Concordia U) 1979 **12** (5), 62

Increasing Trust Improves Productivity (Dwivedi R S, Kurukshetra U) 1985 **18** (3), 82

Management in the 21st Century (Makridakis S) 1989 **22** (2), 37

Managing Change (Worcester R M, Market & Opinion Research Intl) 1970 **3** (1), 31

Managing Strategic Change: An Integrated Approach (Carnall C A, The Mgt Coll Henley-on Thames) 1986 **19** (6), 105

Managing Toxic Wastes—After Bhopal and Sandoz (Mahon J F, Kelley P C, Boston U Sch of Mgt) 1987 **20** (4), 50

The Privatization of British Telecom—Its Impact on Management (Morley W B, British Telecom) 1986 **19** (6), 124

The Scott Bader Commonwealth: Putting People First (Bader G, Scott Bader Co Ltd) 1986 **19** (6), 66

Strategic Management and Artificial Intelligence (Holloway C, Coll of Business Admin) 1983 **16** (5), 89

Using Critical Success Factors in Planning (Jenster Per V, McIntire Sch of Commerce, Virginia) 1987 **20** (4), 102

Why Ownership Matters (Chappell P) 1986 **19** (6), 130

MANAGEMENT BUY-OUTS

The Incentive Effects of Ownership and Control in Management Buy-outs (Green S) 1988 **21** (1), 26

MANAGEMENT BY OBJECTIVES

Corporate Planning and Management by Objectives (Haines W R, Consultant) 1977 **10** (4), 13

Corporate Planning and Management by Objectives (Humble J W, Urwick Orr and Partners) 1969 **1** (4), 36

MBO: The Fad That Changed Management (Seyna E J, Eastman Kodak Company, New York) 1986 **19** (6), 116

Planning and Management by Objectives (Migliore R H, Tulsa U) 1976 **9** (4), 58

MANAGEMENT CONTROL

Controlling Overseas Insurance Subsidiaries (Petroni G) 1989 **22** (4), 106

Decision Support System: A New Tool for Strategic Management (Yoo S, Bowling Green State U Ohio; Digman, L A, U of Nebraska) 1987 **20** (2), 114

Defining the Role of the Board (Demb A, Chouet D, Lossius T, Neubauer F) 1989 **22** (1), 61

Designing an Effective Financial Planning and Control System (Cowen S S, Middaugh II J K) 1988 **21** (6), 83

Economic Impact Reports—Management Controls for the 1980's (Shorrock J, Dobson S, Honeywell) 1979 **12** (6), 26

How Successful Companies Manage Diverse Businesses (Calori R, CESMA) 1988 **21** (3), 80

The Incentive Effects of Ownership and Control in Management Buy-outs (Green S) 1988 **21** (1), 26

Management Control for Effective Corporate Planning (Rhodes D, Wright M and Jarrett M, Nottingham U) 1984 **17** (4), 115

Managing the Diversified Corporation: The Tensions Facing the Chief Executive (Goold M, Campbell A) 1988 **21** (4), 12

Strategic Control of Factory Automation (Meredith J R) 1987 **20** (6), 106

MANAGEMENT DEVELOPMENT

Accelerated Development for Women Managers (Beck J) 1988 **21** (3), 75

Business Policy and Management Development in Large American and European Concerns (Petroni G, Consultant) 1978 **11** (3), 26

Force Field Analysis—A Framework for Strategic Thinking (Ajimal K S, Consultant) 1985 **18** (5), 55

Implementing Corporate Strategy: Using Management Education and Training (Hussey D E, Harbridge Consulting) 1985 **18** (5), 28

Integrating Planning and Management Development (Dill W R, New York U) 1975 **8** (5), 8

Management in the Eighties: How is the Job Changing? (Wissema J G, Winkel J M M van de, Shell Nederland) 1981 **14** (4), 21

Managerial Manpower Planning—A Systematic Approach (Ray K, Northants CC) 1977 **10** (2), 21

Managing Strategic Change in a Mature Business (Whipp R, Rosenfield R, Pettigrew A) 1989 **22** (6), 92

Performance Review: Key to Effective Planning (Berry S J, Carleton Board of Education) 1979 **12** (6), 17

Planning for Executive Development at J.R. Geigy, SA (Niederhausern W von, J.R. Geigy) 1970 **3** (1), 63

Planning for the Older Manager—Collaborative Research in Norwegian Business (Joynt P, Norwegian Sch of Mgt) 1987 **20** (3), 35

MANAGEMENT EDUCATION

The Oracle that Failed (Stander A, Rickards T, Manchester Business Sch) 1975 **8** (5), 13

MANAGEMENT INFORMATION SYSTEMS

Bayer Reorganizes in Response to Growth (Vossberg H, Bayer) 1985 **18** (6), 13

Design Your Own Management Information Systems (Ehrlemark U, Lund U) 1984 **17** (2), 85

Designing Communication Support Systems for Strategic Planning (Charalambides L C) 1988 **21** (6), 93

Developing an Information Systems Strategy (Hayward R G, Massey U Palmerston North New Zealand) 1987 **20** (2), 100

Developing Strategies for Management Information Systems (Tozer E E, Consultant) 1986 **19** (4), 31

Integrating Information Systems into Business Strategies (Ward J M, Cranfield Sch of Mgt) 1987 **20** (3), 79

Introducing Management Information Systems for Corporate Planning and Control (Kashyap R N, R N Kashyap Assocs) 1973 **6** (1), 28

Is Your Information System Mature Enough for Computerized Planning? (Brightman H J, Harris S E, Georgia State U) 1985 **18** (5), 68

Key Issues in Managing Information (Sizer R, BCS) 1983 **16** (5), 10

Management Information Systems for Corporate Planning Control (Kashyap R N, Consultant) 1972 **5** (2), 25

Management Information Systems (Green J F, Urwick Dynamics) 1970 **2** (4), 74

Management Information Systems in Planning (Sethi N K, St. John's U) 1978 **11** (3), 75

A Management Strategy for Information Processing 1. The Segas Case (Collins A C, South Eastern Gas) 1983 **16** (5), 29

A Management Strategy for Information Processing (Collins A C, South Eastern Gas) 1983 **16** (6), 21

Strategic Planning for MIS (Shrivastava P, New York U) 1983 **16** (5), 19

Using Critical Success Factors in Planning (Jenster Per V, McIntire Sch of Commerce, Virginia) 1987 **20** (4), 102

MANAGEMENT PHILOSOPHY

Assessing Your Competitor's People and Organization (Ball R, Cresap, McCormick & Paget) 1987 **20** (2), 32

Japanese Management Philosophy: Can it be Exported? (Kono T, Gakushuin U) 1982 **15** (3), 90

MANAGEMENT SCIENCE

Management Science and Strategic Planning (Wagle B, IBM) 1971 **3** (3), 26

MANAGERS

The Female Manager—The Pressures and the Problems (Cooper G L, Davidson M J, UMIST) 1983 **16** (1), 10

MANPOWER PLANNING

Avoiding Skill Shortages in the New Technologies (Pearson R, U of Sussex) 1985 **18** (4), 33

A Critique of some Techniques of Manpower Forecasting at National and Sectoral Levels (Helps I G, Nat Economic Devel Office) 1973 **6** (2), 75

Developing a Manpower Strategy for an Industry (Moss A, Consultant) 1980 **13** (3), 69

Engineering Manpower Planning in an Airline (Subramaniam S, Indian Inst of Mgt) 1977 **10** (4), 56

How to Computerize Your Personnel Planning (Ward S C, U of Southampton) 1987 **20** (4), 88

Identifying Managerial Potential for Manpower Planning (Barnett G G, Edgars Stores) 1975 **8** (5), 66

Management Stocktaking: An Approach to Manpower Planning in Banking (Hoyle M H, Stubbs R J, Nat Westminster Bank) 1970 **2** (3), 18

Manpower in Corporate Planning (Bell D J, United Dominions Trust) 1976 **9** (2), 31

Manpower Planning at National and Company Level (Cox J, DTI) 1971 **3** (4), 27

Manpower Planning and Individual Goals (Gohl J, Oppelland H J, Researchers) 1979 **12** (6), 29

A Manpower Planning Model for Organizational Effectiveness (Kahalas H, Leininger W E, Virginia Poly Inst & State U) 1975 **8** (4), 85

Manpower Studies for Industrial Sectors (Venning M, EITB) 1974 **7** (3), 27

Personnel Policy and Manpower Planning in Banking (Lyons T P, Williams & Glyn's Bank) 1979 **12** (5), 2

Planning of Medical Manpower (Pizman A, Neuman Y, Tel-Aviv U) 1976 **9** (1), 44

Strategic Planning for Human Resources—Let's Get Started (Nkomo S M) 1988 **21** (1), 66

MANPOWER *see* **LABOUR SUPPLY**

MANUFACTURING

Computer-aided Design and Manufacturing—A Managers Guide (Burrows B C, Futures Information Assocs) 1986 **19** (5), 76

How Sumitomo Transformed Dunlop Tyres (Radford G D) 1989 **22** (3), 28

How U.S. and Japanese CEO's Spend Their Time (Kudo H, Tachikawa T, Suzuki N) 1988 **21** (6), 79

Measuring Manufacturing Performance—The DAP Concept (Leckie A H, Consultant) 1973 **6** (4), 52

Planning for Better Channel Management (Hardy K G, Magrath A J) 1988 **21** (6), 30

Planning for Manufacturing Technology (Swamidass P M, U of Missouri) 1987 **20** (5), 125

Quality Circles: From Introduction to Integration (Dale B G, U of Manchester; Lees J, Inst of Science and Technology) 1987 **20** (1), 78

Strategic Control of Factory Automation (Meredith J R) 1987 **20** (6), 106

Three Simple Steps to Determine Optimum Plant Capacity (Cameron D, Burmah Oil) 1974 **7** (1), 40

Turnaround of a Cable Company (Gopal R) 1989 **22** (1), 98

MANUFACTURING STRATEGY

Achieving Japanese Productivity and Quality Levels at a U.S. Plant (Ishikure K) 1988 **21** (5), 10

Australian Industry: Sophisticated Planning and Weak R & D? (Christodoulou C) 1988 **21** (1), 82

Building a Competitive Advantage Through Information Technology (Jackson C) 1989 **22** (4), 29

Competing Against Low Cost Cutlery Imports (Grant R M) 1989 **22** (5), 59

Creating a Manufacturing Strategy to Suit Your Business (Pendlebury J) 1987 **20** (6), 35

An Information System for Just-In-Time (Yoo S) 1989 **22** (6), 117

Japanese Manufacturing: Strategy and Practice (Bolwijn P T, Brinkman S, Philips Intl BV) 1987 **20** (1), 25

Make or Buy—A Key Strategic Issue (Ford D, U of Bath; Farmer D, Henley—The Mgt Coll) 1986 **19** (5), 54

Managing a Successful Turnaround (Zimmerman F M) 1989 **22** (3), 105

Manufacturing Resource Planning: An Information Systems Model (Adams F P, Cox J F, Auburn U) 1985 **18** (2), 86

Manufacturing Technology as a Competitive Weapon (Blois K J, Templeton Coll Oxford) 1986 **19** (4), 63

Planning for Manufacturing Technology (Swamidass P M, U of Missouri) 1987 **20** (5), 125

Smaller Car Firms — Will They Survive? (Rhys G) 1989 **22** (5), 22

A Strategic Perspective for Make or Buy Descisions (Jaunch L R, Wilson H K, Sthn Illinois U) 1979 **12** (6), 56

Strategic Planning for Power Equipment Manufacture (Shah R K D) 1989 **22** (5), 98

Strategy Alternatives for Vehicle Component Manufacturers (Carr C) 1988 **21** (4), 86

MARKET DEFINITION
How to Define Your Market Segment (Roberts K J, Stategic Planning Inst London) 1986 **19** (4), 53

MARKET FORECASTING
The Dangerous Quest for Certainty in Market Forecasting (Abt R, Borja M, Menke M M, Pezier J P, Ciba-Geigy) 1979 **12** (2), 52

Forecasting the Market Demand for Waste Paper (Turner R K, Grace R P, Leicester U) 1977 **10** (3), 30

Forecasting the Market for Ships (Nielsen K S, Kristensen N E, Bastiansen E, Skytte P, B & W Diesels) 1982 **15** (4), 70

Forecasting and Research for Supply Markets—Commodity Buying Systems (Kingsman B G, Lancaster U and Commodity Systems) 1974 **7** (5), 24

MARKET RESEARCH
Analysing Business Opportunities in North Sea Oil (Briers R, Industrial Market Research Ltd) 1976 **9** (1), 53

Making Corporate Planning Work in Developing Countries (Haines W R) 1988 **21** (2), 91

Market Research for 'Out of Town' Shopping Centres (Hillier T J, Bradford U) 1972 **5** (3), 53

MARKET SHARE
Does Market Share Lead to Profitability? (Bourantas D, Athens Sch of Economics and Business Science; Mandes Y, Technical U of Athens) 1987 **20** (5), 102

Importance of Relative Market Share in Strategic Planning—A Case Study (Delombre J, Bruzelius B, SKF) 1977 **10** (4), 2

Market Share—Key to Higher Profitability? (Newton J K, Lancaster U) 1983 **16** (1), 37

Successful Businesses Compete on Quality—Not Costs (Luchs R, Strategic Planning Inst) 1986 **19** (1), 12

Using IT for Competitive Advantage at Thomson Holidays (Palmer C) 1988 **21** (6), 26

MARKET STRUCTURE
1992: A European Market for Cars? (Perrin-Pelletier F) 1988 **21** (3), 27

Market Concentration—Challenge to Corporate Planning (Blois K J, Loughborough U) 1980 **13** (4), 56

MARKETING
Building a Customer-orientated Organization (Cornish F) 1988 **21** (3), 105

Buying is Marketing Too—Japan's Influence on the Australian Coal Trade (Dowling G, U of New South Wales) 1987 **20** (1), 35

Competitive Superiority Through Data Base Marketing (Shaw B, Stone M) 1988 **21** (5), 24

Creating a Successful Marketing Strategy for UNI Insurance (Overland T) 1989 **22** (4), 25

Database Marketing for Competitive Advantage (Stone M, Taba Midas; Shaw R, Arthur Andersen) 1987 **20** (2), 12

Designing a Long Range Marketing Strategy for Services (Gronroos C, Swedish Sch of Economics and Business Administration) 1980 **13** (2), 36

Environmental Pressures and Marketing in the 1970's (Healy D F, Delaware U) 1975 **8** (3), 41

French 'Savoir-Faire' in Selling Arms: A New Way of Doing Business? (Anastassopoulos J-P, Dussauge P, Hautes Etudes Commerciales) 1985 **18** (5), 13

From Food to Freezers to Freight, Marketing is Vital (Lovell R G, Ntl Freight Consortium Dist Grp) 1986 **19** (5), 40

How Much Customer Service Do You Need? (Metz C K C, Intl Systems Research) 1978 **11** (4), 39

How to Define Your Market Segment (Roberts K J, Stategic Planning Inst London) 1986 **19** (4), 53

The Interaction of Systems Analysis and Marketing Planning (Gladstone E J, Savin Business Machines) 1971 **4** (1), 35

Japanese Marketing Strategies in the United Kingdom (Wong V, Saunders J, Doyle P) 1987 **20** (6), 54

Japan's Drive for the European Car Market—Lessons from U.S. Experience (Wray M, Toftech; Norburn D, Imperial Coll, London) 1987 **20** (4), 60

Market Segmentation for Pharmaceuticals (Lidstone J) 1989 **22** (2), 54

Marketing: the Prospects for the 1980s (Mason J B, Alabama U; Resnik A, Portland State U) 1982 **15** (1), 34

Marketing and Airline Corporate Planning (Shuman J C, Babson Coll) 1974 **7** (6), 68

Marketing in Developing Countries: The New Frontier (Varadarajan P R, Texas U) 1984 **17** (6), 118

Marketing Electricity—A Military Approach (Faruqui A, Battelle Columbus, Palo Alto) 1987 **20** (4), 67

Marketing the Key to Organizational Effectiveness (Lawson R W, Sheffield U) 1983 **16** (4), 90

Marketing in Moderation—The Marketing Concept and the Organization's Structure (Baligh H H, Burton R M, Duke U) 1979 **12** (2), 92

Marketing Planning for Colleges and Universities (Smith L R, Wisconsin-Whitewater U; Cavusgil S T, Bradley U) 1984 **17** (6), 104

Marketing Planning and Corporate Planning (Leyshon A M, Littlewoods Ltd) 1976 **9** (1), 29

Marketing Planning in a Service Economy (Chisnall P M, Manchester Business Sch) 1975 **8** (6), 43

Marketing Strategies for Scotch Whisky (Targett D, London Business Sch) 1983 **16** (2), 65

The Marketing Strategy Worksheet—A Practical Planning Tool (Buttle F, U of Surrey) 1985 **18** (4), 80

Marketing the Telephone in a De-regulated Environment (Kane N J A, British Telecom) 1986 **19** (4), 59

The New Marketing—Developing Long-term Interactive Relationships (Gummesson E, U of Stockholm) 1987 **20** (4), 10

New Product Planning at Hitachi (Nishikawa T) 1989 **22** (4), 20

The Planned Marketing of Textiles (Thomas H A, Courtaulds) 1971 **3** (3), 54

Planners and Bureaucrats—Developing the Consultant Client Relationship (Mushkat M, Hong Kong U) 1984 **17** (2), 111

Planning for Better Channel Management (Hardy K G, Magrath A J) 1988 **21** (6), 30

Re-designing Bank Service Systems for Effective Marketing (Gupta Y P, Torkzadeh G) 1988 **21** (6), 38

Risk Analysis and Investment Appraisal in Marketing (Cameron D A, Beecham Research Laboratories) 1972 **5** (4), 43

The Role of Marketing in Evaluating Acquisitions (Nicholls J R, Bath U; Broadbent D A, Royal Melbourne Inst of Technology) 1979 **12** (1), 67

Strategic Marketing (Murray J A, U Coll) 1979 **12** (2), 76

Strategies for Marketing New Computer Products (Stone M, Henley Mgt Coll) 1985 **18** (3), 41

Where Marketing Planning Fails (Greenley G E, North Staffordshire Poly) 1983 **16** (1), 106

Winning Customers Through Employee Involvement (Bailey J, Bristol Mgt Centre) 1984 **17** (4), 79

MARKETING CONCEPT
Marketing in Moderation—The Marketing Concept and the Organization's Structure (Baligh H H, Burton R M, Duke U) 1979 **12** (2), 92

The New Marketing—Developing Long-term Interactive Relationships (Gummesson E, U of Stockholm) 1987 **20** (4), 10

MARKETS
Competing Against Low Cost Cutlery Imports (Grant R M) 1989 **22** (5), 59

Trucks and Road Transport Towards 1992 (Garuzo G) 1988 **21** (4), 45

Waste Paper and the Market Mechanism (Livesey F, Barcena V A, UMIST) 1975 **8** (3), 17

MATERIALS
Energy and Primary Materials (Ray G, Consultant) 1982 **15** (5), 95

MATERIALS MANAGEMENT
Developing Materials Management (Slater A G, British Oxygen) 1979 **12** (1), 28

Raw Materials, Shortages and Producer Power (Ray G F, Nat Inst of Economic & Social Research) 1975 **8** (4), 2

MATHEMATICAL MODELS
Mathematical Models in National Planning (Vandorffy J, Min for Metallurgy and Mechanical Engineering) 1973 **6** (1), 42

MATRIX STRUCTURES
The Flexible Firm (Krijnen H G, Universiteitscomplex Paddepoel) 1979 **12** (2), 63

MBO *see* **MANAGEMENT BY OBJECTIVES**

MEASUREMENT

Vertical Integration in Petrochemicals—1. The Concept and Its Measurement (Burgess A R, Consultant) 1983 **16** (4), 55

MEDIA RESEARCH

A Businessman's Guide to the Media (Long G, News International) 1983 **16** (2), 15

MEDIA SELECTION

A Businessman' s Guide to the Media 1983 **16** (2), 15

MEDICAL CARE

Planning of Medical Manpower (Pizman A, Neumann Y, Tel-Aviv U) 1976 **9** (1), 44

MEDICINE

Medicines in the 1990's: Experience with a Delphi Forecast (Teeling-Smith G, Office of Health Economics) 1971 **3** (4), 69

MERGERS

Acquiring Firms With Higher PE Ratios (Roy A) 1988 **21** (5), 96

Acquisitions: A Directional Policy Matrix Approach (Newton J K, Lancaster U) 1981 **14** (6), 51

Alternatives to Merger—Joint Ventures and Other Strategies (Harrison J S) 1987 **20** (6), 78

Creating Value to Keep the Raiders at Bay (Reimann B C) 1989 **22** (3), 18

Evaluating the Risks in Acquisition (Hertz D B, Thomas H, Illinois U) 1982 **15** (6), 38

How Sumitomo Transformed Dunlop Tyres (Radford G D) 1989 **22** (3), 28

The Human Side of Merger Planning (Shirley R C, New York State U) 1977 **10** (1), 35

Mergers and British Industry (Stacey N A H, Chesham Amalgamations) 1968 **1** (1), 13

Planning Acquisitions and Mergers (Stotland J A, A.T. Kearney Ltd) 1976 **9** (1), 66

Planning for Post-merger Integration—Eight Lessons for Merger Success (De Noble A F, Gustafson L T, Hergert M) 1988 **21** (4), 82

The Prospect for Petrochemicals—Merger and Rationalization? (Walley K H, Shell Chemicals) 1982 **15** (1), 47

The Revolution in Building Societies (Wells G E) 1989 **22** (5), 30

Risk Analysis and the Formulation of Acquisition Diversification Strategies (Thomas H, Illinois U) 1983 **16** (2), 28

METHOD STUDY

Method Change at B.O.C. (Bayley W J, British Oxygen) 1972 **5** (2), 40

MEXICO

Forecasting Mexico's Oil Potential (Uri J D, US Govt) 1982 **15** (4), 86

MICROCOMPUTERS

Installing a Computerized Planning System in Ghana (Babington E A, Peat Marwick McLintock) 1987 **20** (4), 110

Microcomputers—The Breakthrough in Computer modelling (Harrison F L, Glasgow U) 1983 **16** (5), 94

MICROELECTRONICS INDUSTRY

Management and the Micro-Electronic Revolution—Part 1—Book Review Article (Twiss B C, Bradford U) 1981 **14** (5), 101

Management and the Micro-Electronic Revolution—Part 11—Book Review Article (Twiss B C, Bradford U) 1981 **14** (6), 83

MINERAL RESOURCES

BHP Reorganizes for Global Competition (Lewis G, Clark J, Moss B) 1988 **21** (3), 18

Corporate Planning in the Mineral Industry (Wright V C, Noranda Mines Ltd) 1976 **9** (2), 19

Strategic Alternatives for Australian Iron-Ore Producers (Frost F, Australian Inst of Technology) 1986 **19** (1), 89

MINING INDUSTRY

The Use of Simulations for Market Forecasting—A Case Study in the Mining Industry (Lloyd-Jacob D, Consolidated Gold Fields) 1969 **2** (1), 76

MISSION STATEMENTS

Defining the Role of the Board (Demb A, Chouet D, Lossius T, Neubauer F) 1989 **22** (1), 61

How Companies Define Their Mission (David F R) 1989 **22** (1), 90

MODELS

An Appreciation of Alternative Sales Forecasting Models: Recent Techniques Based on Historical Data (Briscoe G, Hirst M, Warwick U) 1973 **6** (3), 79

Business and Government—A New Partnership? (Halal W E, George Washington U) 1987 **20** (1), 123

Company Failure or Company Health?— Techniques for Measuring Company Health (Robertson J, Mills R W) 1988 **21** (2), 70

A Concept of an Integrated Transport Model (Swan R T, N.S.W. State Planning Authority) 1974 **7** (5), 17

Corporate Planning and Modelling in a Large Bank (Degueldre J, Banque Bruxelles Lambert) 1980 **13** (4), 43

Designing a Business Scanning System (Calori R) 1989 **22** (1), 69

Financial Planning for New Products Part 1—Basis for Model Formulation (Albala A, Technion) 1977 **10** (4), 61

Five Stages of Growth in Small Business (Scott M, U of Cape Town; Bruce R, Graduate Sch of Business) 1987 **20** (3), 45

Improving the Prospects for Plan Acceptance in Public Organizations (Mushkat M, U of Hong Kong) 1987 **20** (1), 52

Integrating Models into the Planning Process (Naylor T H, Duke U) 1977 **10** (6), 11

Modelling a Make or Buy Decision at ICI (Roe P A, ICI) 1972 **5** (4), 21

A New Product Growth Model with a Dynamic Market Potential (Mahajan V, Peterson R A, Jain A K, Malhotra N, Ohio State U, Texas U, New York State U) 1979 **12** (4), 51

Organizing for Strategic Management—A Conceptual Model (Gummesson E, PA Intl Mgt Consultants) 1974 **7** (2), 13

Practice Problems of Gravity Modelling (Hodges S, MIT; Kennett D, Columbia U) 1973 **6** (4), 41

The Software Life Cycle in Computer Applications (Lehner F) 1989 **22** (5), 38

MONITORING

Achievement Reporting—Controlling Performance Against Objectives (Christopher W F, Hooker Chemicals and Plastics) 1977 **10** (5), 14

MOTOR INDUSTRY

1992: A European Market for Cars? (Perrin-Pelletier F) 1988 **21** (3), 27

Achieving Japanese Productivity and Quality Levels at a U.S. Plant (Ishikure K) 1988 **21** (5), 10

Alternative Fuels for Automobiles—the Medium-Term Realities (Williamson E I, Longley R C M, Chem Systems Intl) 1982 **15** (2), 32

Can Hyundai Go It Alone? (Hyun Y, Lee J) 1989 **22** (2), 63

Corporate Planning at Rolls-Royce Motors Limited (Young R, Rolls-Royce Motors; Hussey D E, Harbridge House Europe) 1977 **10** (2), 2

The European Automobile Industry—Three Possible Scenarios (Hohn S, Volkswagenwerk) 1980 **13** (4), 12

A Framework for the Strategic Management of Future Tyre Technology (Lauglaug A S, Goodyear Tyre and Rubber Company) 1987 **20** (5), 21

Getting FIAT Back on the Road (Galimberti F, Chief Economist, Fiat Group) 1986 **19** (1), 25

Government Policy and its Impact on the Motor Industry (Berg M, Society of Motors Manufacturers and Traders) 1985 **18** (6), 40

Japan's Drive for the European Car Market—Lessons from U.S. Experience (Wray M, Toftech; Norburn D, Imperial Coll, London) 1987 **20** (4), 60

Managing a Successful Turnaround (Zimmerman F M) 1989 **22** (3), 105

Planning for Growth in a Japanese Business (Serizawa Y) 1989 **22** (2), 20

Smaller Car Firms — Will They Survive? (Rhys G) 1989 **22** (5), 22

Strategic Alliances with Japanese Firms (Kobayashi N) 1988 **21** (2), 29

Strategies for International Growth in the Automobile Industry (Moulins J-L, U d'Aix-Marseille) 1978 **11** (1), 34

Strategy Alternatives for Vehicle Component Manufacturers (Carr C) 1988 **21** (4), 86

Technology Planning at General Motors (Koerner E) 1989 **22** (2), 9

MULTINATIONAL COMPANIES

Anatomy of a Long Range Plan (Smalter D J, Intl Minerals and Chemical Corp) 1969 **1** (3), 2

Building Competitive Strength in International Markets (Hitt M A, Ireland R D, Texas A & M U; Mays W A, Baylor U Texas) 1987 **20** (1), 115

Business Planning at Union Carbide (Rush K, Union Carbide Corp) 1968 **1** (2), 10

Corporate Planning for Asia, Latin America, and Africa (Dam A van, CPC International Inc) 1972 **5** (4), 2

Corporate Planning in CPC Europe (Champion J R, CPC) 1970 **3** (2), 8

Country-Portfolio Analysis—Assessing Country Risk and Opportunity (Perlitz M, U of Bonn) 1985 **18** (4), 11

Currency Problems in Multinational Long Range Planning (Bruns J, Deutsche Edelstahlwerke) 1970 **3** (2), 71

Dilution of Ownership in Multinational Concerns (Sachdev J C, UMIST) 1977 **10** (5), 33

A Framework for Strategic Planning in Multinational Corporations (Lorange P, Sloan Sch, MIT) 1976 **9** (3), 30

Getting FIAT Back on the Road (Galimberti F, Chief Economist, Fiat Group) 1986 **19** (1), 25

How Marriott Corporation Grew Five-fold in Ten Years (Kennedy C) 1988 **21** (2), 10

Innovation, The Multinational Corporation: Some Implications for National Science Policy (Cordell A J, Science Council Canada) 1973 **6** (3), 22

Inside Europe's Giant Companies: Cultural Revolution at Philips (Turner G) 1986 **19** (4), 12

Inside Europe's Giant Companies: Nestlé Finds a Better Formula (Turner G) 1986 **19** (3), 12

Inside Europe's Giant Companies: Olivetti Goes Bear-hunting (Turner G) 1986 **19** (2), 13

Inside Europes' Giant Companies—Daimler-Benz Goes Top of the League (Turner G) 1986 **19** (5), 12

The Japanese Multinational (Yoshihara H, Kobe U) 1977 **10** (2), 41

Managing the Diversified Corporation: The Tensions Facing the Chief Executive (Goold M, Campbell A) 1988 **21** (4), 12

Managing Toxic Wastes—After Bhopal and Sandoz (Mahon J F, Kelley P C, Boston U Sch of Mgt) 1987 **20** (4), 50

Multinational Business in the 1990s—A Scenario (Schwartz P, Saville J, Shell Intl) 1986 **19** (6), 31

Multinational Corporate Planning: Is it Really Different?—Book Review Article (Hussey D E, Harbridge House Europe) 1980 **13** (2), 105

Multinational Planning Systems (Boulden J B, On-Line Decisions) 1972 **5** (3), 25

Multinational Planning—Developing a Global Approach (Godiwalla H Y, U of Wisconsin) 1986 **19** (2), 110

National or Global?—Control vs Flexibility (Fannin W R, U of Houston; Rodrigues A F, Francis Marion College Sth Carolina) 1986 **19** (5), 84

The New Environment of European Corporations (Lefebvre M, Dor P, Germay J, Verraver J, Strategic and Corporate Europlanners Society) 1978 **11** (1), 15

Opportunities and Pitfalls for Multinational Corporations in a Changed Political Environment (Sethi S P) 1987 **20** (6), 45

Pitfalls in Multi-National Long-Range Planning (Steiner G A, Schollhammer H, California U) 1975 **8** (2), 2

Pitfalls in Planning for Multinational Operations (Brandt W K, Hulbert J M, Columbia U; Richers R, Fundacao Getulio Vargas) 1980 **13** (6), 23

Planning Global Strategies for 3M (Kennedy C) 1988 **21** (1), 9

Planning for a Multi-National Synergy (Rutenberg D P, Carnegie-Mellon U) 1969 **2** (2), 24

Prediction and Practice in Multinational Strategic Planning (Channon D F, Manchester Business Sch) 1976 **9** (2), 50

Product Regrouping can Aid MNE Planning (Kirpalani V H, Concordia U) 1978 **11** (3), 16

The Quest for Quality at Philips, (van Ham K, Philips Intl; Williams R, Erasmus U Rotterdam) 1986 **19** (6), 25

Strategic Leadership through Corporate Planning at ICI (Pink A I H) 1988 **21** (1), 18

Strategic Planning in European Multinationals (Gotcher J W, California State U) 1977 **10** (5), 7

Strategic Planning in IBM (Thoroman D G, IBM) 1971 **4** (1), 1

Strategic Planning for Multinationals—The Views of Government and Scientists (Gotcher J W, California State U) 1981 **14** (1), 23

Strategic Planning System for Multinational Companies (Sethi N K, St. John's U) 1982 **15** (3), 80

Strategies for Global Competition (Lei D) 1989 **22** (1), 102

Strategies for National Competitiveness (Rugman A M, Dalhousie U Nova Scotia) 1987 **20** (3), 92

MULTIOBJECTIVE PROGRAMMING

Multiple Objective Planning for Regional Blood Centres (Kendall K E, Nebraska U) 1980 **13** (4), 98

MULTIPLE CRITERIA DECISION MAKING

Zero-Base Budgeting—dealing with Conflicting Objectives (Lee S M, Nebraska U; Shim J P, Mississippi State U) 1984 **17** (4), 103

N

NATIONAL PLANNING

Development and Planning of Infra Structure (Ray G F, Nat Inst of Economic and Social Research) 1971 **4** (2), 47

Government Economic Planning in the United Kingdom (Marquand J, Civil Servant) 1978 **11** (6), 2

A Health Strategy for Nigeria (Adeyami K S, Petu A O) 1989 **22** (6), 55

How Singapore Makes Central Planning Work (Macdonald, Nat U of Singapore) 1986 **19** (1), 38

India: Can We Eliminate Poverty? (Bhargava P K, Banara Hindu U) 1987 **20** (2), 21

Long-Term Planning in the U.S.S.R. (Kotov F, Nat Economic and Social Research) 1971 **4** (2), 47

Mathematical Models in National Planning (Vandorffy J, Min for Metallurgy and Mechanical Engineering) 1973 **6** (1), 42

National Planning and the French Business Executive (Schollhammer H, UCLA Grad Sch of Business Admin) 1971 **3** (3), 22

National Planning in the United States (Michael S R, Carlisle A E, U of Massachusetts) 1976 **9** (3), 21

A National Strategic Planning Model (Bar-Zakay S N, Israel Aircraft Industries) 1981 **14** (4), 76

New Zealand—a Newcomer to Planning (Wright D, Otago U) 1982 **15** (3), 122

Planning in a Free Market Economy (Kreikebaum H, Grimm U, Johann Wolfgang Goethe U) 1982 **15** (3), 103

Planning in Ireland (FitzGerald G, Eire PM) 1971 **4** (2), 30

Planning in Whitehall—Is it Possible?—Will it Survive? (Razell E J, South Bank Poly) 1980 **13** (1), 34

Plutalist Organization and Consensus in Swedish Planning (Lundberg D, Consultant) 1976 **9** (6), 69

'Titanic Planning' in an Uncertain Environment (Trowbridge A V) 1988 **21** (2), 86

U.S. Industry: Decline and Fall? (Richetto, J P) 1988 **21** (1), 35

NATIONALISED INDUSTRIES *see* **STATE OWNED ENTERPRISE**

NEGOTIATION

Generic Win-Win Negotiating Solutions (Nielsen R P) 1989 **22** (5), 137

NETHERLANDS

Competitive Strategies in the Dutch Insurance Industry (Eppink J, Free U Amsterdam) 1987 **20** (4), 30

How Top Management is Changing Dutch Business (Turner G) 1987 **20** (6), 10

The Internationalization of Dutch Insurance Companies (Eppink D J, Van Rhijn B M) 1988 **21** (5), 54

Planning an Information System at Netherlands Gas (Adriaans W, Hoogakker J T) 1989 **22** (3), 64

NEW INTERNATIONAL ECONOMIC ORDER

The Corporate Role in a North-South Dialogue (Dam A van, Consultant) 1979 **12** (6), 22

NEW PRODUCT DEVELOPMENT

Breakthrough: The Development of the Canon Personal Copier (Yamanouchi T) 1989 **22** (5), 11

Spotting a Market Gap for a New Product (Mattson B E, U of Minnesota) 1985 **18** (1), 87

NEW PRODUCTS

Accelerating Innovation Through Real-time Workshops (Rhodes J D, Thame S) 1988 **21** (5), 41

Analytical Techniques for New Product Planning (Toll R, Metra Consulting Group) 1969 **1** (3), 52

Business Strategies in Small High-technology Companies (Smith J G, Fleck V, Cambridge U) 1987 **20** (2), 61

Directing Technological Development—The Role of the Board (Wilder, STC Technology) 1985 **18** (4), 44

Effective Strategies in Emerging Industries (Calori R, Group ESC Lyon) 1985 **18** (3), 55

Financial Planning for New Products. Part 1—Basis for Model Formulation (Albala A, Technion) 1977 **10** (4), 61

How to get New Products to Market Quicker (Mathot G B M Consultant for Innovation) 1982 **15** (6), 20

The Innovative Firm (Ansoff H I, Vanderbilt U) 1968 **1** (2), 26

A Model for New Product Planning (Albala A, Technion) 1977 **10** (6), 62

A New Product Growth Model with a Dynamic Market Potential (Mahajan V, Peterson R A, Jain A K, Malhotra N, Ohio State U, Texas U, New York State U) 1979 **12** (4), 51

New Product Planning at Hitachi (Nishikawa T) 1989 **22** (4), 20

Strategic Planning and Product Innovation—Some Systematic Approaches (Buij J, TNO Bureau for Product Devel) 1979 **12** (5), 23

Strategies for Marketing New Computer Products (Stone M, Henley Mgt Coll) 1985 **18** (3), 41

Strategies of New Biotechnology Firms (Smith J G, Fleck V) 1988 **21** (3), 51

The Use of Systems Analysis in New Product Development (Zoppoth R C, Xerox) 1972 **5** (1), 23

NEW ZEALAND

New Zealand—a Newcomer to Planning (Wright D, Otago U) 1982 **15** (3), 122

NIGERIA

Corporate Planning In Nigeria (Bedford F A, U of Science & Technology, Port Harcourt Nigeria) 1986 **19** (2), 125

A Health Strategy for Nigeria (Adeyami K S, Petu A O) 1989 **22** (6), 55

Planning in Nigerian Business (Adegbite O, Enterprise Consulting Group, Nigeria) 1986 **19** (4), 98

NON-PROFIT ORGANIZATIONS

Corporate Strategy in Catholic Religious Orders (Goghlan D, Coll of Industrial Relations, Dublin) 1987 **20** (1), 44

Environmental Forecasting and Non-Profit Professional Organizations (Jain S C, Connecticut U; Singhvi S S, Armco Steel) 1977 **10** (3), 50

Making Planning Relevant to Public Agency Management (Barkdoll G L, Dept of Health) 1976 **9** (1), 59

Planning for the Physically Handicapped (Kenny B, Richards G, Clarke-Hill C) 1989 **22** (2), 91

Strategic Issues for Charities and Philanthropies (Harvey J W, McCrohan K F) 1988 **21** (6), 44

Strategic Management of Public and Non-Market Corporations (Ruffat J, Strategies & Structures) 1983 **16** (2), 74

A Strategic Planning Process for Public and Non-profit Organizations (Bryson J M) 1988 **21** (1), 73

Strategic Planning for the World Wildlife Fund (Medley G J) 1988 **21** (1), 46

NORTH AMERICA

The Current State of Planning in North America: Introduction to the Special Issue (Wilson I, Consultant) 1983 **16** (3), 2

NORTH SEA OIL

Analysing Business Opportunities in North Sea Oil (Briers R, Industrial Market Research Ltd) 1976 **9** (1), 53

NORTH—SOUTH DIALOGUE *see* NEW INTERNATIONAL ECONOMIC ORDER

NORWAY

The Norwegian State Railways—Profit Motivated Enterprise or a Community Service? (Norden R F, Norwegian State Railways) 1978 **11** (2), 13

Planning for the Older Manager—Collaborative Research in Norwegian Business (Joynt P, Norwegian Sch of Mgt) 1987 **20** (3), 35

NUCLEAR POWER INDUSTRY

The Hazards of Nuclear Power Generation—The Case for Survival (Fisher S T, F T Fisher's) 1983 **16** (1), 77

Strategic Planning for British Nuclear Fuels Ltd (Geary N R, B.N.F.L.) 1973 **6** (3), 2

O

OBJECTIVES

Achievement Reporting—Controlling Performance Against Objectives (Christopher W F, Hooker Chemicals and Plastics) 1977 **10** (5), 14

The Choice of Corporate Objectives (Cantley M F, Lancaster U) 1970 **3** (1), 36

Defining Corporate Objectives (Argenti J, Barnet Lime) 1969 **1** (3), 24

Establishing a Financial Objective—A Practical Approach (Allen D, Cadbury Schweppes) 1979 **12** (6), 11

Formulating Corporate Objectives and Strategies (Krijnen H G, Groningen U) 1977 **10** (4), 78

Organization for Business Objectives (Havemann E, Royal Dutch Shell) 1969 **2** (2), 14

Setting Corporate Objectives as a Basis for Action (Pearson G J, Clay Cross) 1979 **12** (4), 13

Setting Corporate Objectives (Redwood H, Fisons) 1977 **10** (6), 2

Setting Corporate Objectives Using Market Required Earnings (Walsh C, Irish Mgt Inst; Mock E, FFIN-ECON Inc) 1979 **12** (5), 54

Setting Objectives in Terms of Added Value (Wood E G, Sheffield City Poly) 1979 **12** (4), 2

OCEAN RESOURCES

Corporate Long Range Planning for Ocean Oriented Industries (Moore J J, Modern Mgt) 1971 **4** (2), 7

OECD

The U.K. and its OECD Competitors (Norse D, DOE) 1982 **15** (5), 131

OFFICE MANAGEMENT

Designing Communication Support Systems for Strategic Planning (Charalambides L C) 1988 **21** (6), 93

Managing the Growth of Electronic Office Information Systems (Hirschhein R A, London Sch of Economics) 1983 **16** (6), 59

The Strategic Design of Buildings (Nutt B) 1988 **21** (4), 130

OFFSHORE INDUSTRY

The Management of Offshore Resources—Some Implications of the 200-Mile Limit (Puccini D S, Fisheries & Oceans; Marley-Clarke B W G, Corporate Services) 1979 **12** (5), 8

OIL INDUSTRY

Forecasting Mexico's Oil Potential (Uri N D, US Govt) 1982 **15** (4), 86

How the Rip Van Winkle Approach Helps Oil Executives Plan (Finizza A J, Atlantic Richfield) 1985 **18** (1), 59

Long Range Planning at Continental Oil (Cecil J B, Continental Oil) 1971 **4** (1), 54

Planning for Esso Greece — The Impact of Nationalization (Labroukos N S, Lioukas S) 1989 **22** (4), 98

Third World Oil and Gas—Underexplored and Underdeveloped (Odell P R, Economic Geography Inst) 1981 **14** (1), 10

OLD AGE PLANNING

Keeping People Alive—The Implications for Planning (Hillman H, Surrey U) 1969 **2** (1), 40

OPERATIONAL RESEARCH

Corporate Planning and Operations Research: Do They Go Together? (LaForge L, Clemson U; Wood D R, Virginia Commonwealth U) 1982 **15** (3), 152

Operational Research and Bank Planning (Blumberg L F, Cotter L, Consultants) 1975 **8** (5), 29

ORGANIZATION

Getting Management Commitment to Planning a New Approach (Humphrey A S, Business Planning & Devel) 1974 **7** (1), 45

Human and Organization Problems in Corporate Planning (Wilson A C B, GKN) 1972 **5** (1), 67

Organization for Business Objectives (Havemann E, Royal Dutch Shell) 1969 **2** (2), 14

Organization for Long Range Planning—A Survey of German Companies (Keppler W, Bamberger I, Gabele E, Rutgerswerke A G; Inst de Gestion de Rennes) 1979 **12** (5), 69

Organization of the Planning Department in a Divisionalized Concern (Friedrich A, Land A van't, Portmund) 1974 **7** (2), 27

Organization for Technological Change (Ward E P, New Product Mgt Group) 1981 **14** (4), 121

Organizing the Corporate Planning Function (Denning B W, London Grad Sch of Business Studies) 1969 **1** (4), 67
Reorganization for Export at Ideal Standard (Paterson R R, Ideal-Standard) 1970 **3** (2), 65
Tackling the Human Problems in Planning (Lenz R T, Lyles M A, Consultants) 1981 **14** (2), 72

ORGANIZATION DEVELOPMENT

From Organization Development to Corporate Development at Trebor (Chapman A, Trebor) 1985 **18** (4), 50

ORGANIZATIONAL BEHAVIOUR

Acquisitions—Techniques for Measuring Strategic Fit (Clarke C J, Smith Trust) 1987 **20** (3), 12
Business Strategies in Small High-technology Companies (Smith J G, Fleck V, Cambridge U) 1987 **20** (2), 61
Corporate Culture and Strategy—The Problem of Strategic Fit (Scholz C, Saarland U) 1987 **20** (4), 78
How NASA moved from R & D to Operations (Hunsucker J L, Brah S A, Santos D L) 1989 **22** (6), 38
The Incentive Effects of Ownership and Control in Management Buy-outs (Green S) 1988 **21** (1), 26
Planning for Technology as a Corporate Resource (van Gunsteren L A, Erasmus U Rotterdam, Rotterdam Consulting Group) 1987 **20** (2), 51
The Roles of Formal Strategic Planning (Langley A) 1988 **21** (3), 40
Strategy, Organizational Culture and Symbolism (Green S) 1988 **21** (4), 121
Success Through Culture Change in a Japanese Brewery (Nakajo T, Kono T) 1989 **22** (6), 29

ORGANIZATIONAL CHANGE

Bayer Reorganizes in Response to Growth (Vossberg H, Bayer) 1985 **18** (6), 13
BHP Reorganizes for Global Competition (Lewis G, Clark J, Moss B) 1988 **21** (3), 18
Careers for the 21st Century (Handy C) 1988 **21** (3), 90
Change in Management and the Management of Change (Wilmot R W) 1987 **20** (6), 23
Changing the Corporate Culture of Rank Xerox (Chapman P) 1988 **21** (2), 23
Developing an Enterprise Culture at British Telecom (Brunnen D J) 1989 **22** (2), 27
Forecasting Organizational Changes (Elbing A O, IMEDE Man Devel Inst) 1974 **7** (6), 43
How Top Management is Changing Dutch Business (Turner G) 1987 **20** (6), 10
Managing Organizational Change—A Strategic Approach (McEwen N, Carmichael C, Short D, Steel A) 1988 **21** (6), 71
Planning for Post-merger Integration—Eight Lessons for Merger Success (De Noble A F, Gustafson L T, Hergert M) 1988 **21** (4), 82
Strategic Development as a Means of Organizational Change: Four Case Histories (Green J, Chemical and Allied Products; Jones T, Industry Training Board) 1981 **14** (3), 58
Strategic Planning as an Organizational Change Process—Some Guidelines from Practice (Taylor D E, Business and Mgt Devel) 1979 **12** (5), 43
Success Through Culture Change in a Japanese Brewery (Nakajo T, Kono T) 1989 **22** (6), 29
The Transformation of AT & T (Kennedy C) 1989 **22** (3), 10

ORGANIZATIONAL DESIGN

Creating a Productive Culture at Shell Chemicals (Thornley I A) 1988 **21** (3), 34
Designing an Effective Financial Planning and Control System (Cowen S S, Middaugh II J K) 1988 **21** (6), 83
Designing Innovating Systems (Radosevich R, New Mexico U) 1977 **10** (2), 79
International Strategies of Dutch Insurance Companies (Eppink D J, van Rhijn B M) 1989 **22** (1), 41
Quality Circles: From Introduction to Integration (Dale B G, U of Manchester; Lees J, Inst of Science and Technology) 1987 **20** (1), 78
Re-designing Bank Service Systems for Effective Marketing (Gupta Y P, Torkzadeh G) 1988 **21** (6), 38
Strategic Planning Could Improve Your Share Price (Welch J B, Northeastern U) 1984 **17** (2), 144
Strategic Planning for the World Wildlife Fund (Medley G J) 1988 **21** (1), 46

ORGANIZATIONAL DEVELOPMENT

A Complete Guide to Company Growth and Development (Danielsson C, Swedish Sch of Economics and Business Administration) 1982 **15** (6), 8
Increasing Trust Improves Productivity (Dwivedi R S, Kurukshetra U) 1985 **18** (3), 82
Planning for Changes in Stages of Corporate Development (Leontiades M, Rutgers U) 1979 **12** (6), 70

ORGANIZATIONAL EFFECTIVENESS

Building a Customer-orientated Organization (Cornish F) 1988 **21** (3), 105
Business Synergy Does Not Always Pay Off (Mahajan V, Wind Y) 1988 **21** (1), 59
Can Bureaucracies Become More Flexible and Responsive (Longford M D, Dept of Health and Social Security) 1986 **19** (1), 99
Creating a Climate for Innovation (Humble J, Jones G) 1989 **22** (4), 46
How Leaders Use Goals (Molz R, Clarkson U) 1987 **20** (5), 91
Improving the Prospects for Plan Acceptance in Public Organizations (Mushkat M, U of Hong Kong) 1987 **20** (1), 52
Linking Organizational Effectiveness and Environmental Change (Shipper F, Arizona State U) 1983 **16** (3), 99
Managing the Diversified Corporation: The Tensions Facing the Chief Executive (Goold M, Campbell A) 1988 **21** (4), 12
Marketing the Key to Organizational Effectiveness (Lawson R W, Sheffield U) 1983 **16** (4), 90
Pay for Performance — An Instrument of Strategy (Murphy T) 1989 **22** (4), 40
Setting up Corporate Goals and Measuring Organizational Effectiveness—A Practical Approach (Mendelow A L, Pittsburgh U) 1983 **16** (1), 70
Using Critical Success Factors in Planning (Jenster Per V, McIntire Sch of Commerce, Virginia) 1987 **20** (4), 102
Why Europeans are Weak in Asia—An Organizational Perspective (Lasserre P) 1988 **21** (4), 25

ORGANIZATIONAL PERFORMANCE

Long Range Planning and Organizational Performance (Karger D W, Malik Z A, Rensselaer Poly Inst) 1975 **8** (6), 60

ORGANIZATIONAL STRUCTURE

The Aston Programmes I, II and III. Advances in Organization Theory—An Overview of Some Recent Literature—Book Review Article (Grinyer P H, London Business Sch) 1978 **11** (6), 89
The Energy Manager and His Corporate Role (Bowonder B, Coll of India) 1984 **17** (4), 74
The Flexible Firm (Krijnen H G, Universiteitscomplex Paddepoel) 1979 **12** (2), 63
How Successful Companies Manage Diverse Businesses (Calori R, CESMA) 1988 **21** (3), 80
Japanese Manufacturing: Strategy and Practice (Bolwijn P T, Brinkman S, Philips Intl BV) 1987 **20** (1), 25
Linking Organization Structures and Processes to Business Strategy (Cowherd D M, Luchs R H) 1988 **21** (5), 47
Marketing in Moderation—The Marketing Concept and the Organization's Structure (Baligh H H, Burton R M, Duke U) 1979 **12** (2), 92
Planning for Technology as a Corporate Resource (van Gunsteren L A, Erasmus U Rotterdam, Rotterdam Consulting Group) 1987 **20** (2), 51
Systematic Planning and Re-organization (Janzen L T, Nordisk Aluminium Industri) 1971 **4** (2), 58

P

PAPER AND PULP INDUSTRY

Forecasting the Market Demand for Waste Paper (Turner R K, Grace R P, Leicester U) 1977 **10** (3), 30
Long Range Planning of Paper and Board Supplies (Vincent J D, Reed International) 1980 **13** (2), 60
A Note on Forecasting the Market Demand for Waste Paper (Livesey F, Consultant) 1978 **11** (1), 87
Policy Experiments with a Paper Industry Model (Price D H R, Thillainathan V, Bradford U) 1981 **14** (1), 73

Waste Paper—Case for Government Action (Whiting P L, Thames Board Mills) 1975 **8** (5), 23

PARTICIPATION

Decentralized Administration and Citizen Participation in Community Planning (Jackson R, Waterloo U) 1972 **5** (1), 16

Participation in Planning (Berschin H H, Brown, Boveri) 1973 **6** (4), 25

Participation in Planning—A Study of Two Organizations in The Netherlands (Dyson R G, Warwick U) 1978 **11** (4), 61

Participative Planning at Swiss Reinsurance (Odermatt H K, Swiss Reinsurance) 1978 **11** (5), 11

Planning Participation in Public Decision Making (Davies J, Newcastle upon Tyne U) 1970 **2** (4), 23

Public Participation in Planning—A Research Report (Benwell M, Centre for Transport Studies) 1980 **13** (4), 71

Strategic Planning and Participation: A Contradiction in Terms (Kloeze H J, Molenkamp A, Roelofs F J W, Consultants) 1980 **13** (5), 10

PAY

Narrowing the Gap—Equal Pay in Britain 1970–1986 (Tzannatos Z, U of Buckingham) 1987 **20** (2), 69

Pay for Performance — An Instrument of Strategy (Murphy T) 1989 **22** (4), 40

PENSION FUNDS

Investment Strategies for Pension Funds (in an Age of Inflation) (Skelton J D, Bradford U) 1973 **6** (4), 47

PENSIONS

Planning for Pensions in Inflation (Stuart C F, Standard Life Assur) 1975 **8** (6), 13

PERFORMANCE APPRAISAL

Assessing Performance in Libraries (Karunaratne N D, Queensland U) 1978 **11** (2), 66

The Impact of Key Success Factors on Company Performance (Vasconcellos e Sá J) 1988 **21** (6), 56

Pay for Performance — An Instrument of Strategy (Murphy T) 1989 **22** (4), 40

Planning for Strategic Performance in Local Government (McGill R) 1988 **21** (5), 77

PERFORMANCE MEASUREMENT

Linking Organization Structures and Processes to Business Strategy (Cowherd D M, Luchs R H) 1988 **21** (5), 47

Measuring Manufacturing Performance—The DAP Concept (Leckie A H, Consultant) 1973 **6** (4), 52

PERIODICALS

The Journal Readership Survey (Horne A, Horne Nunn) 1980 **13** (3), 40

PERSONNEL MANAGEMENT

Controlling and Evaluating Personnel Strategy (Newton D, Shell UK) 1969 **1** (4), 24

How to Computerize Your Personnel Planning (Ward S C, U of Southampton) 1987 **20** (4), 88

Implementing Strategies for Human Resources (Zabriskie N, Huellmantel A) 1989 **22** (2), 70

Long Range Planning of Managers (Ford H P, Shell Intl) 1968 **1** (1), 18

Managing Organizational Change—A Strategic Approach (McEwen N, Carmichael C, Short D, Steel A) 1988 **21** (6), 71

Personnel Administration in 1980: A Delphi Study (Lachmann O, Danish Inst of Graduate Engineers) 1972 **5** (2), 21

Personnel Planning and Information Systems (Domsch M, Wirtschaft U) 1971 **4** (2), 12

Personnel Planning—A Strategic View (Swart J M M de, Akzo Nederland br) 1979 **12** (3), 8

Personnel Policy and Manpower Planning in Banking (Lyons T P, Williams & Glyn's Bank) 1979 **12** (5), 2

Personnel and Training Policies—Some Lessons for Western Companies (Brown G F, Read A R, Consultants) 1984 **17** (2), 48

Planning the Deployment of Clergy (King M, Loughborough U; Smith D K, Exeter U) 1982 **15** (2), 104

Planning for Executive Development at J. R. Geigy, SA (Niederhausern W von, J.R. Geigy) 1970 **3** (1), 63

Planning for Personal Development (Poulsen A, Consultant) 1977 **10** (5), 86

Reducing Personnel Turnover and Improving Morale (Kohl J P, Stephens D B) 1989 **22** (4), 125

Should You Have a Payment System Based on Added Value? (Swannack A R, Inbucon/AIC) 1982 **15** (1), 76

Tackling the Human Problems in Planning (Lenz R T, Lyles M A, Consultants) 1981 **14** (2), 72

Woolworth's Drive for Excellence (Rose D) 1989 **22** (1), 28

PETROCHEMICALS

Predicting Plant Closures in European Industry (Baden-Fuller C, Longley R) 1988 **21** (1), 90

The Prospect for Petrochemicals—Merger and Rationalization? (Walley K H, Shell Chemicals) 1982 **15** (1), 47

Vertical Integration in Petrochemicals: Part 3. An Analysis of Ten Companies (Burgess A R, Consultant) 1983 **16** (4), 55

Vertical Integration in Petrochemicals—1. The Concept and Its Measurement (Burgess A R, Consultant) 1983 **16** (4), 55

Vertical Integration in Petrochemicals—2. Strategies and Problems (Burgess A R, Consultant) 1983 **16** (6), 29

PHARMACEUTICAL INDUSTRY

The Future for Pharmaceuticals in a Health Care Crisis (Redwood H) 1989 **22** (1), 18

Market Segmentation for Pharmaceuticals (Lidstone J) 1989 **22** (2), 54

The Roles of Formal Strategic Planning (Langley A) 1988 **21** (3), 40

Social Impact: The Pharmaceutical Industry (James B G, Consultant) 1978 **11** (1), 2

PLANNING

Alternative Plans for London Dockland: Not Force but Seduction (Ledgerwood G, Anglian Regional Mgt Centre) 1980 **13** (6), 46

An Approach to Simulation Model Development for Improved Planning (McKenney J L, Harvard U) 1970 **2** (3), 56

Computerised Industrial Forecasting for Planning in Central Government (Wells J D, DTI) 1971 **4** (2), 41

Coordinating Business Strategy and Technical Planning (Frohman A L, Boston U; Biotondo D, Bendix Corporation) 1981 **14** (6), 58

Corporate Planning and Modelling in a Large Bank (Degueldre J, Banque Bruxelles Lambert) 1980 **13** (4), 43

Corporate Planning Takes off in Singapore (Hou Wee C, Farley J U, Lee S K) 1989 **22** (2), 78

The Current State of Planning in North America: Introduction to the Special Issue (Wilson I, Consultant) 1983 **16** (3), 2

Defence Planning: The Uncertainty Factor (Moulton J L, Consultant) 1971 **3** (4), 50

Designing Communication Support Systems for Strategic Planning (Charalambides L C) 1988 **21** (6), 93

Designing an Effective Financial Planning and Control System (Cowen S S, Middaugh II J K) 1988 **21** (6), 83

Developing Corporate Strategy Through Planning, Programming, and Budgeting (Dougharty L A, Rand Corp) 1970 **2** (3), 24

Development Planning—An Adaptive Approach (Sachdeva P S, Indian Institute of Mgt) 1984 **17** (4), 96

The Directors' Role in Planning: What Information Do They Need? (Aram J D and Cowen S S, Case Wstrn Reserve U Ohio) 1986 **19** (2), 117

Does Planning Pay? The Effect of Planning on Success of Acquisitions in American Firms (Ansoff H I, Avner J, Brandenburg R G, Porter F E, Radosevich R, Vanderbilt U) 1970 **3** (2), 2

Ecology, Pollution and Business: A Proposed Planning Solution (Kahalas H, Groves D L, New York U) 1978 **11** (6), 62

The Effect of Technological Change on Planning for International Transport (Harding A, Nat Ports Council) 1969 **2** (1), 30

The Energy Market and Energy Planning (Robinson C, Surrey U) 1976 **9** (6), 30

Energy Planning in India (Venu S, Inst of Financial Mgt and Research) 1982 **15** (3), 146

Evaluating Alternative Strategies Using Scenarios (Whipple III W) 1989 **22** (3), 82

Everywhere, Planners are in Pain (Brown A, Weiner, Edrich, Brown) 1983 **16** (3), 18

Exploratory Planning in an Electronics Industry (Geradin L A, Look Out Studies) 1973 **6** (3), 72

Failings in U.K. Transport Planning (Jolliffe J K, Atkins Planning) 1977 **10** (1), 73

Financial Modelling for Planning in the U.K. (Grinyer P H, St Andrews U) 1983 **16** (5), 58

Foresight Activities in the U.S.A.: Time for a Re-Assessment (Lederman L L, Nat Science Foundation) 1984 **17** (3), 41

The Future from the Top: Presidential Perspectives on Planning—Part Three (Rosen S, Marketing and Planning Group Inc) 1974 **7** (4), 73

The Future from the Top: Presidential Perspectives on Planning—Part Two (Rosen S, Marketing and Planning Group) 1974 **7** (3), 34

Getting Management Commitment to Planning a New Approach (Humphrey A S, Business Planning & Devel) 1974 **7** (1), 45

How Danish Companies Plan (Ackelsberg R, Harris W C) 1989 **22** (6), 111

How Managers Plan—The Analysis of Managers' Activities (Snyder N, Glueck W F, Georgia U) 1980 **13** (1), 70

How Scenarios Trigger Strategic Thinking (Millett S M) 1988 **21** (5), 61

How to Computerize Your Personnel Planning (Ward S C, U of Southampton) 1987 **20** (4), 88

The Human Side of Merger Planning (Shirley R C, New York State U) 1977 **10** (1), 35

Improving Health Care Planning—Some Lessons from Immunization (Fottler M D, Alabama U) 1984 **17** (4), 88

Improving the Prospects for Plan Acceptance in Public Organizations (Mushkat M, U of Hong Kong) 1987 **20** (1), 52

India: Can We Eliminate Poverty? (Bhargava P K, Banara Hindu U) 1987 **20** (2), 21

Installing a Computerized Planning System in Ghana (Babington E A, Peat Marwick McLintock) 1987 **20** (4), 110

Integrated Planning for Health Care Organizations Especially Hospitals (Karger D W, West Florida U; Vora J A, St Cloud State Coll) 1979 **12** (1), 91

Integrating Forecasting and Planning (Makridakis S, INSEAD, Wheelwright S, Harvard U) 1973 **6** (3), 53

Interactive Planning—The Way to Develop Commitment (Lahr M L, Battelle Columbus Div) 1983 **16** (4), 31

Involving Managers in System-improvement Planning (Goldstein S G M, U of Western Australia) 1981 **14** (1), 93

Joint Planning for an Independent World (Dam A Van, Consultant) 1975 **8** (6), 8

Land-Use Planning in a World of Shrinking Resources (Coleman A, London U) 1978 **11** (1), 47

The Lost Art of Planning (Cartwright T J) 1987 **20** (2), 92

Making Planning More Effective (Dyson R G, Warwick U; Foster M J, Kingston Poly) 1983 **16** (6), 68

Making Planning Relevant to Public Agency Management (Barkdoll G L, Dept of Health) 1976 **9** (1), 59

Market Planning at the National Coal Board (Edwards M J, The Nat Coal Board) 1986 **19** (3), 46

Marketing Planning in India—A Survey (Kapoor M C, Singh J D, Delhi U) 1981 **14** (3), 97

Materials Developments and Planning—Future Implications in the Engineering and Chemical Industries (Locke B, Nat Research Devel Corp) 1969 **2** (1), 66

A Model for Long Range Planning in Higher Education (McKay C W, Cutting G D, Houston U) 1974 **7** (5), 58

The Motor Freight Industry—A Case against Planning (Kallman E A, Shapiro H J, New York U) 1978 **11** (1), 81

Operations Research and Bank Planning (Blumberg L F, Cotter L, Consultants) 1975 **8** (5), 29

An Organizational Study Approach to Planning Problems in an Industrial-Military Activity (Weston F C, Colorado State U) 1973 **6** (4), 58

Paradoxes in Planning (Robinson J, Shell UK) 1986 **19** (6), 21

Participative Planning at Swiss Reinsurance (Odermatt H K, Swiss Reinsurance) 1978 **11** (5), 11

Participative Planning for a Public Service (Grewe T, Marshall J, O'Toole D E) 1989 **22** (1), 110

People and Pollution: The Challenge to Planning (Hutchinson C, Consultant) 1970 **2** (3), 2

Planned Divestment—A Five-step Approach (Clarke C J, Gall, Francois, Wallace Smith Trust) 1987 **20** (1), 17

Planning for Banking—The Indian Experience (Godse V T, Nat Inst of Bank Management, Bombay) 1986 **19** (1), 105

Planning for Better Channel Management (Hardy K G, Magrath A J) 1988 **21** (6), 30

Planning in British Railways (Long R A, British Railways Board) 1969 **2** (2), 72

Planning for Business with China (Patten A J Van, Bronson & Bronson & McKinnon) 1974 **7** (4), 27

Planning a Computer Network: The Octopus Experience (Fletcher J G, California U) 1975 **8** (3), 72

Planning and Economics (Semister L, Bradford U) 1971 **4** (32), 63

Planning for Electricity Generation in India (Patel R R, Bharat Heavy Electrical) 1983 **16** (4), 61

Planning for Executive Development at J.R. Geigy, SA (Niederhausern W von, J.R. Geigy) 1970 **3** (1), 63

Planning the Future Raw Material Supply (Wright R W, Rio Tinto Zinc) 1976 **9** (1), 12

Planning in a German Steel Company (Friedrich A, Hoesch AG) 1972 **5** (4), 78

Planning for Giro (Singer A, Nat Giro) 1976 **9** (3), 38

Planning Global Strategies for 3M (Kennedy C) 1988 **21** (1), 9

Planning for Growth (Armenakis A A, Burgh H B, Auburn Tech Assistance Cntr, Alabama) 1986 **19** (3), 93

Planning for Growth in a Japanese Business (Serizawa Y) 1989 **22** (2), 20

Planning and Health Care—The Approach in a Reorganized NHS (Donald B L, Manchester U) 1974 **7** (6), 33

Planning for Hospitals: No Focus, No Strategy (Thakur M, U of Texas) 1985 **18** (6), 77

Planning an Information System at Netherlands Gas (Adriaans W, Hoogakker J T) 1989 **22** (3), 64

Planning Information Technology and the Post-Industrial Society (Burrows B C, Futures Information Assocs) 1986 **19** (2), 79

Planning for Innovation (Locke H B, Wilson A, Grossfield K, NRDC) 1974 **7** (2), 19

Planning for Job Creation (Falk N, Urban and Economic Devel) 1980 **13** (2), 20

Planning for Job Creation (May G, Green H, Leeds Poly) 1984 **17** (1), 100

Planning for Leisure in Sweden (Tobe E I, Consultant) 1971 **4** (1), 50

Planning for Leisure (Turnbull P, Exeter County Hall) 1975 **8** (5), 55

Planning for Local Government—A Grass-Roots Approach (Kemp R L, City Administrator of Placentia) 1985 **18** (6), 91

Planning for Manufacturing Technology (Swamidass P M, U of Missouri) 1987 **20** (5), 125

Planning in the Ministry of Industry and Tourism (Barrows D, Min of Industry and Tourism) 1979 **12** (6), 37

Planning for a Multi-National Synergy (Rutenberg D P, Carnegie-Mellon U) 1969 **2** (2), 24

Planning for a New International Economic Order? (Dam A van, Consultant) 1976 **9** (5), 57

Planning in Nigerian Business (Adegbite O, Enterprising Consulting Group, Nigeria) 1986 **19** (4), 98

Planning for Personal Development (Poulsen A, Consultant) 1977 **10** (5), 86

Planning for the Physically Handicapped (Kenny B, Richards G, Clarke-Hill C) 1989 **22** (2), 91

Planning for Post-merger Integration—Eight Lessons for Merger Success (De Noble A F, Gustafson L T, Hergert M) 1988 **21** (4), 82

Planning for a Professional Association (Ayal I, Faculty of Mgt, Tel Aviv) 1986 **19** (3), 51

Planning Research and Development at Hitachi (Kuwahara Y, Okada O, Horikoshi H) 1989 **22** (3), 54

Planning and Social Change (Walding P, LLewelyn-Davies Weeks Forestier-Walker & Bor) 1974 **7** (5), 51

Planning for Strategic Performance in Local Government (McGill R) 1988 **21** (5), 77

A Planning System for the British Prison Department (Garrett J, AIC Management Consultants; Home N, Home Office) 1972 **5** (3), 36

Planning for Technology as a Corporate Resource (van Gunsteren L A, Erasmus U Rotterdam, Rotterdam Consulting Group) 1987 **20** (2), 51

Planning for the U.S. Political Cycle (Marcus A A, Mevorach B) 1988 **21** (4), 50

Planning for a University, Using Interactive Forecasting (Moore L F, Charach L, British Columbia U) 1980 **13** (3), 109

Planning vs Strategy: Which will Win? (Carpenter M A, Gen Electric Company, Connecticut) 1986 **19** (6), 50

Planning for Water Resources (Perret D, Thames Water Authority) 1977 **10** (2), 65

Planning in West German Industry (Strigel W H, IFO-Inst for Econ Research) 1970 **3** (1), 9

Policy Planning and Central-Local Relations (Hinings B, U of Alberta; Leach S, Ranson S, Skelcher C, U of Birmingham) 1985 **18** (2), 38

Public Participation in Planning—A Research Report (Benwell M, Centre for Transport Studies) 1980 **13** (4), 71

Public Planning and Political Strategy (Rondinelli D A, The East-West Center, Hawaii) 1976 **9** (2), 75

R.O.C.E. As a Tool for Planning and Control (Bishop E B, Burmah Oil) 1969 **2** (2), 80

Realistic Planning for Transportation — A Flexible Approach (Khan A M) 1989 **22** (5), 128

The Roles of Formal Strategic Planning (Langley A) 1988 **21** (3), 40

Scenario Planning—What Style Should You Use? (Huss W R, Xenergy; Honton E J, Battelle Columbus) 1987 **20** (4), 21

Seventh World Planning Congress—A Report (Reid A, Consultant) 1979 **12** (2), 114

Strategic Leadership through Corporate Planning at ICI (Pink A I H) 1988 **21** (1), 18

Strategic Planning in Banks — Does it Pay? (Gup B E, Whitehead D D) 1989 **22** (1), 124

Strategy—The Key to Planning in the Public Corporation (Smith J G, City U) 1981 **14** (6), 24

Systemic Health Planning (Sepulveda C R, UN Asia and Pacific Devel Inst) 1979 **12** (3), 62

Systems Analysis and Planning for the Criminal Justice System (Blumstein A, Carnegie-Mellor U) 1972 **5** (4), 61

Testing Plans Against Alternative Futures (Boshoff H) 1989 **22** (5), 69

University Planning: An Organization Model (Mazze E M, Virginia Poly Inst and State U) 1971 **4** (2), 55

The Use of Comupters in Town Planning (Wood P, Liverpool City Planning Dept) 1971 **3** (3), 59

The Use of Games in Planning (Armstrong R H R, Hobson M, Birmingham U) 1972 **5** (1), 62

Using Critical Success Factors in Planning (Jenster Per V, McIntire Sch of Commerce, Virginia) 1987 **20** (4), 102

Water Supply—The Case for Joint Planning (Dam A van, Soc for Intl Devel) 1978 **11** (1), 69

Where Marketing Planning Fails (Greenley G E, North Staffordshire Poly) 1983 **16** (1), 106

Why Has Planning Failed? (Pennington M W, Golightly Intl) 1972 **5** (1), 2

Why Planning in State Enterprises Doesn't Work (Javidan M, Dastmalchian A) 1988 **21** (3), 98

Will Hong Kong's Entrepreneurs Move to Planning? (Warrington M B, Napier Coll) 1982 **15** (3), 157

PLANNING MODELS

Building Scenarios for an Electric Utility (Goldfarb D L, Huss W R) 1988 **21** (2), 78

Creative Strategic Planning Using Imagery (Maddox N, Stetson U; Anthony W P, Florida State U; Wheatley Jr W, U of West Florida) 1987 **20** (5), 118

Developing a Corporate Planning Model for a Small Company (Kluyver C A de, Purdue U; McNally G M, Canterbury U) 1982 **15** (1), 97

Developing Planning Models (Holloway C, Gulf Oil) 1974 **7** (1), 52

Developing a Practical Planning System for a Steel Business (Rozman R, Slovenske Zelezarne) 1986 **19** (2), 90

Energy Modeling as a Tool for Planning (Kopelman J B, Weaver N I, SRI Energy Center) 1978 **11** (1), 25

An Environmental Scanning System for Business Planning (Narchal R M, Kittappa K, Bhattacharya P) 1987 **20** (6), 96

How Belgian Businesses Make Strategic Planning Work (Caeldries F, van Dierdonck R) 1988 **21** (2), 41

How Managers Decide to Use Planning Models (Blanning R W, Pennsylvania U) 1980 **13** (2), 32

How to Design a Financial Planning Model (Hayen R L, Nebraska U) 1983 **16** (5), 111

Is Your Information System Mature Enough for Computerized Planning? (Brightman H J, Harris S E, Georgia State U) 1985 **18** (5), 68

A Model for New Product Planning (Albala A, Technion) 1977 **10** (6), 62

Modelling for Corporate Planning—Book Review Article (Power P D, Macgregor J M, EPS) 1980 **13** (3), 125

A Modelling System for Local Government Resource Planning (Howard K, Wagle B V, Bradford U) 1978 **11** (4), 77

Policy Experiments with a Paper Industry Model (Price D H R, Thillainathan V, Bradford U) 1981 **14** (1), 73

A Practical Approach to Strategy Development (Schwaninger M, St Gall Graduate Sch of Economics) 1987 **20** (5), 74

Quantifying Level of Investment in Growth and Renewal (Ziemer D R, Texas Instruments) 1976 **9** (4), 2

Strategic Planning and the Chief Executive (Forman R) 1988 **21** (4), 57

Strategic Planning for Hospitals—A Health-needs Approach (Champagne F, Contandriopoulos A-P, Larouche D, Clemenhagen C, Barbir C, U of Montreal) 1987 **20** (3), 77

Strategic Planning for Human Resources—Let's Get Started (Nkomo S M) 1988 **21** (1), 66

A Strategic Planning Process for Public and Non-profit Organizations (Bryson J M) 1988 **21** (1), 73

The Use of a Model in Long Term Planning—A Case History (Mann C W, Harold Whitehead & Partners) 1978 **11** (5), 55

PLANT LOCATION

Design and Location of Plant—A Case Study (Warner F, Cremer and Warner) 1969 **1** (3), 68

Plant Location—The International Perspective (Leontiades J C, EIASM) 1974 **7** (1), 10

PLASTICS INDUSTRY

What the New GATT Trade Agreement Means for Plastics (Christopher W F, Consultant) 1980 **13** (1), 77

POLICY

Energy Policy: Government vs Industry (Jones P, Electricity Council) 1987 **20** (1), 12

Lessons of Privatization (Lord King) 1987 **20** (6), 18

The Thatcher Revolution — Radical Policies in a Changing Society (Worcester R M) 1989 **22** (4), 72

U.K. Competition Policy Evaluated (Pass C L, Sparkes J R, Bradford) 1983 **16** (4), 76

POLICY MAKING

Alcohol: Is it Time to Say 'When'? (Steele D W, Action on Alcohol Abuse) 1987 **20** (5), 86

Managing Public Policy Issues (Barrows D S, Morris S) 1989 **22** (6), 66

National Policy Making in a Global Economy: The Case for U.S. Economic Planning (Bolling R, Boston Coll; Krauthoff L C, U.S. Government) 1983 **16** (3), 25

Rationality in Policy Making: Two Concepts Not One (Regan D E, London Sch of Economics) 1978 **11** (5), 83

U.S. Firms' Responses to Regulation: Stonewalling and Opportunism (Marcus A A) 1987 **20** (3), 98

POLITICAL RISKS

Assessing Country Risk for Foreign Investment Decisions (Leavy B, Nat Inst for Higher Education Dublin) 1984 **17** (3), 141

Country-Portfolio Analysis—Assessing Country Risk and Opportunity (Perlitz M, U of Bonn) 1985 **18** (4), 11

The Evaluation of Country Risk and Economic Potential (Kern D, Nat Westminster Bank) 1985 **18** (3), 17

The Identification and Assessment of Political Risk in the International Environment (Lloyd B, Commonwealth Devel) 1974 **7** (6), 24

POLITICS

Long Range Planning in a Politicized Environment (Windsor D, Greanias G, Texas U Sch of Administration) 1983 **16** (3), 82

Planning for the U.S. Political Cycle (Marcus A A, Mevorach B) 1988 **21** (4), 50

Population Policies and the Contemporary Political Scene (Loraine J A, Usher Inst) 1975 **8** (6), 2

Strategic Planning for Social and Political Change (Taylor B, Administrative Staff Coll Henley) 1974 **7** (1), 33

The Thatcher Revolution — Radical Policies in a Changing Society (Worcester R M) 1989 **22** (4), 72

POLLUTION

Ecology, Pollution and Business: A Proposed Planning Solution (Kahalas H, Groves D L, New York U) 1978 **11** (6), 62

Managing Toxic Wastes—After Bhopal and Sandoz (Mahon J F, Kelley P C, Boston U Sch of Mgt) 1987 **20** (4), 50

People and Pollution: The Challenge to Planning (Hutchinson C, Consultant) 1970 **2** (3), 2

POPULATION

Population Policies and the Contemporary Political Scene (Loraine J A, Usher Inst) 1975 **8** (6), 2

PORTFOLIO MANAGEMENT

The Business Portfolio Approach—Where it Falls Down in Practice (Bettis R A, Texas U Sch of Business; Hall W K, Michigan U Sch of Business Admin) 1983 **16** (2), 95

A Commonsense Approach to Portfolio Planning (Linneman R E, Philadelphia Sch of Mgt Science; Thomas M J, Lancaster U) 1982 **15** (2), 77

Creating Value to Keep the Raiders at Bay (Reimann B C) 1989 **22** (3), 18

How Successful Companies Manage Diverse Businesses (Calori R, CESMA) 1988 **21** (3), 80

The Internationalization of Dutch Insurance Companies (Eppink D J, Van Rhijn B M) 1988 **21** (5), 54

Pitfalls in Portfolio Planning (Coate M B, U.S. Government) 1983 **16** (3), 47

Pitfalls in Using Portfolio Techniques—Assessing Risk and Potential (Derkinderen F G J, Netherlands Sch of Business; Crum R L, Florida U) 1984 **17** (2), 129

Portfolio Analysis: Practical Experience with the Directional Policy Matrix (Hussey D E, Harbridge House Europe) 1978 **11** (4), 2

Portfolio Analysis in Practice (Walker R F, Consultant) 1984 **17** (3), 63

Portfolio Analysis and the Product Life Cycle (Barksdale H C, Harris C E, Georgia U) 1982 **15** (6), 74

Portfolio Analysis for the Small Firm (Bamberger I, Rennes U) 1982 **15** (6), 49

Portfolio Theory—A Planning Tool (Gup B E, Tulsa U) 1977 **10** (3), 10

Portfolio Planning at Akzo (Tieleman T M, Akzo) 1981 **14** (6), 17

Risk Return Approach to Product Portfolio Strategy (Cardozo R N, U of Minnesota; Wind J, U of Pennsylvania) 1985 **18** (2), 77

Strategy and the 'Business Portfolio' (Hedley B D, Boston Consulting) 1977 **10** (1), 9

Strategy, Cross Subsidization and the 'Business Portfolio' (Lofthouse S, Capel-Cure Myers) 1978 **11** (4), 58

PORTS

Alternative Plans for London Dockland: Not Force but Seduction (Ledgerwood G, Anglian Regional Mgt Centre) 1980 **13** (6), 46

POST OFFICE

How Will the British Post Office Cope with Technological Change (Corby M E, Mail Users' Assoc) 1982 **15** (6), 58

PRICE POLICY

Pricing Policies and Corporate Strategy (May R, British Printing Corp) 1970 **2** (4), 49

PRICING

The Experience Effect and Pricing for Agricultural Products (Ribon B, Consultant) 1981 **14** (4), 65

PRIVATE SECTOR

Lessons of Privatization (Lord King) 1987 **20** (6), 18

Privatization — A Cure for all Ills? (Hammer R M, Hinterhuber H H, Lorentz J) 1989 **22** (6), 19

The State of Private Sector Strategic Planning in Canada (Frederick G D, Consultant) 1983 **16** (3), 40

PROBLEM FORMULATION

Accelerating Innovation Through Real-time Workshops (Rhodes J D, Thame S) 1988 **21** (5), 41

Creative Strategic Planning Using Imagery (Maddox N, Stetson U; Anthony W P, Florida State U; Wheatley Jr W, U of West Florida) 1987 **20** (5), 118

Diagnosing Long-Term Information Problems (White M, Ashridge Mgt Coll; Leigh A, London Borough of Hammersmith) 1974 **7** (1), 27

A Tough Future for Australian Business (Laczniak E R, Pecotich A, Carroll B) 1989 **22** (1), 48

PROCESS ENGINEERING

The Future Size of Process Plant (Ball D F, Pearson A W, R & D Research) 1976 **9** (4), 18

PRODUCT DEVELOPMENT

Accelerating Innovation Through Real-time Workshops (Rhodes J D, Thame S) 1988 **21** (5), 41

Analytical Techniques for New Product Planning (Toll R, Metra Consulting Group) 1969 **1** (3), 52

Breakthrough: The Development of the Canon Personal Copier (Yamanouchi T) 1989 **22** (5), 11

Building a Competitive Advantage Through Information Technology (Jackson C) 1989 **22** (4), 29

Corporate Product Planning: A Vector Analysis Approach (Mazze E M, Hamelman P W, Kucheman W H, Virginia Poly Inst and State U) 1973 **6** (2), 35

Creating a Climate for Innovation (Humble J, Jones G) 1989 **22** (4), 46

GE's High-tech Strategy (Koerner E) 1989 **22** (4), 11

Materials Developments and Planning—Future Implications in the Engineering and Chemical Industries (Locke B, Nat Research Development Corp.) 1969 **2** (1), 66

A Model for New Product Planning (Albala A, Technion) 1877 **10** (6), 62

New Product Planning at Hitachi (Nishikawa T) 1989 **22** (4), 20

Planning Research and Development at Hitachi (Kuwahara Y, Okada O, Horikoshi H) 1989 **22** (3), 54

Product Forecasting: The BAC 3–11 Airliner (Thomas C H, BAC) 1970 **2** (4), 36

Product Planning at Perkins Engines Group (Kraushar C A A, Perkins Engines Group) 1968 **1** (2), 15

Product Planning—We're Still Getting it Upside Down (Pilditch J, AID) 1981 **14** (5), 20

Strategic Alliances—Guidelines for Success (Devlin G, Bleackley M) 1988 **21** (5), 18

Strategies for New Product Development (Buggie F D, Strategic Innovations Incorporated) 1982 **15** (2), 22

The Use of Futures Research in Product Planning (Morris G K, Matrix Corporate Affairs Consultants) 1982 **15** (6), 67

PRODUCT LIFE CYCLE

Can Industries De-Mature—Applying New Technologies to Mature Industries (Dowdy W L, Nikolchev J, SRI Intl) 1986 **19** (2), 38

Portfolio Analysis and the Product Life Cycle (Barksdale H C, Harris C E, Georgia U) 1982 **15** (6), 74

Strategies for Declining Industrial Markets (Robinson S J Q, Shell UK Ltd) 1986 **19** (2), 72

Strategies for Mature Business (Schofield M, Arnold D) 1988 **21** (5), 69

PRODUCT PLANNING *see* **PRODUCT DEVELOPMENT**

PRODUCTION

Automated Manufacturing—Why is it Taking so Long? (Ross M H, Arthur D Little) 1981 **14** (3), 28

PRODUCTION MANAGEMENT

Manufacturing Planning with Companies at Honeywell (Cross K, Honeywell Information Systems) 1984 **17** (6), 66

Quality Circles—Are they Working in British Factories (Dale B G, UMIST) 1984 **17** (6), 50

Technology Planning at General Motors (Koerner E) 1989 **22** (2), 9

PRODUCTION PLANNING

Developing and Implementing a Strategy for Production (Twiss B C, Bradford U) 1974 **7** (2), 31

Long Range Planning for Production (Corke D K, P-E Consulting Group) 1970 **3** (2), 27

Production Strategy Decisions—A Simulation Model Approach (Bell J A, Mullard) 1970 **2** (4), 62

PRODUCTION POLICY

Developing a Product Market Strategy (Foster D W, Planning for Growth) 1970 **2** (3), 70

PRODUCTIVITY

Achieving Japanese Productivity and Quality Levels at a U.S. Plant (Ishikure K) 1988 **21** (5), 10

Incomes, Productivity and Planning (Blakeman L T, Ford Motor Co) 1969 **1** (4), 10

Planning for Increased Productivity (Withers R M J, Urwick Technology Mgt) 1978 **11** (4), 16

Planning for Productivity (Smith G, Consultant) 1980 **13** (2), 52

Planning—Satisfaction and Productivity (Groves D L, Kahalas H and Lamb F, Virginia Poly and State U) 1976 **9** (4), 52

Productivity: Lessons from Japan (Keegan W J, New York U) 1975 **8** (2), 61

Productivity: What is it? (Coates J B, Aston U) 1980 **13** (4), 90

Productivity Improvement Through Reduced Labour Turnover (Rothwell S, Henley Centre) 1982 **15** (2), 67

Productivity Planning: a Central Issue for Australian Management (Cameron M J, Australian Paper Manufacturers) 1982 **15** (3), 157

Raising Productivity in Customer Services (Potts G W) 1988 **21** (2), 15

PROFITABILITY

Assessing the Performance of a Development Bank (Jain P K) 1989 **22** (6), 100

Business Synergy Does Not Always Pay Off (Mahajan V, Wind Y) 1988 **21** (1), 59

Does Market Share Lead to Profitability? (Bourantas D, Athens Sch of Economics and Business Science; Mandes Y, Technical U of Athens) 1987 **20** (5), 102

Market Share—Key to Higher Profitability? (Newton J K, Lancaster U) 1983 **16** (1), 37

Strategic Planning in Banks — Does it Pay? (Gup B E, Whitehead D D) 1989 **22** (1), 124

PROJECT EVALUATION

Corporate Planning and Project Evaluation in Urban Transport (Tyson W J, Manchester U; Cochrane R I D, GMPIE) 1981 **14** (5), 62

Project Selection and Evaluation (Johnstone R D, Consultant) 1972 **5** (3), 40

PROJECT MANAGEMENT

Effective Planning and Control of Large Projects—Using Work Breakdown Structure (Lanford H W, Wright State U; McCann T M, ANALYTICS) 1983 **16** (2), 51

Measuring Performance in Capital Project Management (Snowdon M, Cleveland Project Services) 1980 **13** (4), 51

Some Problems in Managing Complex Development Projects (Martyn A S, Seawolf) 1975 **8** (2), 13

PROJECT PLANNING

Effective Planning and Control of Large Projects—Using Work Breakdown Structure (Lanford H W, Wright State U; McCann T M, ANALYTICS) 1983 **16** (2), 51

Linear Programming Techniques in R & D Project Planning (Allen D H, Nottingham U) 1974 **7** (1), 61

Planned Euthanasia for Old Projects (Hutchinson A C, ICI) 1971 **4** (2), 17

Planning Development Projects: Lessons from Developing Countries (Rondinelli D A, Syracuse U) 1979 **12** (3), 48

PROPERTY DEVELOPMENT

Information Technology—Its Impact on Property (Burrows B C, Futures Information Associates) 1984 **17** (4), 60

The Strategic Design of Buildings (Nutt B) 1988 **21** (4), 130

PSYCHOLOGY

Psychological Aspects of Planning (Taylor R N, U of British Columbia) 1976 **9** (2), 66

Psychological Perspectives on the Future (Kay H, Exeter U) 1975 **8** (2), 51

PUBLIC AFFAIRS

Communicating Corporate Strategy — The Payoffs and the Risks (Higgins R B, Diffenbach J) 1989 **22** (3), 133

Corporate Strategies for Political Action (Gram H A, Crawford R L, Concordia U) 1979 **12** (5), 62

Growth in Activist Groups: How Can Business Cope? (Pattakos A N) 1989 **22** (3), 98

The Public Affairs Function in American Corporations: Development and Relations with Corporate Planning (Post J E, Murray E A, Dickie R, Mahon J F, Boston U) 1982 **15** (2), 12

Public Participation in Corporate Planning—Strategic Management in a Kibitzer's World (Dill W R, New York U) 1975 **8** (1), 57

Strategic Planning for Public Relations (Slatter S St. P, London Business Sch) 1980 **13** (3), 57

PUBLIC CORPORATIONS *see* **STATE OWNED ENTERPRISE**

PUBLIC EXPENDITURE

What Should we Spend on Health Care? (Hardie M C, King's Fund Centre) 1974 **7** (1), 2

PUBLIC POLICY

Corporate Strategy and Public Policy in Saudi Arabia (Luqmani M, Yavas U, Quraeshi Z A) 1989 **22** (4), 79

A Critique of some Techniques of Manpower Forecasting at National and Sectoral Level (Helps I G, Nat Economic Devel Office) 1973 **6** (2), 75

The Dynamics of Policy Change (Friend J K, Inst for Operational Research) 1976 **9** (5), 40

Forecasting the Impact of Public Policies (Renfro W L, Policy Analysis) 1980 **13** (4), 80

Implementing Public Plans: The Case for Social Marketing (Mushkat M, Hong Kong U) 1980 **13** (4), 24

Managing the Impacts of Large Public Programs (Yavitz B, Columbia U; Schnee J E, Rutgers U) 1977 **10** (1), 65

Managing Public Policy Issues (Barrows D S, Morris S) 1989 **22** (6), 66

Planning in a Free Market Economy (Kreikebaum H, Grimm U, Johann Wolfgang Goethe U) 1982 **15** (3), 103

Planning Participation in Public Decision Making (Davies J, Newcastle upon Tyne U) 1970 **2** (4), 23

Sector Policy in Government (Marshall R, DOE) 1974 **7** (4), 2

PUBLIC RELATIONS *see* **PUBLIC AFFAIRS**

PUBLIC SECTOR

Decision Making in the Public Sector—A Logical Model (Kahalas H, Virginia Poly Inst and State U) 1976 **9** (3), 75

Participative Planning for a Public Service (Grewe T, Marshall J, O'Toole D E) 1989 **22** (1), 110

Public Planning and Political Strategy (Rondinelli D A, The Far East-West Center, Hawaii) 1976 **9** (2), 75

A Strategic Planning Process for Public and Non-profit Organizations (Bryson J M) 1988 **21** (1), 73

Strategic Planning for a Public Sector Enterprise (Karagozoglu N, Seglund R) 1989 **22** (2), 121

Turnaround Strategies for Economic Development (Allen D N, Plosila W H) 1988 **21** (3), 59

PURCHASING

Competitive Analysis—Its Role in Purchasing (Farmer D, Henley Mgt and Advisory Service) 1984 **17** (3), 72

Competitive Procurement Strategies: Building Strength and Reducing Vulnerability (Spekman R E, Norwegian Sch of Economics) 1985 **18** (1), 94

The Impact of Supply Markets on Corporate Planning (Farmer D, Consultant) 1972 **5** (1), 10

The Marketing Approach to Purchasing (Davies O, Ciba-Geigy) 1974 **7** (3), 2

Planning and Control of Purchasing Performance: A New Concept (Dobson S M, Shorrock J E T, Honeywell) 1980 **13** (3), 30

Raw Materials, Shortages and Producer Power (Ray G F, Nat Inst of Economic & Social Research) 1975 **8** (4), 2

A Strategic Perspective for Make or Buy Decisions (Jauch L R, Wilson H K, Sthn Illinois U) 1979 **12** (6), 56

see also **BUYING**

Q

QUALITY CIRCLES

Achieving Japanese Productivity and Quality Levels at a U.S. Plant (Ishikure K) 1988 **21** (5), 10

Changing the Corporate Culture of Rank Xerox (Chapman P) 1988 **21** (2), 23

Quality Circles: From Introduction to Integration (Dale B G, U of Manchester; Lees J, Inst of Science and Technology) 1987 **20** (1), 78

Quality Circles—Are they Working in British Factories (Dale B G, UMIST) 1984 **17** (6), 50

Success Through Culture Change in a Japanese Brewery (Nakajo T, Kono T) 1989 **22** (6), 29

QUALITY MANAGEMENT

How British Industry is Making Decisions on Product Quality (Duncalf A J, Preston Poly; Dale B G, U of Manchester) 1985 **18** (5), 81

Making Quality a Fundamental Part of Strategy (Ross J E, Florida Atlantic U; Shetty Y K, Utah State U) 1985 **18** (1), 53

Quality Control—Learning From the Japanese (Trevor M, Policy Studies Inst) 1986 **19** (5), 46

The Quest for Quality at Philips, (van Ham K, Philips Intl; Williams R, Erasmus U Rotterdam) 1986 **19** (6), 25

Successful Businesses Compete on Quality—Not Costs (Luchs R, Strategic Planning Inst) 1986 **19** (1), 12

R

R & D EVALUATION

Credibility and the Assessment of R & D Projects (Allen D H, Nottingham U) 1972 **5** (2), 53

Evaluating Basic Research Strategies (Menke M M, Resource Planning; Gelzer J, CIBA-GEIGY; Pezier J P, SRI) 1981 **14** (3), 44

R & D PLANNING

Australian Industry: Sophisticated Planning and Weak R & D? (Christodoulou C) 1988 **21** (1), 82

Financial Planning and Control of Industrial Research and Development (Pessemier E A, Krannet H C, Purdue U) 1970 **3** (2), 32

Getting a Quicker Pay-off From R & D (van den Kroonenberg H H) 1989 **22** (5), 51

How Much Basic Research is Enough?—A Problem in Resource Allocation (Hill K M, Brookes L G, Hunt H, UK Atomic Energy Authority and Min of Tech) 1969 **1** (3), 38

How NASA moved from R & D to Operations (Hunsucker J L, Brah S A, Santos D L) 1989 **22** (6), 38

Innovation by Design (Locke H B, NRDC) 1976 **9** (4), 34

Investment and Planning in R & D (Locke B, NRDC) 1974 **7** (3), 12

Linear Programming Techniques in R & D Project Planning (Allen D H, Nottingham U) 1974 **7** (1), 61

New Jobs in Energy Research and Development—A Survey (Davis D L, Houston U) 1977 **10** (4), 51

The Organization of Corporate R & D Planning (Domsch M, SCS) 1978 **11** (3), 67

Planning Research and Development at Hitachi (Kuwahara Y, Okada O, Horikoshi H) 1989 **22** (3), 54

Planning of Research and Development (Pearson A, Manchester Business Sch) 1972 **5** (1), 56

Planning for Research and Development—The Impact on Society (Kahalas H, Virginia Poly Inst & State U) 1975 **8** (6), 37

Planning for Technology as a Corporate Resource (van Gunsteren L A, Erasmus U Rotterdam, Rotterdam Consulting Group) 1987 **20** (2), 51

R & D and Corporate Planning in Government (Peretz D, Inter-Bank Research Organisation) 1972 **5** (4), 67

Selecting R & D Projects for Development (Ramsey J E, James Madison U) 1981 **14** (1), 83

The Strategic Management of R & D, Part II—Organizing for Integration (Petroni G, Udine U) 1983 **16** (2), 65

Strategic Planning for Research and Development (Bemelmans T, Eindhoven U) 1979 **12** (2), 33

Strategic Planning and Research and Development—Can we Integrate Them? (Petroni G, Udine U) 1983 **16** (1), 15

Strategy for Research and Development (Twiss B C, Bradford U) 1970 **3** (1), 57

The Uncertainties of Planning Major Research and Development (Binning K G H, Min of Tech, Atomic Energy Authority) 1969 **1** (4), 48

RAIL TRANSPORT

Corporate Planning in the Canadian National Railways (Maroti E, Canadian Nat Railways) 1970 **3** (1), 21

Corporate Planning in Indian Railways—A Case Study (Subramaniam S, Indian Inst of Mgt) 1979 **12** (3), 91

The Norwegian State Railways—Profit Motivated Enterprise or a Community Service? (Norden R F, Norwegian State Railways) 1978 **11** (2), 13

Optimising Railway Strategies (Detmold P, Canadian Transport Commission) 1969 **1** (3), 74

Planning in British Railways (Long R A, British Railways Board) 1969 **2** (2), 72

Strategic Planning for Information Systems at British Rail (Mainelli M R, Miller, D R) 1988 **21** (4), 65

The Transformation of a Railroad (Johnson W B, ICI) 1976 **9** (6), 18

RATE OF RETURN

Assessing the Performance of a Development Bank (Jain P K) 1989 **22** (6), 100

Capital Budgeting—The State of the Art (Mills R W) 1988 **21** (4), 76

Does Market Share Lead to Profitability? (Bourantas D, Athens Sch of Economics and Business Science; Mandes Y, Technical U of Athens) 1987 **20** (5), 102

Linking Organization Structures and Processes to Business Strategy (Cowherd D M, Luchs R H) 1988 **21** (5), 47

Rate of Return on New Invested Capital — Its Relationship to Corporate Earnings Growth Rate and Equity Market Values (Moore C S, Ethyle Corp) 1972 **5** (4), 33

Why Different Divisions Require Different Hurdle Rates (Andrews G S, Firer C, U of the Witwatersrand) 1987 **20** (5), 62

RATIONALITY

Rationality in Policy Making: Two Concepts Not one (Regan D E, London Sch of Economics) 1978 **11** (5), 83

RATIONALIZATION

Creating a Productive Culture at Shell Chemicals (Thornley I A) 1988 **21** (3), 34

Rationalizing Branch Banking (Kitching D W C, Midland Bank) 1982 **15** (1), 53

RECESSION

Can Recessions be Predicted? (Majani B, Aussedat-Rey; Makridakis S, INSEAD) 1977 **10** (2), 31

Innovation: The Way Out of the Recessions? (Smith F M, Ciba-Geigy) 1982 **15** (1), 19

REGIONAL DEVELOPMENT

Regional Development—Alternatives for New England (Howell J M, First Nat Bank) 1976 **9** (5), 72

REGIONAL PLANNING

Milton Keynes: A Model for Regenerating our Cities? (Burrows B, Futures Information Assocs) 1987 **20** (1), 67

The Modern Approach to Sub-Regional Planning (Thorburn A, Notts and Derbys Sub-Regional Study) 1970 **2** (3), 60

Regional Planning in China—A Systems Engineering Approach (Yuji W, Quanli C, Hunan Academy of Social Studies) 1987 **20** (1), 99

Regional Planning Regulations in the United States (Holmberg S R, American U) 1978 **11** (5), 72

Urban and Regional Planning—A Systems View (Burrows B C, Literature Survey) 1980 **13** (2), 67

REGIONAL POLICY

Long Range Planning and Regional Policy 1. Britain—A European Pioneer (Despicht N, Sussex U) 1970 **2** (4), 28

Long Range Planning and Regional Policy 2. France and Italy—Latecomers to the Industrial Urban Scene (Despicht N, Sussex U) 1970 **3** (1), 75

Promoting Small Business in Northern Ireland (Birley S, Cranfield Sch of Mgt; Bridge S, Local Enterprise Development Unit, Belfast) 1987 **20** (6), 71

REGULATION

Airline Deregulation: Why the Supporters Lost Out (Marcus A A, U of Minnesota Sch of Mgt) 1987 **20** (1), 90

RELOCATION

Credibility and the Assessment of R & D Projects (Allen D H, Nottingham U) 1972 **5** (2), 53

Relocation or Dislocation?—A Planned Approach to Location (Lederer T F, Inbucon Mgt Consultants) 1980 **13** (6), 10

RESOURCE ALLOCATION

How Much Basic Research is Enough?—A Problem in Resource Allocation (Hill K M, Brookes L G and Hunt H, UK Atomic Energy Authority and Min of Tech) 1969 **1** (3), 38

RESOURCE MANAGEMENT

Avoiding Dependence on Suppliers and Distributors (Bourantas D) 1989 **22** (3), 140

Framework for Making Resource Use Decisions: An Application to Subdivisions Development (Miller W W, Ching C T K, Benesch G N) 1978 **11** (1), 72

A Modelling System for Local Government Resource Planning (Howard K, Wagle B V, Bradford U) 1978 **11** (4), 77

Resource Management Schemes (Benfitto M T, Hager R B, Lapointe F A, US Army Electronics Command) 1975 **8** (3), 46

Resource Planning for Technology-Oriented Companies (Gansler J S, Consultant) 1973 **6** (4), 17

RETAILING
Competitive Strategies in Retailing (Walters D, Knee D) 1989 **22** (6), 74
Food Retailing in the Eighties—Technological Opportunities and Social Constraints (MacLaurin I, Tesco Stores) 1982 **15** (1), 40
The Impact of Retailers on Financial Services (Bliss M) 1988 **21** (1), 55
The Influence of Retailing Trends on the Food Industry (Tanburn J, Booler McConnell) 1975 **8** (3), 10
Planning and Performance in Australian Retailing (Burt D N, Naval Postgraduate Sch) 1978 **11** (3), 62
Strategic Planning Catches on in U.S. Retailers (Rosenbloom B, Tripuraneni R V, Drexel U) 1985 **18** (4), 55
Woolworth's Drive for Excellence (Rose D) 1989 **22** (1), 28

RISK
The Control of Bank Exposure to Risk (Moore V, Consultant) 1979 **12** (5), 35

RISK ANALYSIS
Assessing Country Risk for Foreign Investment Decisions (Leavy B, Nat Inst for Higher Education Dublin) 1984 **17** (3), 141
Assessing the Risks in Acquisitions—The Risk-Chance Analysis (Neuburger K) 1986 **19** (3), 41
Country-Portfolio Analysis—Assessing Country Risk and Opportunity (Perlitz M, U of Bonn) 1985 **18** (4), 11
Essay Review Article: Risk, Uncertainty and Risk Analysis (Brauers Prof Dr W K, U of Antwerp) 1986 **19** (6), 139
The Evaluation of Country Risk and Economic Potential (Kern D, Nat Westminster Bank) 1985 **18** (3), 17
A Formal Model for Long Range Planning: 2. The Assessment of Opportunity and Risk (Hetrick J C, Arthur D Little) 1969 **1** (4), 54
The Identification and Assessment of Political Risk in the International Environment (Lloyd B, Commonwealth Devel) 1974 **7** (6), 24
Pitfalls in Using Portfolio Techniques—Assessing Risk and Potential (Derkinderen F G J, Netherlands Sch of Business; Crum R L, Florida U) 1984 **17** (2), 129
A Practical Approach to Risk and Sensitivity Analyses (Singhvi S S, Armco) 1980 **13** (1), 12
Risk Analysis and the Formulation of Acquisition Diversification Strategies (Thomas H, Illinois U) 1983 **16** (2), 28
Risk Analysis and Investment Appraisal in Marketing (Cameron D A, Beecham Research Laboratories) 1972 **5** (4), 43
Risk Analysis in Plant Design (Cameron D A, Beecham Research Laboratories) 1973 **6** (3), 30
Risk-Decision Analysis in Weapons System Acquisitions (Cuff J D, Consultant) 1973 **6** (1), 49
Strategic Thinking Supported by Risk Analysis (Wagner G R, Execucom) 1980 **13** (3), 61
Why Risk Analysis Isn't Working (Hall W K, Michigan U) 1975 **8** (6), 25

RISK MANAGEMENT
Foreign Exchange Risk Management (Donaldson J A, ICI) 1979 **12** (3), 22
Planning for Emergencies-Lessons From the Chemical Industry (Kharbanda O P, Stallworthy E A) 1989 **22** (1), 83
Risk Management in Corporate Planning (Haner F T, Business Environment Risk) 1981 **14** (6), 12

RISK MEASUREMENT
Evaluating the Risks in Acquisition (Hertz D B, Thomas H, Illinois U) 1982 **15** (6), 38

ROAD CONSTRUCTION
Assessing Trunk Roads—The Conservationist Viewpoint (Taitz L, Harman R, Conservation Society) 1979 **12** (1), 56

ROAD TRANSPORT
Planning Problems of State Road Transport—India (Subramaniam S, Indian Inst of Mgt) 1976 **9** (1), 77
Realistic Planning for Transportation — A Flexible Approach (Khan A M) 1989 **22** (5), 128
Road Transport and the Environment (Cottee B, Nat Freight Corporation) 1978 **11** (2), 39
Trucks and Road Transport Towards 1992 (Garuzo G) 1988 **21** (4), 45

RURAL AREAS
The Breakdown in Rural Communities—Can We Stop it? (Richetto J P, Alabama U) 1983 **16** (1), 97

India: Can We Eliminate Poverty? (Bhargava P K, Banara Hindu U) 1987 **20** (2), 21

S

SAFETY
Health and Safty Regulations—A Key Issue for the Board (Simeons C, Consultant) 1986 **19** (3), 86
Planning for Emergencies—Lessons From the Chemical Industry (Kharbanda O P, Stallworthy E A) 1989 **22** (1), 83
Safety in Commercial Aviation—The Long-Term Trends (Shaw R R, IATA) 1976 **9** (6), 24

SALES FORECASTING
An Appreciation of Alternative Sales Forecasting Models: Recent Techniques Based on Historical Data (Briscoe G, Hirst M, Warwick U) 1973 **6** (3), 79
Sales Forecasting—Using a Combination of Approaches (Doyle P, Fenwick I) 1976 **9** (3), 60

SAUDI ARABIA
Corporate Strategy and Public Policy in Saudi Arabia (Luqmani M, Yavas U, Quraeshi Z A) 1989 **22** (4), 79

SCENARIOS
Building Scenarios for an Electric Utility (Goldfarb D L, Huss W R) 1988 **21** (2), 78
Creative Strategic Planning Using Imagery (Maddox N, Stetson U; Anthony W P, Florida State U; Wheatley Jr W, U of West Florida) 1987 **20** (5), 118
Developing Inflation Scenarios (Lanzenauer C H von, Western Ontario U; Sprung M R, Confederation Life Insurance) 1982 **15** (4), 37
Energy Scenarios—The Sizewell Experience (Hankinson G A, Kingston Poly) 1986 **19** (5), 94
The European Automobile Industry—Three Possible Scenarios (Hohn S, Volkswagenwerk) 1980 **13** (4), 12
Evaluating Alternative Strategies Using Scenarios (Whipple III W) 1989 **22** (3), 82
Generating Future Scenarios—Their Use in Strategic Planning (Nair K, Sarin R L, Purdue U) 1979 **12** (3), 57
How the Rip Van Winkle Approach Helps Oil Executives Plan (Finizza A J, Atlantic Richfield) 1985 **18** (1), 59
How Scenarios Trigger Strategic Thinking (Millett S M) 1988 **21** (5), 61
How to Develop and Use Scenarios (Schnaars S P, City U of New York) 1987 **20** (1), 105
Industrial Applications of Cross-Impact Analysis (Fontela E, Geneva U) 1976 **9** (4), 29
Multinational Business in the 1990s—A Scenario (Schwartz P, Saville J, Shell Intl) 1986 **19** (6), 31
Scenario Planning for Australia (Galer G, Shell; Kasper W, New South Wales U) 1982 **15** (4), 50
Scenario Planning—What Style Should You Use? (Huss W R, Xenergy; Honton E J, Battelle Columbus) 1987 **20** (4), 21
Scenarios in Europe—Who Uses Them and Why? (Malaska P, Meristo T, Turku Sch of Economics; Malmivirta M, Neste Oy; Hansen S-O, Farmos Group) 1984 **17** (5), 45
Scenarios for the Indian Iron and Steel Industry (Rao T R, Mineral Devel Board) 1984 **17** (4), 91
Scenarios, Past, Present and Future (Zentner R D, Shell Oil) 1982 **15** (3), 12
Three Energy Scenarios for the United Kingdom (Chapman P F, Open U) 1976 **9** (2), 2
The Use of Multiple Scenarios by U.S. Industrial Companies: A Comparison Study, 1977—1981 (Linneman R E, Klein H E, Temple U) 1983 **16** (6), 94
The Use of Multiple Scenarios by U.S. Industrial Companies (Linneman R E, Klein H E, Philadelphia U) 1979 **12** (1), 83
The Use of Scenarios in Corporate Planning—Eight Case Histories (Klein H E, Linneman R E, Temple U) 1980 **13** (1), 12
Using Scenarios to Develop Strategies (Leemhuis J P, Shell Nederland) 1985 **18** (2), 30

SENSITIVITY ANALYSIS
Capital Budgeting—The State of the Art (Mills R W) 1988 **21** (4), 76

A Practical Approach to Risk and Sensitivity Analyses (Singhvi S S, Armco) 1980 **13** (1), 12

SERVICE INDUSTRIES
Building a Customer-orientated Organization (Cornish F) 1988 **21** (3), 105
Competitive Strategies for Service Businesses (Wilson I) 1988 **21** (6), 10
Creating a Successful Marketing Strategy for UNI Insurance (Overland T) 1989 **22** (4), 25
Designing a Long Range Marketing Strategy for Services (Gronroos C, Swedish Sch of Economics and Business Administration) 1980 **13** (2), 36
The Impact of Retailers on Financial Services (Bliss M) 1988 **21** (1), 55
Japan's New Industrial Era—II. The New Information and Services Industries (Yamamoto S, Ind Bank of Japan Ltd) 1986 **19** (2), 65
Marketing Planning in a Service Economy (Chisnall P M, Manchester Business Sch) 1975 **8** (6), 43
New Opportunities in Global Services (Trondsen E, SRI Intl; Edfelt R, San Jose State U) 1987 **20** (5), 53
Raising Productivity in Customer Services (Potts G W) 1988 **21** (2), 15
Re-designing Bank Service Systems for Effective Marketing (Gupta Y P, Torkzadeh G) 1988 **21** (6), 38
Re-positioning a Leading Stockbroker (Dorwin K) 1988 **21** (6), 13
The Service Sector Revolution: The Automation of Services (Collier D A, Virginia U) 1983 **16** (6), 10
Setting Goals in a Professional Service Firm (Keeney R L, Intl Inst for Applied Systems Analysis; Nair K, Wood-Clyde Consultants) 1976 **9** (3), 54
Strategic Management of Consumer Services (Allen M) 1988 **21** (6), 20

SHARE OWNERSHIP
Dilution of Ownership in Multinational Concerns (Sachdev J C, UMIST) 1977 **10** (5), 33
The Future Pattern of U.K. Share Ownership (Dobbins R, Greenwood M, Bradford U) 1975 **8** (4), 81

SHARE PRICES
Creating Value to Keep the Raiders at Bay (Reimann B C) 1989 **22** (3), 18
Strategic Credibility — The Basis of a Strong Share Price (Higgins R B, Diffenbach J) 1989 **22** (6), 10
Strategic Planning Could Improve Your Share Price (Welch J B, Northeastern U) 1984 **17** (2), 144

SHAREHOLDERS
The Fisons Shareholder Survey (Redwood H, Fisons) 1971 **3** (3), 2
The Incentive Effects of Ownership and Control in Management Buy-outs (Green S) 1988 **21** (1), 26
Strategic Credibility — The Basis of a Strong Share Price (Higgins R B, Diffenbach J) 1989 **22** (6), 10

SHIPBUILDING INDUSTRY
Forecasting the Market for Ships (Nielsen K S, Kristensen N E, Bastiansen E, Skytte P, B & W Diesels) 1982 **15** (4), 70

SHIPPING INDUSTRY
Developing a Data Base for Planning—A Shipping Industry Case (Tomlinson D S, Panocean-Anco) 1980 **13** (6), 42
Long-Term Planning for Indian Shipping (Kumar S P, Indian Inst of Mgt) 1976 **9** (6), 63

SHOPPING CENTRES
Market Research for 'Out of Town' Shopping Centres (Hillier T J, Bradford U) 1972 **5** (3), 53

SIMULATION
Canadian Industrial Policy—Simulation and Analysis (Thompson W, Vertinsky I, Kane J, British Columbia U) 1973 **6** (4), 66
The Use of Simulations for Market Forecasting—A Case Study in the Mining Industry (Lloyd-Jacob D, Consolidated Gold Fields) 1969 **2** (1), 76

SIMULATION MODELS
An Approach to Simulation Model Development for Improved Planning (McKenney J L, Harvard U) 1970 **2** (3), 56
Computer Based Corporate Modelling—Book Review Article (Nutt W O, Estercrete) 1984 **17** (1), 114
A Computer-Based Modelling System for Electric Utility Planning (Ben-Yaacov G Z, Electricity Supply Commission) 1978 **11** (6), 30

The Design of Computer-Based Planning and Modelling Systems (Naylor T H, Duke U; Mansfield M J, Social Systems) 1977 **10** (1), 16
Designing Computer Models that Work (Collins M R, MacGregor J M, EPS Consultants) 1980 **13** (6), 60
Experience with Corporate Simulation Models—A Survey (Naylor T H, Duke U) 1976 **9** (2), 94
Managerial Attitudes Towards Computer Models for Planning and Control (Higgins J C, Finn R, Bradford U) 1976 **9** (6), 107
Microcomputers—The Breakthrough in Computer modelling (Harrison F L, Glasgow U) 1983 **16** (5), 94
Production Strategy Decisions—A Simulation Model Approach (Bell J A, Mullard) 1970 **2** (4), 62
A Simulation System for Corporate Planning (Craig G D, Waikato U) 1980 **13** (5), 43
Using Computer Models in Corporate Planning (Kumar R, Vrat P) 1989 **22** (2), 114
What Users Think About Computer Models (MacGregor J M, EPS Consultants) 1983 **16** (5), 45
World Energy Resources and the Limitations of Computer Modelling (Chesshire J H, Surrey A J, Sussex U) 1975 **8** (3), 54
see also **MODELS**

SINGAPORE
Corporate Planning Takes off in Singapore (Hou Wee C, Farley J U, Lee S K) 1989 **22** (2), 78
How Singapore Makes Central Planning Work (Macdonald I, Nat U of Singapore) 1986 **19** (1), 38
The Second Decade—The Economic Outlook for a Developing Nation (Shelley R, Hume Industries) 1976 **9** (4), 66
Strategies for Tourism in Singapore (Cheong W K, Khem G S) 1988 **21** (4), 36

SINGLE EUROPEAN MARKET
1992: The Implications for Management (Mitchell D) 1989 **22** (1), 32
Strategies for a Pan European Market (Vandermerwe S) 1989 **22** (3), 45
Towards 1992: A Strategy for Training (Day D) 1989 **22** (6), 48

SMALL BUSINESS
Business Strategies in Small High-technology Companies (Smith J G, Fleck V, Cambridge U) 1987 **20** (2), 61
Corporate Planning in Small Companies—A Survey (Shuman J G, Babson Coll) 1975 **8** (5), 81
Developing Competitive Advantage in Small and Medium-size Firms (Bamberger I) 1989 **22** (5), 80
Developing a Corporate Planning Model for a Small Company (Kluyver C A de, Purdue U; McNally G M, Canterbury U) 1982 **15** (1), 97
Dynamic Planning for the Smaller Company—A Case History (House W C, Arkansas U) 1979 **12** (3), 38
Encouraging Entrepreneurs in Developing Countries (El-Namaki M S S) 1988 **21** (4), 98
Federated Marketing—A Practical Approach to Export for the Smaller Company or Division (Claxton C, Europa Industrial Projects) 1979 **12** (6), 43
Financing the Smaller Company (Dimson E, London Business Sch) 1978 **11** (6), 9
Five Stages of Growth in Small Business (Scott M, U of Cape Town; Bruce R, Graduate Sch of Business) 1987 **20** (3), 45
How Elf Aquitaine Provides Technological Assistance to Small Businesses (Turbil J-P, Elf Aquitaine) 1986 **19** (3), 59
How Large and Small Firms Can Grow Together (Wilson P, Gorb P, London Business Sch) 1983 **16** (2), 19
Long Range Planning for the Small Firm (Forbes A M, Natal U) 1974 **7** (2), 43
'Minimum Level of Activity'—A Quick Method of Assessing Growth Potential in the Smaller Business (Marmuse C, I.A.E. Lille) 1983 **16** (1), 84
Planning in the Smaller Company (Foster D, Planning for Growth) 1971 **4** (1), 71
Portfolio Analysis for the Small Firm (Bamberger I, Rennes U) 1982 **15** (6), 49
Promoting Small Business in Northern Ireland (Birley S, Cranfield Sch of Mgt; Bridge S, Local Enterprise Development Unit, Belfast) 1987 **20** (6), 71
The Role of Strategic Planning in Small Businesses (Unni V K, Illinois State U) 1981 **14** (2), 54

Shirt-Sleeved Approach to Long Range Planning for the Smaller Growing Corporation—Book Review Article (Teager R H, Consultant) 1980 **13** (6), 83

Small Businesses Do Plan and It Pays Off (Ackelsberg R, Shippensburg U; Arlow P, Youngstown State U) 1985 **18** (5), 61

Strategic Management: New Ventures and Small Business (Cooper A C, Krannert Graduate Sch of India) 1981 **14** (5), 39

Strategic Planning in Small and Medium-sized Companies (Hoorn Th. P van, Consultant) 1979 **12** (2), 84

Strategic Planning in Smaller Rapid Growth Companies (Shuman J C, Shaw J J, Sussman G, Bentley Coll and Providence Coll) 1985 **18** (6), 48

Strategy and Flexibility in the Smaller Business (MacMillan I C, South Africa U) 1975 **8** (3), 62

Strategy Formulation for the Smaller Firm—A Practical Approach (Nagal A, Eindhoven U) 1981 **14** (4), 115

SOCIAL CHANGE

Changing Values and Lifestyles (Mitchell A, MacNulty C, SRI Intl) 1981 **14** (2), 37

Community Without Consensus?—Book Review Article (Vickers G, FUTURES) 1981 **14** (2), 90

Forecasting the Impact of Social Change (Morris G K, Matrix Consultants) 1975 **8** (3), 64

Marital Breakdown and the Future of Marriage (Dominian J, Marriage Research Centre) 1984 **17** (2), 77

Planning and Social Change (Walding P, LLewelyn-Davies Weeks Forestier-Walker & Bor) 1974 **7** (5), 51

Social Innovation—Management's New Dimension (Drucker P F) 1987 **20** (6), 29

Social Trends: Urgent Issues for Management (Shanks M, Nat Consumer Council) 1982 **15** (1), 12

Strategic Planning for Social and Political Change (Taylor B, Administrative Staff Coll) 1974 **7** (1), 33

Will 1990 Mark the End of the Will to Work—Or the Right to Manage? (Carter A, Foy N, STC) 1981 **14** (2), 42

SOCIAL ECONOMICS

The Social and Psychological Causes of Inflation (Daniel W W, PEP) 1977 **10** (3), 37

SOCIAL ENVIRONMENT

Alcohol: Is it Time to Say 'When'? (Steele D W, Action on Alcohol Abuse) 1987 **20** (5), 86

The Crisis in the Jails (Shaw S, Prison Reform Trust) 1986 **19** (3), 27

Key Social Issues for European Business (Taylor B, Henley Mgt Coll; Ferro L, Turin Centre for Mgt Devel) 1983 **16** (1), 42

Management and The Social Environment (Sadler P, Ashridge Mgt Coll) 1975 **8** (4), 18

Social Impact: The Pharmaceutical Industry (James B G, Consultant) 1978 **11** (1), 2

SOCIAL FORECASTING

Is There a Future for Social Forecasting? (Holroyd P, Bradford U) 1980 **13** (5), 29

Social Forecasting: An Integral Part of Corporate Planning? (Higgins J C, Romano D, Bradford U) 1980 **13** (2), 82

Social Forecasting for Company Planning—Book Review Article (MacNulty C A R, Consultant) 1983 **16** (2), 118

Social Forecasting in U.S. Corporations—A Survey (Newgren K E, Florida State U; Carroll A B, Georgia U) 1979 **12** (4), 59

Social Futures: Individualism or Social Harmony (de Vulpian A, Corry C, Taylor Nelson Group) 1986 **19** (5), 33

Sociological and Cultural Forecasting (Hargreaves B J A, Matrix Consulting) 1978 **11** (3), 49

SOCIAL MARKETING

Implementing Public Plans: The Case for Social Marketing (Mushkat M, Hong Kong U) 1980 **13** (4), 24

SOCIAL RESPONSIBILITY

Business and Government—A New Partnership? (Halal W E, George Washington U) 1987 **20** (1), 123

Corporate Planning for Social Responsibility (Challen P, South London Industrial Mission) 1974 **7** (3), 38

Defining Social Responsibility (Feldberg M, Cape Town U) 1974 **7** (4), 39

Ethics and Social Responsibility in Local Government (Amos F J C, Birmingham U) 1982 **15** (2), 121

Keeping People Alive—The Implications for Planning (Hillman H, Surrey U) 1969 **2** (1), 40

Planning for Corporate Social Programs—Problems and Guidelines (Gray E R, Lousiana State U) 1981 **14** (2), 49

The Role of Business in Society (Kempner T, Hawkins K, MacMillan K, Bradford U) 1970 **2** (4), 2

Setting Operational Goals for Corporate Social Responsibility (Carroll A B, Georgia U) 1978 **11** (2), 35

SOCIAL RESPONSIBILITY OF BUSINESS *see* **BUSINESS RESPONSIBILITY**

SOCIAL SERVICES

Goal Setting and Efficiency in Social Service Agencies (Keating B P, Notre Dame U; Keating M O, St. Mary's Coll) 1981 **14** (1), 40

SOCIAL STRUCTURE

Middle Class Decline in Post-industrial Society (Simmie J, Brady R) 1989 **22** (4), 52

Social System Needs Assessment (Morasky R L, Amick D, Montana U) 1978 **11** (2), 47

SOCIETY

Middle Class Decline in Post-industrial Society (Simmie J, Brady R) 1989 **22** (4), 52

Planning for Research and Development—The Impact on Society (Kahalas H, Virginia Poly Inst & State U) 1975 **8** (6), 37

The Programmable Society and the Individual as a Unit of Data (Butler D, Cox G, Diebold Group) 1974 **7** (5), 43

The Thatcher Revolution — Radical Policies in a Changing Society (Worcester R M) 1989 **22** (4), 72

'Titanic Planning' in an Uncertain Environment (Trowbridge A V) 1988 **21** (2), 86

SOLAR ENERGY

Solar Energy: Where Policy-makers and Conservationists Disagree (Shama A, Jacobs K, Solar Energy Research Inst) 1982 **15** (1), 63

SOUTH AFRICA

Corporate Planning in South African Companies (Woodburn T L, Grey Mann Associates) 1984 **17** (1), 84

Planning for Heavy Industry in South Africa (Kieser P J, African Explosives & Chemical Industries) 1972 **5** (1), 78

'Titanic Planning' in an Uncertain Environment (Trowbridge A V) 1988 **21** (2), 86

STAFFING

Reducing Personnel Turnover and Improving Morale (Kohl J P, Stephens D B) 1989 **22** (4), 125

Staffing Long Range Planning Groups (Litschert R J, Nicholson E A, Virginia Poly Inst and State U) 1972 **5** (1), 37

STATE OWNED ENTERPRISES

Business Planning in Tanzanian State Enterprises (El-Namaki M S S) 1977 **10** (5), 52

Corporate Planning as a Control System in United Kingdom Nationalized Industries (Harris D J, Davies B C L, Bath U) 1981 **14** (1), 15

Corporate Planning in Hungarian Companies (Csath M) 1989 **22** (4), 89

Corporate Strategy and Public Policy in Saudi Arabia (Luqmani M, Yavas U, Quraeshi Z A) 1989 **22** (4), 79

Improving the Prospects for Plan Acceptance in Public Organizations (Mushkat M, U of Hong Kong) 1987 **20** (1), 52

Keeping it Simple: A Case Study in Corporate Planning (Sedgwick A, NCB) 1978 **11** (1), 10

Key Strategic Issues for Public Corporations (Subramaniam S, Balasubramaniam R, Admin Staff Coll of India) 1974 **7** (5), 39

Lessons of Privatization (Lord King) 1987 **20** (6), 18

Planning in British Railways (Long R A, British Railways Board) 1969 **2** (2), 72

Planning for Esso Greece — The Impact of Nationalization (Labroukos N S, Lioukas S) 1989 **22** (4), 98

Planning in a Nationalised Industry (Kingshott A L, BSC) 1975 **8** (5), 58

Planning for Strategic Performance in Local Government (McGill R) 1988 **21** (5), 77

Strategic Management of Public and Non-market Corporations (Ruffat J, Strategies & Structures) 1983 **16** (2), 74

Strategy—The Key to Planning in the Public Corporation (Smith J G, City U) 1981 **14** (6), 24

Why Planning in State Enterprises Doesn't Work (Javidan M, Dastmalchian A) 1988 **21** (3), 98

STEEL INDUSTRY

Developing a Practical Planning System for a Steel Business (Rozman R, Slovenske Zelezarne) 1986 **19** (2), 90

India—The Plan for Steel (Rao R, Iron Ore Board) 1978 **11** (4), 22

Planning in a German Steel Company (Friedrich A, Hoesch A G) 1972 **5** (4), 78

Scenarios for the Indian Iron and Steel Company (Rao T R, Mineral Devel Board) 1984 **17** (4), 91

The Future of the Stock Exchange (Hollis J D, Stock Exchange) 1975 **8** (6), 65

STRATEGIC ALLIANCES

Can Hyundai Go It Alone? (Hyun Y, Lee J) 1989 **22** (2), 63

Managing Technology Alliances (Nueno P, Oosterveld J) 1988 **21** (3), 11

Strategic Alliances with Japanese Firms (Kobayashi N) 1988 **21** (2), 29

Strategic Alliances—Guidelines for Success (Devlin G, Bleackley M) 1988 **21** (5), 18

Strategies for Global Competition (Lei D) 1989 **22** (1), 102

STRATEGIC MANAGEMENT

Competing Against Low Cost Cutlery Imports (Grant R M) 1989 **22** (5), 59

Competitive Strategies in Retailing (Walters D, Knee D) 1989 **22** (6), 74

Corporate Culture and Strategy—The Problem of Strategic Fit (Scholz C, Saarland U) 1987 **20** (4), 78

Decision Support System: A New Tool for Strategic Management (Yoo S, Bowling Green State U Ohio; Digman L A, U of Nebraska) 1987 **20** (2), 114

Developing a Company's Strategic Management Capacity (Houlden B T, U of Warwick) 1986 **19** (5), 89

Developing Strategic Thinking (Mason J, Consultant) 1986 **19** (3), 72

A Framework for the Strategic Management of Future Tyre Technology (Lauglaug A S, Goodyear Tyre and Rubber Company) 1987 **20** (5), 21

Helping Managers to Develop Strategies (Skipton M D, Kingston Poly) 1985 **18** (2), 56

How Successful Companies Manage Diverse Businesses (Calori R, CESMA) 1988 **21** (3), 80

The Impact of Key Success Factors on Company Performance (Vasconcellos e Sá J) 1988 **21** (6), 56

Managing the Diversified Corporation: The Tensions Facing the Chief Executive (Goold M, Campbell A) 1988 **21** (4), 12

Managing Diversity: Strategy and Control in Diversified British Companies (Goold M, Campbell A, London Business Sch) 1987 **20** (5), 42

Managing Strategic Change: An Integrated Approach (Carnall C A, The Mgt Coll Henley-on-Thames) 1986 **19** (6), 105

Managing Strategic Change in a Mature Business (Whipp R, Rosenfield R, Pettigrew A) 1989 **22** (6), 92

Managing Technology Alliances (Nueno P, Oosterveld J) 1988 **21** (3), 11

Organizing for Strategic Management (Nagel A, Eindhoven U) 1984 **17** (4), 71

Organizing for Strategic Management—A Case Study (Gummesson E, PA Intl Mgt Consultants) 1974 **7** (2), 13

Privatization — A Cure for all Ills? (Hammer R M, Hinterhuber H H, Lorentz J) 1989 **22** (6), 19

Regaining Your Competitive Edge (Naylor M E, General Motors) 1985 **18** (1), 30

The Stategic Management of Technology: Corporate Fad or Strategic Necessity (Wilson I, American Editor) 1986 **19** (2), 21

Strategic Control of Factory Automation (Meredith J R) 1987 **20** (6), 106

Strategic Management: Lessons from Success and Failure (Hussey D E, Harbridge House Europe) 1984 **17** (1), 43

Strategic Management: A New Managerial Concept for an Era of Rapid Change (Frankenhoff W P, Granger C H, Wm E Hill) 1971 **3** (3), 7

Strategic Management: New Ventures and Small; Business (Cooper A C, Krannert Graduate Sch U) 1981 **14** (5), 39

Strategic Management of Consumer Services (Allen M) 1988 **21** (6), 20

Strategic Management in a Firm of Consulting Engineers (TenDam H, Consultant; Siffert C, Promon Engenharia) 1984 **17** (4), 21

Strategic Management in a Government Agency (TenDam H, Mgt Consultant) 1986 **19** (4), 78

Strategic Management in Major Japanese Hightech Companies (Nakamura G-I, Asia U Tokyo) 1986 **19** (6), 82

Strategic Management Step by Step (Green G J L, Jones E G, Consultants) 1982 **15** (3), 61

Strategic Planning for Power Equipment Manufacture (Shah R K D) 1989 **22** (5), 98

Strategies for Declining Businesses—Survival in the Fur Business (Siomkos G, Shrivastava P) 1987 **20** (6), 84

Strategies for Mature Business (Schofield M, Arnold D) 1988 **21** (5), 69

Strategy in Action—Techniques for Implementing Strategy (Reed R, Buckley M R) 1988 **21** (3), 67

Strategy Alternatives for Vehicle Component Manufacturers (Carr C) 1988 **21** (4), 86

Strategy as a System of Expedients (Hinterhuber H, Popp W) 1988 **21** (4), 107

Successfully Implementing Strategic Decisions (Alexander L D, Virginia Tech) 1985 **18** (3), 91

Technology Planning at General Motors (Koerner E) 1989 **22** (2), 9

'Titanic Planning' in an Uncertain Environment (Trowbridge A V) 1988 **21** (2), 86

Towards Better Strategic Management (Irwin P H, Urwick, Currie & Partners) 1974 **7** (6), 64

Using Critical Success Factors in Planning (Jenster Per V, McIntire Sch of Commerce, Virginia) 1987 **20** (4), 102

Using Finance for Competitive Advantage (Clarke C J) 1988 **21** (2), 63

Why Planning in State Enterprises Doesn't Work (Javidan M, Dastmalchian A) 1988 **21** (3), 98

Woolworth's Drive for Excellence (Rose D) 1989 **22** (1), 28

see also **STRATEGIC PLANNING**

STRATEGIC MAPPING

Mapping Competitive Groups in the Clothing Industry (McNamee P, McHugh M) 1989 **22** (5), 89

Strategic Mapping—a Tool for Corporate Planners (Vesper V D, Consultant) 1979 **12** (6), 75

STRATEGIC PLANNING

1992: The Implications for Management (Mitchell D) 1989 **22** (1), 32

Acquisitions—Techniques for Measuring Strategic Fit (Clarke C J, Smith Trust) 1987 **20** (3), 12

Alliance: The New Strategic Focus (James B G, Ciba-Geigy) 1985 **18** (3), 76

Alternatives to Merger—Joint Ventures and Other Strategies (Harrison J S) 1987 **20** (6), 78

Artificial Intelligence: A Way Through the Strategic Planning Crisis? (Orsini J-F, Consultant) 1986 **19** (4), 71

Assessing Your Competitor's People and Organization (Ball R, Cresap, McCormick & Paget) 1987 **20** (2), 32

Australian Industry: Sophisticated Planning and Weak R & D? (Christodoulou C) 1988 **21** (1), 82

Bank Management and Strategic Planning for the 1980s (Mason J B, Mayer M L, Alabama U) 1979 **12** (4), 35

Betting The Bank on Technology Strategic Planning at Bank of America (Raphael D E, Bank of America) 1986 **19** (2), 23

BHP Reorganizes for Global Competition (Lewis G, Clark J, Moss B) 1988 **21** (3), 18

Building a Strategic Data Base (Szewczak E J) 1988 **21** (2), 97

Business Strategies in Small High-technology Companies (Smith J G, Fleck V, Cambridge U) 1987 **20** (2), 61

Business Synergy Does Not Always Pay Off (Mahajan V, Wind Y) 1988 **21** (1), 59

Can Technology be Managed Strategically? (Sethi N K, St. John's U Jamaica, New York; Movsesian B, City U of New York; Hickey K D, NCR Corp) 1985 **18** (4), 89

Changing the Corporate Culture of Rank Xerox (Chapman P) 1988 **21** (2), 23

Comparison of Strategic Planning in Large Corporations and Government (East R J, H.M. Treasury) 1972 **5** (2), 2

Competing with AT & T (Reichert Smith K, GTE Sprint) 1985 **18** (1), 47

Competitive Analysis Using Matrix Displays (McNamee P, Ulster U) 1984 **17** (3), 98

Competitive Strategies for Service Businesses (Wilson I) 1988 **21** (6), 10

Competitive Strategies in U.S. Banking (Sontheimer C K, Thorn R S, U of Pittsburgh) 1986 **19** (1), 113

The Components of Strategic Planning (Kudla R J, Arizona State U) 1978 **11** (6), 48

Computer Assisted Strategic Planning (Holloway C, Pearce J A, South Carolina U) 1982 **15** (4), 56

Corporate Development—Preferred Strategies in U.K. Companies (Littler D A, U of Manchester; Sweeting R C, UMIST) 1987 **20** (2), 125

Corporate Strategic Planning in Practice (Malmlow E G, B & S Corporate Devel AG) 1972 **5** (3), 2

Corporate Strategic Planning in a University (Thomas R, Bath U) 1980 **13** (5), 70

Corporate Strategy and Entrepreneurial Vision (Shirley S) 1989 **22** (6), 107

Corporate Strategy and Public Policy in Saudi Arabia (Luqmani M, Yavas U, Quraeshi Z A) 1989 **22** (4), 79

Creating a Manufacturing Strategy to Suit Your Business (Pendlebury A J) 1987 **20** (6), 35

Creative Strategic Planning Using Imagery (Maddox N, Stetson U; Anthony W P, Florida State U; Wheatley Jr W, U of West Florida) 1987 **20** (5), 118

The Dangers of Centralized Economic Planning (Duncombe H L, General Motors Corp) 1976 **9** (3), 16

The Decision-Making Process for Strategic Adaptation (Ronchi L, Rome U) 1980 **13** (1), 48

Designing a Business Scanning System (Calori R) 1989 **22** (1), 69

Designing Communication Support Systems for Strategic Planning (Charalambides L C) 1988 **21** (6), 93

Designing Information Systems for Strategic Decisions (Hayes R L, Radosevich R, Vanderbilt U) 1974 **7** (4), 45

Developing an Information Systems Strategy (Hayward R G, Massey U Palmerston North New Zealand) 1987 **20** (2), 100

Developing Knowledge-based Systems for Strategic Corporate Planning (Mockler R J, Dologite D G) 1988 **21** (1), 97

Developing A Planning Culture for More Effective Strategic Planning (Cleland D I, King W R, Pittsburgh U) 1974 **7** (3), 70

Developing Systems for Strategic Planning (Ruggles R L, IBM) 1971 **3** (4), 39

The Directional Policy Matrix—Tool for Strategic Planning (Robinson S J Q, Hichens R E, Wade D P, Shell Chemicals; Shell Intl) 1978 **11** (3), 8

Does Strategic Planning Improve Company Performance (Greenley G E, U of Birmingham) 1986 **19** (2), 101

An Early Warning System for Strategic Planning (Reinhardt W A, Volvo) 1984 **17** (4), 25

Effective Strategies in Emerging Industries (Calori R, Group ESC Lyon) 1985 **18** (3), 55

Environmental Scanning and Forecasting in Strategic Planning—The State of the Art (Fahey L, King W R, Narayanan V K, Pittsburgh U) 1981 **14** (1), 32

Evaluating Alternative Approaches to Strategic Planning (Holloway C, Pittsburgh U; King W R, U of Sth Carolina) 1979 **12** (4), 74

Exit Barriers and Strategic Position in Declining Markets (Rafferty J) 1987 **20** (2), 86

The Federal Government as a Source of Strategic Planning Information (Noya L E De, US Govt Printing Office) 1980 **13** (5), 100

Financial Issues in Strategic Planning (Zettergren L, Consultant) 1975 **8** (3), 23

Financial Planning Using Goal Programming (Batson R G) 1989 **22** (5), 112

Force Field Analysis: A New Way to Evaluate your Strategy (Thomas J, Middle Tennessee State U) 1985 **18** (6), 54

Force Field Analysis—A Framework for Strategic Thinking (Ajimal K S, Consultant) 1985 **18** (5), 55

Formal Strategic Planning in the United States Today (Steiner G A, Kunin H & E, UCLA) 1983 **16** (3), 2

A Framework for Strategic Analysis (Ziemer D R, Mavcock P D, Texas Instruments) 1973 **6** (2), 6

A Framework for the Strategic Management of Future Tyre Technology (Lauglaug A S, Goodyear Tyre and Rubber Company) 1987 **20** (5), 21

A Framework for Strategic Planning in Multinational Corporations (Lorange P, Sloan Sch, MIT) 1976 **9** (3), 30

A Fundamental Approach to Strategy Development (Hedley B, Boston Consulting) 1976 **9** (6), 2

Future Forecasting for Strategic Planning at General Electric (Wilson I H, Gen Electric) 1973 **6** (2), 39

Generating Future Scenarios—Their Use in Strategic Planning (Nair K, Sarin R L, Purdue U) 1979 **12** (3), 57

Helping Managers to Develop Strategies (Skipton M D, Kingston Poly) 1985 **18** (2), 56

Horizons For Strategic Planning (Friedman Y, Segev E, Tel-Aviv U) 1976 **9** (5), 84

How Belgian Businesses Make Strategic Planning Work (Caeldries F, van Dierdonck R) 1988 **21** (2), 41

How Companies Define Their Mission (David F R) 1989 **22** (1), 90

How Danish Companies Plan (Ackelsberg R, Harris W C) 1989 **22** (6), 111

How the Japanese Came to Dominate the Machine Tool Business (Rendeiro J O, Sussex U) 1985 **18** (3), 62

How Scenarios Trigger Strategic Thinking (Millett S M) 1988 **21** (5), 61

How Strategic Decisions are Made (Mazzolini R, Columbia U) 1981 **14** (3), 85

How to Integrate Strategic Planning into your Management Process (Naylor T H, Duke U) 1981 **14** (5), 56

Identifting Strategic Issues (Murphy J J) 1989 **22** (2), 101

Identifying and Using Critical Success Factors (Leidecker J K, Bruno A V, Santa Clara U) 1984 **17** (1), 23

Implementing Strategies for Human Resources (Zabriskie N, Huellmantel A) 1989 **22** (2), 70

Importance of Relative Market Share in Strategic Planning—A Case Study (Delombre J, Bruzelius B, SKF) 1977 **10** (4), 2

Information for More Effective Strategic Planning (King W R, Cleland D I, Pittsburgh U) 1977 **10** (1), 59

Integrating Information Systems into Business Strategies (Ward J M, Cranfield Sch of Mgt) 1987 **20** (3), 79

Issues Management in an Uncertain Environment (Arrington C B, Sawaya R N, Atlantic Richfield) 1984 **17** (6), 17

Key Strategic Issues for German Companies (Hohn S, Volkswagen AG) 1986 **19** (6), 38

Long-Range Strategic Planning: Is it for Everyone? (Carlson T S, California State U) 1978 **11** (3), 54

Making Strategic Planning Work in Local Government (Rider R W, Hawaii Government) 1983 **16** (3), 73

Management Science and Strategic Planning (Wagle B, IBM) 1971 **3** (3), 26

A Management Strategy for Information Processing (Collins A C, South Eastern Gas) 1983 **16** (6), 21

The Management of Strategy (Salveson M E, Pepperdine U) 1974 **7** (1), 19

Managing Diversity: Strategy and Control in Diversified British Companies (Goold M, Campbell A, London Business Sch) 1987 **20** (5), 42

Managing Organizational Change—A Strategic Approach (McEwen N, Carmichael C, Short D, Steel A) 1988 **21** (6), 71

Manufacturing Resource Planning: An Information Systems Model (Adams F P, Cox J F, Auburn U) 1985 **18** (2), 86

Market Segmentation for Pharmaceuticals (Lidstone J) 1989 **22** (2), 54

Marketing Strategies for Scotch Whisky (Targett D, London Business Sch) 1983 **16** (2), 65

Multinational Planning—Developing a Global Approach (Godiwalla H Y, U of Wisconsin-Whitewater, U.S.A) 1986 **19** (2), 110

A National Strategic Planning Model (Bar-Zakay S N, Israel Aircraft Industries) 1981 **14** (4), 76

Participative Planning for a Public Service (Grewe T, Marshall J, O'Toole D E) 1989 **22** (1), 110

PIMS: A Tool for Developing Competitive Strategy (Wakerly R G, PIMS Associates) 1984 **17** (3), 92

Pitfalls in Planning for Multinational Operations (Brandt W K, Hulbert J M, Columbia U; Richers R, Fundacao Getulio Vargas) 1980 **13** (6), 23

Planning for Better Channel Management (Hardy K G, Magrath A J) 1988 **21** (6), 30

Planning Global Strategies for 3M (Kennedy C) 1988 **21** (1), 9

Planning for Strategic Decision Support Systems (King W R, Pittsburgh U) 1983 **16** (5), 73

Planning for Strategic Flexibility (Eppink D J, Free U) 1978 **11** (4), 9

Planning Strategy for World Markets (Leontiades J, Pennsylvania U) 1970 **3** (2), 40

Planning for Technology as a Corporate Resource (van Gunsteren L A, Erasmus U Rotterdam, Rotterdam Consulting Group) 1987 **20** (2), 51

Planning for the U.S. Political Cycle (Marcus A A, Mevorach B) 1988 **21** (4), 50

Portfolio Analysis: Practical Experience with the Directional Policy Matrix (Hussey D E, Harbridge House Europe) 1978 **11** (4), 2

A Practical Approach to Strategy Development (Schwaninger M, St Gall Graduate Sch of Economics) 1987 **20** (5), 74

Prediction and Practice in Multinational Strategic Planning (Channon D F, Manchester Business Sch) 1976 **9** (2), 50

Raising Productivity in Customer Services (Potts G W) 1988 **21** (2), 15

Re-positioning a Leading Stockbroker (Dorwin K) 1988 **21** (6), 13

Reforming the Strategic Planning Process: Integration of Social and Business Needs (Wilson I H, G.E.C.) 1974 **7** (5), 2

The Role of Strategic Planning in Small Businesses (Unni V K, Illinois State U) 1981 **14** (2), 54

The Role of Trade Unions in Strategic Planning (Mills L, National Union of Bank Employees) 1978 **11** (5), 78

The Roles of Formal Strategic Planning (Langley A) 1988 **21** (3), 40

Spotting a Market Gap for a New Product (Mattson B E, U of Minnesota) 1985 **18** (1), 87

The State of Private Sector Strategic Planning in Canada (Frederick G D, Consultant) 1983 **16** (3), 40

Strategic Alliances—Guidelines for Success (Devlin G, Bleackley M) 1988 **21** (5), 18

Strategic Alternatives for Australia Iron-Ore Producers (Frost F, Australian Inst of Technology) 1986 **19** (1), 89

Strategic Assessment—A Rational Response to University Cutbacks (Dube C S, Brown A W, New York State U) 1983 **16** (2), 105

Strategic Control: A New Task for Top Management (Horovitz J H, Ecole Superieure des Sciences Economiques et Commerciales) 1979 **12** (3), 2

Strategic Decision Making in Large European Firms (Guoy M, French Embassy) 1978 **11** (3), 41

Strategic Development as a Means of Organizational Change: Four Case Histories (Green J, Chemical and Allied Products; Jones T, Industry Training Board) 1981 **14** (3), 58

The Strategic Dimension of Computer Systems Planning (Kriebel C H, Carnegie-Mellon U) 1968 **1** (1), 7

The Strategic Divestment Decision (Davis J B, Vanderbilt U) 1974 **7** (1), 15

Strategic Issues for Charities and Philanthropies (Harvey J W, McCrohan K F) 1988 **21** (6), 44

Strategic Issues for the Trustee Savings Banks (Marshall I, TSB Group) 1985 **18** (4), 39

Strategic Leadership through Corporate Planning at ICI (Pink A I H) 1988 **21** (1), 18

Strategic Management of Consumer Services (Allen M) 1988 **21** (6), 20

Strategic Management of Public and Non-Market Corporations (Ruffat J, Strategies & Structures) 1983 **16** (2), 74

The Strategic Management of R & D. Part II—Organizing for Integration (Petroni G, Udine U) 1983 **16** (2), 65

Strategic Mapping—A Tool for Corporate Planners (Vesper V D, Consultant) 1979 **12** (6), 75

Strategic Planning in 21 U K Companies (Grinyer P H, Norburn D, City U and London Graduate Business Sch) 1974 **7** (4), 80

Strategic Planning: One Workable Approach (McConnell J D, Stanford Res Inst) 1971 **4** (2), 2

Strategic Planning in an Age of Uncertainty (Menke M M, SRI) 1979 **12** (4), 27

Strategic Planning for the Armed Forces (Russell Colonel W N, Canadian National Defence HQ) 1986 **19** (4), 41

Strategic Planning at the Copenhagen Telephone Company (Allesen-Holm J, Copenhagen Telephone Co) 1985 **18** (3), 68

Strategic Planning in Banks — Does it Pay? (Gup B E, Whitehead D D) 1989 **22** (1), 124

Strategic Planning for British Nuclear Fuels (Geary N R, B.N.F.L.) 1973 **6** (3), 2

Strategic Planning Catches on in U.S. Retailers (Rosenbloom B, Tripuraneni R V, Drexel U) 1985 **18** (4), 55

Strategic Planning in a Changing Corporate Environment (Amara R, Institute for the Future) 1979 **12** (1), 2

Strategic Planning and the Chief Executive (Forman R) 1988 **21** (4), 57

Strategic Planning for Commodities and Specialities (Unger L, Consultant) 1983 **16** (4), 12

Strategic Planning and Consensus Building for External Relations— Five Cases (Nielsen R P, Boston Coll) 1983 **16** (6), 74

Strategic Planning for Corporate Growth in Developing Countries (Dam A van, Corn Products Latin America) 1969 **2** (1), 9

Strategic Planning Could Improve Your Share Price (Welch J B, Northeastern U) 1984 **17** (2), 144

Strategic Planning for Distribution (La Londe B J, Ohio State U) 1971 **4** (2), 23

Strategic Planning for Endgame (Harrigan K R, Columbia U) 1982 **15** (6), 45

Strategic Planning in European Multinationals (Gotcher J W, California State U) 1977 **10** (5), 7

Strategic Planning in Government-Dependent Businesses (Ramamurti R, Northeastern U, Boston, USA) 1986 **19** (3), 62

Strategic Planning for Hospitals—A Health-needs Approach (Champagne F, Contandriopoulos A-P, Larouche D, Clemenhagen C, Barbir C, U of Montreal) 1987 **20** (3), 77

Strategic Planning for Human Resources—Let's Get Started (Nkomo S M) 1988 **21** (1), 66

Strategic Planning in IBM (Thoroman D G, IBM) 1971 **4** (1), 1

Strategic Planning and Inflation (Hussey D E, Harbridge House Europe) 1976 **9** (2), 24

Strategic Planning for Information Systems at British Rail (Mainelli M R, Miller D R) 1988 **21** (4), 65

Strategic Planning for International Business (Hussey D E, Wander) 1972 **5** (2), 16

Strategic Planning for Internationalization—The European Dilemma and some Possible Solutions (Franko L G, CEI) 1973 **6** (2), 58

The Strategic Planning Matrix—A Quantitative Approach (David F R, Auburn U) 1986 **19** (5), 102

Strategic Planning for MIS (Shrivastava P, New York U) 1983 **16** (5), 19

Strategic Planning for Multinationals—The views of Government and Scientists (Gotcher J W, California State U) 1981 **14** (1), 23

Strategic Planning as an Organizational Change Process—Some Guidelines from Practice (Taylor D E Business and Mgt Devel) 1979 **12** (5), 43

Strategic Planning and Participation: A Contradiction in Terms (Kloeze H J, Molenkamp A, Roelofs F J W, Consultants) 1980 **13** (5), 10

Strategic Planning and Policy Making in Banks (Adolfse J, Vervoordelfonk F, Central Rabobank) 1979 **12** (3), 73

Strategic Planning for Power Equipment Manufacture (Shah R K D) 1989 **22** (5), 98

A Strategic Planning Process for Public and Non-profit Organizations (Bryson J M) 1988 **21** (1), 73

Strategic Planning and Product Innovarion—Some Systematic Approaches (Buij J, TNO Bureau for Product Devel) 1979 **12** (5), 23

Strategic Planning for Public Relations (Slatter S St. P, London Business Sch) 1980 **13** (3), 57

Strategic Planning for a Public Sector Enterprise (Karagozoglu N, Seglund R) 1989 **22** (2), 121

Strategic Planning in a Rapidly Changing Environment—Book Review Article (Argenti J, Consultant) 1979 **12** (5), 110

Strategic Planning for Research and Development (Bemelmans T, Eindhoven U) 1979 **12** (2), 33

Strategic Planning and Research and Development—Can we Integrate Them? (Petroni G, Udine U) 1983 **16** (1), 15

Strategic Planning for Resources (Taylor B, Administrative Staff Coll Henley) 1974 **7** (4), 12

Strategic Planning in the Scottish Health Service—A Mixed-Scanning Approach (Wiseman C, Scottish Inst for Operational Research) 1979 **12** (2), 103

Strategic Planning in Small and Medium-sized Companies (Hoorn Th. P van, Consultant) 1979 **12** (2), 84

Strategic Planning in Smaller Rapid Growth Companies (Shuman J C, Shaw J J, Sussman G, Bentley Coll and Providence Coll) 1985 **18** (6), 48

Strategic Planning for Social and Political Change (Taylor B, Administrative Staff Coll Henley) 1974 **7** (1), 33

Strategic Planning System for Multinational Companies (Sethi N K, St. John's U) 1982 **15** (3), 80

Strategic Planning in Tanzania (Mrema, E L, Tanzania Wood Industry Corp) 1987 **20** (3), 105

Strategic Planning for Telecommunications—A Systems Approach (Chakraborty S, New Telephone Co.) 1981 **14** (5), 46

Strategic Planning in the Thomas Cook Group (Davies A H T, Thomas Cook Group) 1981 **14** (5), 27

Strategic Planning in a Turbulent International Environment (Ringbakk K-A, Dartmouth Coll) 1976 **9** (3), 2

Strategic Planning for Water—A Case History (Mohanty R P, Nat Inst of Training in Industrial Engineering) 1984 **17** (4), 79

Strategic Planning for the World Wildlife Fund (Medley G J) 1988 **21** (1), 46

Strategic Planning—A Contingency Approach—Part 1. The Strategic Analysis (Ghosh B C, Nee A Y C, Singapore U) 1983 **16** (4), 93

Strategic Planning—A Contingency Approach—Part 2. The Plan (Ghosh B C, Nee A Y C, Nat U of Singapore) 1983 **16** (6), 46

Strategic Planning—A New Arrival in Hungarian Industry (Csath M, National Mgt Devel Centre) 1983 **16** (2), 85

Strategic Planning—Myth or Reality?—A Chief Executive's View (Ford T M, Emhart Corporation) 1981 **14** (6), 9

Strategic Planning—Which Style do you Need? (Taylor B, Henley Mgt Coll) 1984 **17** (3), 51

Strategic Thinking in Insurance (Howard E F) 1989 **22** (5), 76

Strategic Thinking Supported by Risk Analysis (Wagner G R, Execucom) 1980 **13** (3), 61

Strategic Thinking—Dealing with Uncertainty (Weber C E, Wisconsin U) 1984 **17** (4), 60

Strategies of New Biotechnology Firms (Smith J G, Fleck V) 1988 **21** (3), 51

Strategies for Planning (Taylor B, Administrative Staff Coll Henley) 1975 **8** (4), 27

Strategy Consulting—A Shooting Star? (Payne A, Lumsden C, Cranfield Sch of Mgt) 1987 **20** (3), 53

A Tough Future for Australian Business (Laczniak E R, Pecotich A, Carroll B) 1989 **22** (1), 48

Turnaround Strategies for Economic Development (Allen D N, Plosila W H) 1988 **21** (3), 59

U.K. Chemicals—Strategic Planning or Industrial Strategy (Caudle P, Chemical Industries Assoc) 1977 **10** (6), 31

Using Strategic Issue Analysis (King W R, Pittsburgh U) 1982 **15** (4), 45

Who Influences Strategic Decisions? (Hegarty W H, Indiana U; Hoffman R C, Coll of William and Mary, Virginia) 1987 **20** (2), 61

Why Don't U.S. Boards Get More Involved in Strategy? (Rosenstein J, U of Texas at Arlington) 1987 **20** (3), 30

Why Planning in State Enterprises Doesn't Work (Javidan M, Dastmalchian A) 1988 **21** (3), 98

Why we Need a Revolution in Strategic Planning (Stubbart C G, U of Massachusetts) 1985 **18** (6), 68

Woolworth's Drive for Excellence (Rose D) 1989 **22** (1), 28

Xerox Charts a New Strategic Direction (Kennedy C) 1989 **22** (1), 10

Zero-based Budgeting—A Technique for Planned Organizational Decline (Pearson J V, Henley; Michael R J, London Borough of Bexley) 1981 **14** (3), 68

STRATEGY

Can Hyundai Go It Alone? (Hyun Y, Lee J) 1989 **22** (2), 63

Communicating Corporate Strategy — The Payoffs and the Risks (Higgins R B, Diffenbach J) 1989 **22** (3), 133

Competitive Strategies in the Dutch Insurance Industry (Eppink J, Free U Amsterdam) 1987 **20** (4), 30

Competitive Strategies for Service Businesses (Wilson I) 1988 **21** (6), 10

Corporate Culture and Strategy—The Problem of Strategic Fit (Scholz C, Saarland U) 1987 **20** (4), 78

Developing Strategic Thinking (Easterby-Smith M, Davies J, Lancaster U) 1983 **16** (4), 39

Developing a Strategy for an Industrial Training Board a Participative Approach (Beavan P R, Green G J L and Russell J G R, Industry Training Board) 1979 **12** (1), 41

Generic Win-Win Negotiating Solutions (Nielsen R P) 1989 **22** (5), 137

GE's High-tech Strategy (Koerner E) 1989 **22** (4), 11

How Companies Define Their Mission (David F R) 1989 **22** (1), 90

Identifying the Levels of Strategy for a College or University (Shirley R C, Trinity U) 1983 **16** (3), 92

Japanese Business Strategy in China (Campbell N, Manchester Business Sch) 1987 **20** (5), 69

Japan's Drive for the European Car Market—Lessons from U.S. Experience (Wray M, Toftech; Norburn D, Imperial Coll, London) 1987 **20** (4), 60

Linking Organization Structures and Processes to Business Strategy (Cowherd D M, Luchs R H) 1988 **21** (5), 47

So What is Strategy? (Evered R, Naval Postgraduate Sch) 1983 **16** (3), 57

Strategic Issues for Charities and Philanthropies (Harvey J W, McCrohan K F) 1988 **21** (6), 44

Strategic Management and Artificial Intelligence (Holloway C, Coll of Business Admin) 1983 **16** (5), 89

Strategies for Global Competition (Lei D) 1989 **22** (1), 102

Strategies for Mature Business (Schofield M, Arnold D) 1988 **21** (5), 69

Strategies for a Pan European Market (Vandermerwe S) 1989 **22** (3), 45

Strategies for Tourism in Singapore (Cheong W K, Khem G S) 1988 **21** (4), 36

Strategy in Action—Techniques for Implementing Strategy (Reed R, Buckley M R) 1988 **21** (3), 67

Strategy Alternatives for Vehicle Component Manufacturers (Carr C) 1988 **21** (4), 86

Strategy, Organizational Culture and Symbolism (Green S) 1988 **21** (4), 121

The Strategy for Organized Technology in the light of Hard-, and Org-Ware Interaction (Dobrov G M, Intl Institute for Applied Systems Analysis) 1979 **12** (4), 79

Strategy as a System of Expedients (Hinterhuber H, Popp W) 1988 **21** (4), 107

Why Planners Don't (Saunders C B, Tuggle F D, Kansas U) 1977 **10** (3), 19

STRATEGY FORMULATION

Aids in Determining Strategy, the Internal Analysis (Croon P, Consultant) 1979 **12** (4), 65

Avoiding Dependence on Suppliers and Distributors (Bourantas D) 1989 **22** (3), 140

Decision Analysis and Strategic Policy Formulation (Bunn D, Thomas H, London Business Sch & Australian Graduate Sch of Mgt) 1977 **10** (6), 23

Developing Strategies: A Practical Approach (Weir G A, Weir Group) 1974 **7** (5), 7

Developing a Strategy for International Business (Fannin W R, U of Houston-Clear Lake; Gilmore C B, U of Maine at Orono) 1986 **19** (3), 81

Evaluating Alternative Strategies Using Scenarios (Whipple III W) 1989 **22** (3), 82

A Frame of Reference for Strategy Development (Patel P, Younger M, Arthur D. Little) 1978 **11** (2), 6

Identifting Strategic Issues (Murphy J J) 1989 **22** (2), 101

Making Corporate Planning Work in Developing Countries (Haines W R) 1988 **21** (2), 91

Marketing Electricity—A Military Approach (Faruqui A, Battelle Columbus, Palo Alto) 1987 **20** (4), 67

New Uses of Delphi in Strategy Formulation (Wedley W C, Simon Fraser U) 1977 **10** (6), 70

Strategic Planning and the Chief Executive (Forman R) 1988 **21** (4), 57

Strategies for Declining Industrial Markets (Robinson S J Q, Shell UK Ltd) 1986 **19** (2), 72

Strategies for International Growth in the Automobile Industry (Moulins J-L, U d'Aix-Marseille) 1978 **11** (1), 34

Strategies for National Competitiveness (Rugman A M, Dalhousie U Nova Scotia) 1987 **20** (3), 92

Strategy Formulation for the Smaller Firm—A Practical Approach (Nagel A, Eindhoven U) 1981 **14** (4), 115

Turnaround and Recovery: What Strategy do You Need, (O'Neill H M, U of Connecticut) 1986 **19** (1), 80

STRATEGY IMPLEMENTATION

Bridging the Awful Gap Between Strategy and Action (Wernham R, British Telecom) 1984 **17** (6), 34

Corporate Culture and Strategy—The Problem of Strategic Fit (Scholz C, Saarland U) 1987 **20** (4), 78

Corporate Long-Range Planning Groups—Some Different Approaches (Litschert R J, Virginia Poly and State U; Nicholson E A, Wright State U) 1974 **7** (4), 62

How to Integrate Strategic Planning into your Management Process (Naylor T H, Duke U) 1981 **14** (5), 56

Implementing Strategies for Human Resources (Zabriskie N, Huellmantel A) 1989 **22** (2), 70

Integrating Planning and Management Development (Dill W R, New York U) 1975 **8** (5), 8

Integrating Planning with Management (Miesing P, New York State U) 1984 **17** (4), 118

A Look at Major Planning Methods: Development, Implementations Strengths and Limitations (Kahalas H, New York State U) 1978 **11** (4), 84

Patterns of Success in German Business (Kruger W) 1989 **22** (2), 106

Plans—Their Preparations and Implementation (Chandler W J, Reed International) 1978 **11** (6), 14

Strategy in Action—Techniques for Implementing Strategy (Reed R, Buckley M R) 1988 **21** (3), 67

Successful Strategies in French High Technology Companies (Calori R, Noel R, Group Ecole Superieure de Commerce de Lyon) 1986 **19** (6), 54

Successfully Implementing Strategic Decisions (Alexander L D, Virginia Tech) 1985 **18** (3), 91

Translating Planning into Action (Cornfield K, STC plc) 1984 **17** (4), 23

Turning Plans into Action—A Case Study (Ahlquist C G, Simon Engineering) 1974 **7** (6), 59

STRUCTURAL ANALYSIS

Designing a Business Scanning System (Calori R) 1989 **22** (1), 69

Wither or Whither London? An Application of Industry Structure Analysis (Burke T, Friends of the Earth; Wilson L, Harbridge House Europe) 1980 **13** (5), 79

SUPPLY MANAGEMENT

Avoiding Dependence on Suppliers and Distributors (Bourantas D) 1989 **22** (3), 140

Planning the Future Raw Material Supply (Wright R W, Rio Tinto Zinc) 1976 **9** (1), 12

SURVEYS

Corporate Planning in Small Companies—A Survey (Shuman J G, Babson Coll) 1975 **8** (5), 81

How are Companies Planning Now?—A Survey (Boulton W R, Georgia U; Franklin S G, Emory U; Lindsay W M, Nthn Kentucky U; Rue L W, Georgian State U) 1982 **15** (1), 82

How French Industry Plans (Montebello M, Buigues P, Institut d'Administration des Enterprises) 1982 **15** (3), 116

How Planning Works in Practice—A Survey of 48 U.K. Companies (Al-Bazzaz S, Grinyer P M, St Andrews U) 1980 **13** (4), 30

Long Range Planning in Large United States Corporations—A Survey (Ang J S, Chua J H, Oklahoma State U) 1979 **12** (2), 99

Organization for Long Range Planning—A Survey of German Companies (Keppler W, Bamberger I, Gabele E, Rutgerswerke A G, Inst de Gestion de Rennes) 1979 **12** (5), 69

Organized Planning in Major U.K. Companies (Taylor B, Irving P, Bradford U) 1971 **3** (4), 10

The Planner's Dual Role—A Survey of U.S. Companies (Lorange P, IMEDE Lausanne) 1973 **6** (1), 13

Planning Procedures in German Companies—Findings and Consequences (Scholz C, Regensburg U) 1984 **17** (6), 94

Strategic Planning in 21 U.K. Companies (Grinyer P H, Norburn D, City U and London Graduate Business Sch) 1974 **7** (4), 80

Will Hong Kong's Entrepreneurs Move to Planning? (Warrington M B, Napier Coll) 1982 **15** (3), 157

SWEDEN

Planning for Leisure in Sweden (Tobe E I, Consultant) 1971 **4** (1), 50

Pluralist Organization and Consensus in Swedish Planning (Lundberg D, Consultant) 1976 **9** (6), 69

Scenarios for Industrial Relations: Sweden Evolves a New Consensus (Jones H G, U of Strathclyde) 1987 **20** (3), 65

Swedish Industrial Policy Planning—A Workshop Report, Stockholm, 6–7 March 1980 (Finlay A W, Society for Long Range Planning) 1980 **13** (6), 55

Town Planning in Sweden: National Officials Versus Local Politicians (Khakee A, Umea U) 1984 **17** (6), 82

SWITZERLAND

Diversification in the Swiss Chemical Industry (Eugster C, J.R. Geigy) 1969 **2** (1), 42

Integrated Long Range Planning at Nestlé (Brey A, Gabsa G, Nestlé) 1972 **5** (2), 44

SYSTEM ANALYSIS

Corporate Planning—A System View (Nadler G, Wisconsin U) 1978 **11** (6), 67

The Interaction of Systems Analysis and Marketing Planning (Gladstone E J, Savin Business Machines) 1971 **4** (1), 35

Regional Planning in China—A Systems Engineering Approach (Yuji W, Quanli C, Hunan Academy of Social Studies) 1987 **20** (1), 99

System Analysis and Planning for the Criminal Justice System (Blumstein A, Carnegie-Mellor U) 1972 **5** (4), 61

The Use of Systems Analysis in New Product Development (Zoppoth R C, Xerox) 1972 **5** (1), 23

SYSTEMS THEORY

Long Range Planning—An Open Systems View (Kahalas H, New York State U) 1977 **10** (5), 78

A Systems Approach to Corporate Development (Wilemon D L, Porter L H, Syracuse U) 1972 **5** (1), 46

The Systems Revolution (Ackoff R L, Pennsylvania U) 1974 **7** (6), 2

T

TAKEOVER *see* **MERGERS**

TANZANIA

Business Planning in Tanzanian State Enterprises (El-Namaki M S S) 1977 **10** (5), 52

Strategic Planning in Tanzania (Mrema E L, Tanzania Wood Industry Corp) 1987 **20** (3), 105

TECHNOLOGICAL CHANGE

Can Industries De-Mature—Applying New Technologies to Mature Industries (Dowdy W L, Nikolchev J, SRI Intl) 1986 **19** (2), 38

Develop Your Technology Strategy (Ford D) 1988 **21** (5), 85

The Effect of Technological Change on Planning for International Transport (Harding A, Nat Ports Council) 1969 **2** (1), 30

A Framework of Decision Making for Technological Change (Cox J G, Essex U) 1978 **11** (1), 53

How Will the British Post Office Cope with Technological Change (Corby M E, Mail Users Assoc) 1982 **15** (6), 58

The Innovative Firm (Ansoff H I, Vanderbilt U) 1968 **1** (2), 26

Investing in CAD: A Case of *ad hoc* Decision-making (Currie W L) 1989 **22** (6), 85

Organization for Technological Change (Ward E P, New Product Mgt Group) 1981 **14** (4), 121

Planning for Manufacturing Technology (Swamidass P M, U of Missouri) 1987 **20** (5), 125

Technological Change: Theory and Practice—Book Review Article (Langrish J, Manchester Poly) 1983 **16** (4), 106

Technological Innovation and Long Range Planning (Zvegintzov M, Nat Res and Devel Corp) 1968 **1** (2), 46

TECHNOLOGICAL FORECASTING

Approaches to Technological Forecasting as a Planning Tool (Lanford H W, Imundo L V, Wright State U) 1974 **7** (4), 49

Data Sources for Trend Extrapolation in Technological Forecasting (Nutt A B, US Air Force, Dayton; Lenz R C, Dayton U; Lanford H W, Cleary M J, Wright State U) 1976 **9** (1), 72

Evaluating Industrial Technological Forecasting (Gechele G B, Instituto per la Ricostruzione Industriale) 1976 **9** (4), 76

Forecasting the Future—Developments in Computers (Wilkes M W, Cambridge U) 1970 **2** (3), 15

How Companies Keep Abreast of Technological Change (Quinn J J, Tech Change Centre) 1985 **18** (2), 69

The Preparation and Deployment of Technological Forecasts (Wills G, Bradford U) 1970 **2** (3), 44

Recent Trends in Long Range Forecasting for Technology-Based Organizations—Book Review Article (Twiss B C, Bradford U) 1979 **12** (2), 120

Scientific-Technological Forecasting in the U.S.S.R (Dobrov G M, Science Investigation Dept) 1971 **3** (3), 13

Technological Forecasting in Corporate Planning (Jantsch E, Consultant) 1968 **1** (1), 40

Technological Forecasting and the Delphi Technique—A Reply (Rowlands D G, Unilever Research Laboratory) 1969 **2** (2), 78

Technological Forecasting as a Guide for Managerial Planning (Jeckovich S, PPG Industries) 1971 **4** (1), 29

Technological Forecasting for Power Generation—A Study Using the Delphi Technique (Garde V D, Patel R R, Bharat Heavy Electricals) 1985 **18** (4), 73

Technological Forecasting in Six Major U.K. Companies (Currill D L, Stevenson, Jordan & Harrison) 1972 **5** (1), 72

Technological Forecasting—a Criticism of the Delphi Technique (Overbury R E, Min of Tech) 1969 **1** (4), 76

TECHNOLOGICAL INNOVATION

Can Technology be Managed Strategically? (Sethi N K, St. John's U Jamaica, New York; Movsesian B, City U of New York; Hickey K D, NCR Corp) 1985 **18** (4), 89

Controlling and Evaluating Personnel Strategy (Newton D, Shell UK) 1969 **1** (4), 24

The Corporate Library as a Source of New Technology (McKinnon L M B, Sanders) 1980 **13** (2), 102

Directing Technological Development—The Role of the Board (Willder, STC Technology) 1985 **18** (4), 44

How Companies Keep Abreast of Technological Change (Quinn J J; Tech Change Centre) 1985 **18** (2), 69

How Will Technology Impact Your Business? (Whaley R, Burrows B, Strategic Planning Society) 1987 **20** (5), 109

Managing Technology Alliances (Nueno P, Oosterveld J) 1988 **21** (3), 11

Planning for Technological Innovation: Part II—Investment in Technological Change in Three Major Industries (Cox J G, Essex U) 1978 **11** (4), 70

Planning for Technological Innovation (Ward E P, New Product Mgt Group) 1981 **14** (2), 59

Planning for Technological Innovation—Part I. Investment in Technology (Cox J G, Essex U) 1977 **10** (6), 40

Some Hints on Financing New Technologies (Shepherdson P, Pilkington Brothers) 1985 **18** (6), 34

Strategies for Global Competition (Lei D) 1989 **22** (1), 102

Technological Innovation in European Industry: The Need for a World Perspective (Pavitt K, O.E.C.D.) 1969 **2** (2), 8

Who Should Plan Technological Innovation? (Petroni G, U of Udine) 1985 **18** (5), 108

TECHNOLOGY

Alternative Technologies and the Rising cost of Energy (Clarke F J P, Harwell Laboratory) 1981 **14** (4), 51

Assessing the Impact of New Technology in Information Systems (Lientz B P, Graduate Sch of Mgt; Chen M, Atlantic Richfield) 1981 **14** (6), 44

Avoiding Skill Shortages in the New Technologies (Pearson R, U of Sussex) 1985 **18** (4), 33

Betting The Bank on Technology—Strategic Planning at Bank of America (Raphael D E, Bank of America) 1986 **19** (2), 23

Can we Plan for New Technology (Fairtlough G, Celltech) 1984 **17** (3), 14

Competing with the Japanese Approach to Technology (Prentice J, Consultant) 1984 **17** (2), 25

Energy Resources and the Impact of New Technologies (Ibrahim S M A, Al-Azhar U) 1980 **13** (4), 63

A Framework for the Strategic Management of Future Tyre Technology (Lauglaug A S, Goodyear Tyre and Rubber Company) 1987 **20** (5), 21

How Will Technology Impact Your Business? (Whaley R, Burrows B, Strategic Planning Society) 1987 **20** (5), 109

Managing Technology Alliances (Nueno P, Oosterveld J) 1988 **21** (3), 11

Manufacturing Technology as a Competitive Weapon (Blois K J, Templeton Coll Oxford) 1986 **19** (4), 63

Planning for Technology as a Corporate Resource (van Gunsteren L A, Erasmus U Rotterdam, Rotterdam Consulting Group) 1987 **20** (2), 51

Seeking Strategic Advantage with Technology?—Focus on Customer Value (Craig R S, Strategic Planning GenRad Inc) 1986 **19** (2), 50

The Stategic Management of Technology: Corporate Fad or Strategic Necessity (Wilson I, American Editor) 1986 **19** (2), 21

The Strategy for Organized Technology in the light of Hard, Soft, and Org-Ware Interaction (Dobrov G M, Intl Institute for Applied Systems Analysis) 1979 **12** (4), 79

Technology Management in Indian Companies (Desai A V, National Council for Applied Economic Research) 1972 **5** (4), 70

Technology Planning at General Motors (Koerner E) 1989 **22** (2), 9

TECHNOLOGY ASSESSMENT

Morphology: A Tool for Exploring New Technology (Shurig R, Ontario Hydro) 1984 **17** (3), 129

Technology Assessment: Need and Motivation of Industry (Oberkampf V, Klockner-Humboldt-Deutz) 1978 **11** (4), 48

TECHNOLOGY STRATEGY

Develop Your Technology Strategy (Ford D) 1988 **21** (5), 85

Who Should Plan Technological Innovation? (Petroni G, U of Udine) 1985 **18** (5), 108

TECHNOLOGY TRANSFER

Civil Spin-off from Defence Research: A Fresh Approach (Herdan B L, Defence Technology Enterprises) 1987 **20** (1), 84

Getting a Quicker Pay-off From R & D (van den Kroonenberg H H) 1989 **22** (5), 51

How Elf Aquitaine Provides Technological Assistance to Small Businesses (Turbil J-P, Elf Aquitaine) 1986 **19** (3), 59

Japanese Business Strategy in China (Campbell N, Manchester Business Sch) 1987 **20** (5), 69

Selecting a Foreign Partner for Technology Transfer (Lasserre P, INSEAD) 1984 **17** (6), 43

Training: Key to Technological Transfer (Lasserre P, INSEAD) 1982 **15** (3), 51

Transferring Technology to Developing Countries — Critical Factors for Success (Madu C N) 1989 **22** (4), 115

TELECOMMUNICATIONS INDUSTRY

Developing an Enterprise Culture at British Telecom (Brunnen D J) 1989 **22** (2), 27

Marketing the Telephone in a De-regulated Environment (Kane N J A, British Telecom) 1986 **19** (4), 59

Strategic Planning for Telecommunications—A Systems Approach (Chakraborty S, New Telephone Co) 1981 **14** (5), 46

Telecommunications and the Customer—Prospects for the 1980s (Lawson F, Post Office Telecommunications) 1980 **13** (6), 70

The Transformation of AT & T (Kennedy C) 1989 **22** (3), 10

TELEVISION

Economic Forecasting for a Television Company (Bennett B C, Trident Management) 1978 **11** (5), 63

Television in the Seventies (Goodman J, Nat Broadcasting Corporation) 1973 **6** (4), 63

TEXTILE INDUSTRY

The Planned Marketing of Textiles (Thomas H A, Courtaulds) 1971 **3** (3), 54

Why Textile and Clothing Industries are Shifting to the Third World (Fitzpatrick J, Consultant) 1983 **16** (6), 42

see also **CLOTHING INDUSTRY**

THINKING

Developing Strategic Thinking (Easterby-Smith M, Davies J, Lancaster U) 1983 **16** (4), 39

THIRD WORLD *see* **UNDERDEVELOPED ECONOMIES**

TOBACCO INDUSTRY

The Impact of the EEC on the U.K. Food, Drink and Tobacco Processing Industry (Nicholls J R, Bath U) 1979 **12** (3), 82

TOP MANAGEMENT
Assessing Your Competitor's People and Organization (Ball R, Cresap, McCormick & Paget) 1987 **20** (2), 32
Decision Analysis for Top Management (Sneddon L M, Sunridge Park Mgt Centre) 1970 **3** (1), 50
Defining the Role of the Board (Demb A, Chouet D, Lossius T, Neubauer F) 1989 **22** (1), 61
How Marriott Corporation Grew Five-fold in Ten Years (Kennedy C) 1988 **21** (2), 10
How Top Management is Changing Dutch Business (Turner G) 1987 **20** (6), 10
How U.S. and Japanese CEO's Spend Their Time (Kudo H, Tachikawa T, Suzuki N) 1988 **21** (6), 79
Selling Long Range Planning to Management (Berteaux R, Solvay) 1969 **2** (2), 32
Top Management's Role in Planning (Steiner G A, U of California) 1969 **1** (4), 2
Who Controls the Board? (Mills G) 1989 **22** (3), 125
Why Don't U.S. Boards Get More Involved in Strategy? (Rosenstein J, U of Texas at Arlington) 1987 **20** (3), 30

TOURISM
Planning in the Ministry of Industry and Tourism (Barrows D, Min of Industry and Tourism) 1979 **12** (6), 37
Strategies for Tourism in Singapore (Cheong W K, Khem G S) 1988 **21** (4), 36
Tourism—Key Issues for the 1980's (Burkart A J, Surrey U) 1982 **15** (4), 91

TOWN PLANNING see **URBAN PLANNING**

TRADE UNIONS
The Role of Trade Unions in Strategic Planning (Mills L, National Union of Bank Employees) 1978 **11** (5), 78

TRAINING
Building a Customer-orientated Organization (Cornish F) 1988 **21** (3), 105
Cost-Benefit Analysis of Training—An Appraisal (Reddy Y R K, Administrative Staff Coll of India) 1979 **12** (6), 50
Creating a Productive Culture at Shell Chemicals (Thornley I A) 1988 **21** (3), 34
Installing a Computerized Planning System in Ghana (Babington E A, Peat Marwick McLintock) 1987 **20** (4), 110
Personnel and Training Policies—Some Lessons for Western Companies (Brown G F, Read A R, Consultants) 1984 **17** (2), 48
Towards 1992: A Strategy for Training (Day D) 1989 **22** (6), 48
Training: Key to Technological Transfer (Lasserre P, INSEAD) 1982 **15** (3), 51

TRANSPORT
A Concept of an Integrated Transport Model (Swan R T, N.S.W. State Planning Authority) 1974 **7** (5), 17
Corporate Planning and Project Evaluation in Urban Transport (Tyson W J, Manchester U; Cochrane R L D, GMPTE) 1981 **14** (5), 62
The Effect of Technological Change on Planning for International Transport (Harding A, Nat Ports Council) 1969 **2** (1), 30
Failings in U.K. Transport Planning (Jolliffe J K, Atkins Planning) 1977 **10** (1), 73
Long Range Planning for London Transport (Ellen E R, London Transport) 1973 **6** (3), 10
Long Range Planning for Transport (Stuart C, British Transport Staff Coll) 1968 **1** (2), 38
A Role for Transport in Canada (Gratwick J, Fahey W R, Schneiderman A, Canadian Ntl Railways) 1976 **9** (1), 38
Trucks and Road Transport Towards 1992 (Garuzo G) 1988 **21** (4), 45

TRANSPORTATION
Realistic Planning for Transportation — A Flexible Approach (Khan A M) 1989 **22** (5), 128
Transportation After Deregulation (Lazarus M, Ashley W C, United Airlines) 1985 **18** (1), 42

TURNAROUND
ICL: Crisis and Swift Recovery (Marwood D C L) 1985 **18** (2), 10
Strategies in Managing Turnaround (Melin L, Linkoping U) 1985 **18** (1), 80

TURNAROUND STRATEGIES
Company Failure or Company Health?—Techniques for Measuring Company Health (Robertson J, Mills R W) 1988 **21** (2), 70
How Sumitomo Transformed Dunlop Tyres (Radford G D) 1989 **22** (3), 28
Managing a Successful Turnaround (Zimmerman F M) 1989 **22** (3), 105
Strategies in Managing Turnaround (Melin L, Linkoping U) 1985 **18** (1), 80
The Turnaround at Italtel (Bellisario M, Italtel) 1985 **18** (6), 21
Turnaround at MFI—From a Troubled Mail-Order Firm to a Leading Furniture Retailer (Seabright J W, Henley Distance Learning) 1985 **18** (4), 27
Turnaround of a Cable Company (Gopal R) 1989 **22** (1), 98
Turnaround and Recovery: What Strategy do You Need? (O'Neill H M, U of Connecticut) 1986 **19** (1), 80
Turnaround Strategies for Economic Development (Allen D N, Plosila W H) 1988 **21** (3), 59
Turnaround—A Painful Learning Process (Zimmerman F M) 1986 **19** (4), 104

U

UNCERTAINTY
Forecasting in Conditions of Uncertainty (Fildes R, Jalland M, Wood D, Manchester Business Sch) 1978 **11** (4), 29
How Corporate Planning Responds to Uncertainty (Harrison F L, Henley Mgt Centre) 1976 **9** (2), 88
Strategy as a System of Expedients (Hinterhuber H, Popp W) 1988 **21** (4), 107

UNDERDEVELOPED ECONOMIES
Can Corporate Planning Invent the Future of the Third World? (Dam A van, Latin America CPC Intl) 1974 **7** (2), 8
Long Range Planning in Under-developed countries—A Case History (Stanbridge P J, Sabi-Limpopo Authority) 1969 **2** (2), 38
Making Corporate Planning Work in Developing Countries (Haines W R) 1988 **21** (2), 91
Third World Oil and Gas—Underexplored and Underdeveloped (Odell P R, Economic Geography Inst) 1981 **14** (1), 10
Why Textile and Clothing Industries are Shifting to the Third World (Fitzpatrick J, Consultant) 1983 **16** (6), 42
see **DEVELOPING COUNTRIES**

UNEMPLOYMENT
Creative Crisis: New Patterns of Growth and Employment (Godet M, Auguste Comte Institute) 1981 **14** (5), 12
Manpower and Unemployment in the U.K. (Lawrence J, ICI) 1979 **12** (5), 16
Measuring Unemployment (Joseph K, Centre for Policy Studies) 1976 **9** (3), 12
What is to be Done About Unemployment? (Hanagan P, Reuters) 1982 **15** (2), 46

UNITED KINGDOM
Diversification as a Factor in U.K. Industrial Strategy (Constable J, British Inst of Mgt) 1986 **19** (1), 52
Financial Modelling for Planning in the U.K. (Grinyer P H, St Andrews U) 1983 **16** (5), 58
Japanese Marketing Strategies in the United Kingdom (Wong V, Saunders J, Doyle P) 1987 **20** (6), 54
Management Buy-outs in Britain—A Monograph (Wright M, Coyne J, Robbie K, Centre for Mgt Buy-out Research, Nottingham) 1987 **20** (4), 38
National Programmes to Promote Youth Training (Atkinson K N, Manpower Services Commission) 1985 **18** (3), 26
Promoting Small Business in Northern Ireland (Birley S, Cranfield Sch of Mgt; Bridge S, Local Enterprise Unit, Belfast) 1987 **20** (6), 71
The Stock Exchange After the Big Bang (Valentine S) 1988 **21** (2), 35
The Thatcher Revolution — Radical Policies in a Changing Society (Worcester R M) 1989 **22** (4), 72
U.K. Competition Policy Evaluated (Pass C L, Sparkes J R, Bradford U) 1983 **16** (4), 76

UNITED STATES OF AMERICA see **USA**

UNIVERSITIES

Corporate Strategic Planning in a University (Thomas R, Bath U) 1980 **13** (5), 70

Getting a Quicker Pay-off From R & D (van den Kroonenberg H H) 1989 **22** (5), 51

How Belgian Businesses Make Strategic Planning Work (Caeldries F, van Dierdonck R) 1988 **21** (2), 41

Long Range Planning for Universities (Doyle P, Lynch J E, Bradford U) 1976 **9** (6), 39

Marketing Planning for Colleges and Universities (Smith L R, Wisconsin-Whitewater U; Cavusgil S T, Bradley U) 1984 **17** (6), 104

Planning for University: Using Interactive Forecasting (Moore L F, Charach L, British Columbia U) 1980 **13** (3), 109

UNIVERSITY ADMINISTRATION

Identifying the Levels of Strategy for a College or University (Shirley R C, Trinity U) 1983 **16** (3), 92

Strategic Assessment—A Rational Response to University Administration (Dube C S, Brown A W, New York State U) 1983 **16** (2), 105

University Planning: An Organization Model (McLaughlin E M, Virginia Poly Inst and State U) 1971 **4** (2), 55

URBAN AREAS

Controlling the Urban System (McLaughlin J B, Leicester and Leicestershire Sub Regional Planning Survey) 1970 **3** (2), 61

URBAN DEVELOPMENT

Research and Planning Inputs to Metropolitan Development System (Rao B B, Narayanamurthy S G, Indian Inst of Mgt) 1977 **10** (5), 71

URBAN PLANNING

Analytical Methods in Town Planning (Ben-Shahar H, Mazor A, Pines D, Israel Inst of Urban Studies) 1970 **3** (1), 42

Corporate Planning for a Town—A Case History (Paine R E, Stockport Met Borough) 1975 **8** (5), 39

The Delphi Method and Urbanization (Marley-Clarke B, Environment Canada) 1974 **7** (6), 81

Milton Keynes: A Model for Regenerating our Cities? (Burrows B, Futures Information Assocs) 1987 **20** (1), 67

Planning Without Vision—Roots of the Urban Disaster (Schneider K R, Consultant) 1977 **10** (3), 71

Town Planning in Sweden: National Officials Versus Local Politicians (Khakee A, Umea U) 1984 **17** (6), 8282

Urban Management—Some Models for Policy Making (Low N, Melbourne U) 1979 **12** (5), 91

Urban Planning in India (Subramaniam S, Balasubramaniam R, Administrative Staff Coll India) 1974 **7** (2), 39

Urban and Regional Planning—A Systems View (Burrows B C, Literature Survey) 1980 **13** (2), 67

The Use of Computers in Town Planning (Wood P, Liverpool City Planning Dept) 1971 **3** (3), 59

URBAN SOCIOLOGY

The Crisis of Urban Living (James J R, Sheffield U) 1971 **3** (4), 44

USA

Achieving Japanese Productivity and Quality Levels at a U.S. Plant (Ishikure K) 1988 **21** (5), 10

Acquiring Companies in the U.S.A. (Adler H S, Peat Marwick Group New York; Sneath C G, Peat Marwick London) 1987 **20** (2), 42

Building Scenarios for an Electric Utility (Goldfarb D L, Huss W R) 1988 **21** (2), 78

Competitive Strategies in U.S. Banking (Sontheimer C K, Thorn R S, U of Pittsburgh) 1986 **19** (1), 113

Corporate Environmental Analysis in Large U.S. Corporations (Diffenbach J, Boston U) 1983 **16** (3), 107

Corporate Planning in the U.S. Regional Airline Industry (Shuman J C, Babson Coll) 1973 **6** (4), 35

Does Planning Pay? The Effect of Planning on Success of Acquisitions in American Firms (Ansoff H I, Avner J, Brandenburg R G, Porter F E, Radosevich R, Vanderbilt U) 1970 **3** (2), 2

Entering the 21st Century: The Global 2000 Report to the President—Book Review Article (Nutt W O, Consultant) 1983 **16** (3), 120

Environmental Scanning in U.S. Corporations (Jain S C, Connecticut U) 1984 **17** (2), 117

Foreign Competition for the U.S. Banking World (Rabino S, Northeastern U) 1984 **17** (3), 115

Foresight Activities in the U.S.A.: Time for a Re-Assessment (Lederman L L, National Science Foundation) 1984 **17** (3), 41

Formal Planning in Major U.S. Corporations (Henry H W, Tennessee U) 1977 **10** (5), 40

Formal Strategic Planning in the United States Today (Steiner G A, Kunin H & E, UCLA) 1983 **16** (3), 2

The Future of U.S. Government—Corporate Relations (Fleming J E, U of Sthn California) 1979 **12** (4), 20

How Belgian Businesses Make Strategic Planning Work (Caeldries F, van Dierdonck R) 1988 **21** (2), 41

How U.S. and Japanese CEO's Spend Their Time (Kudo H, Tachikawa T, Suzuki N) 1988 **21** (6), 79

Integrated Distribution Management—The American Perspective (La Londe B J, Ohio State U) 1969 **2** (2), 61

Japan's Drive for the European Car Market—Lessons from U.S. Experience (Wray M, Toftech; Norburn D, Imperial Coll, London) 1987 **20** (4), 60

Long Range Planning in Large United States Banks (Wood D R, Virginia Commonwealth U) 1980 **13** (3), 91

Long Range Planning in Large United States Corporations—A Survey (Ang J S, Chua J H, Oklahoma State U) 1979 **12** (2), 99

Long Range Planning in the U.S.A.—N.I.C.B. Survey (Brown J K, Sands S S, Thompson G C, Nat Industrial Conference Board) 1969 **1** (3), 44

Long Range Planning—Japan-USA—A Comparative Study (Kono T, Gakushuin U) 1976 **9** (5), 61

National Planning in the United States (Michael S R, Carlisle A E, Massachusetts U) 1976 **9** (3), 21

National Policy Making in a Global Economy: The Case for U.S. Economic Planning (Bolling R, Boston Coll; Krauthoff L C, U.S. Government) 1983 **16** (3), 25

Organised Planning in Major U.S. Companies (Ringbakk K A, C.E.I) 1969 **2** (2), 46

The Planner's Dual Role—A Survey of U.S. Companies (Lorange P, IMEDE Lausanne) 1973 **6** (1), 13

Planning for Growth in Leading U.S. Companies (Worcester R M, Market and Opinion Research Intl) 1970 **2** (3), 8

Planning for the U.S. Political Cycle (Marcus A A, Mevorach B) 1988 **21** (4), 50

The Public Affairs Function in American Corporations: Development and Relations with Corporate Planning (Post J E, Murray E A, Dickie R, Mahon J F, Boston U) 1982 **15** (2), 12

Regional Development—Alternatives for New England (Howell J M, First Nat Bank) 1976 **9** (5), 72

Regional Planning Regulations in the United States (Holmberg S R, American U) 1978 **11** (5), 72

Social Forecasting in U.S. Corporations—A Survey (Newgren K E, Florida State U; Carroll A B, Georgia U) 1979 **12** (4), 59

Strategic Issues for Charities and Philanthropies (Harvey J W, McCrohan K F) 1988 **21** (6), 44

Strategies of the United States Airlines (Huffmire D W, Connecticut U) 1975 **8** (2), 72

Technology Planning at General Motors (Koerner E) 1989 **22** (2), 9

Turnaround Strategies for Economic Development (Allen D N, Plosila W H) 1988 **21** (3), 59

U.S. Firms' Responses to Regulation: Stonewalling and Opportunism (Marcus A A) 1987 **20** (3), 98

U.S. Industry: Decline and Fall? (Richetto J P) 1988 **21** (1), 35

The Use of Multiple Scenarios by U.S. Industrial Companies: A Comparison Study, 1977–1981 (Linneman R E, Klein H E, Temple U) 1983 **16** (6), 94

The Use of Multiple Scenarios by U.S. Industrial Companies (Linneman R E, Klein H E, Philadelphia U) 1979 **12** (1), 83

Why Don't U.S. Boards Get More Involved in Strategy? (Rosenstein J, U of Texas at Arlington) 1987 **20** (3), 30

USSR

Long-Term Planning in the U.S.S.R. (Kotov F, Nat Economic Planning Dept State Planning Committee) 1975 **8** (4), 61

Scientific-Technological Forecasting in the U.S.S.R. (Dobrov G M, Science Investigation Dept) 1971 **3** (3), 13

V

VALUE ADDED

Assessing Company Strength Using Added Value (Bryant J) 1989 **22** (3), 34

Setting Objectives in Terms of Added Value (Wood E G, Sheffield City Poly) 1979 **12** (4), 2

VALUES

Values in Forecasting and Planning (Redmond W H, Houston U) 1978 **11** (3), 22

Values and Future's Research (Croft W, NASA) 1977 **10** (6), 51

VENTURE CAPITAL

The External Corporate Venture Capital Fund—A Valuable Vehicle for Growth (Bleicher K, Paul H) 1987 **20** (6), 64

Some Hints on Financing New Technologies (Shepherdson P, Pilkington Brothers 1985 **18** (6), 34

VENTURE MANAGEMENT

New Venture Development at Du Pont (Cohen A B, Du Pont de Nemours) 1970 **2** (4), 7

New Venture Management in a Electric Utility (Harrell G D, Michigan State U; Murray G O, Utility Technical Inc) 1986 **19** (2), 57

Strategic Management: New Ventures and Small Business (Cooper A C, Krannert Graduate Sch of India) 1981 **14** (5), 39

Venture Management—Success or Failure? (Burrows B C, Milton Keynes Devel Corporation) 1982 **15** (6), 84

VERTICAL INTEGRATION

Make or Buy—A Key Stragegic Issue (Ford D, U of Bath; Farmer D, Henley—The Mgt Coll) 1986 **19** (5), 54

Vertical Integration in Petrochemicals: Part 3. An Analysis of Ten Companies (Burgess A R, Consultant) 1984 **17** (1), 54

Vertical Integration in Petrochemicals—1. The Concept and Its Measurement (Burgess A R, Consultant) 1983 **16** (4), 55

Vertical Integration in Petrochemicals—2. Strategies and Problems (Burgess A R, Consultant) 1983 **16** (6), 29

W

WAR

Can Business Learn from Wargames? (Ginter P M, Rucks A C, Alabama U) 1984 **17** (3), 123

WASTE

A Note on Forecasting the Market Demand for Waste Paper (Livesey F, Consultant) 1978 **11** (1), 87

Waste Paper and the Market Mechanism (Livesey F, Barcena V A, UMIST) 1975 **8** (3), 17

WASTE DISPOSALS

Managing Toxic Wastes—After Bhopal and Sandoz (Mahon J F, Kelley P C, Boston U Sch of Mgt) 1987 **20** (4), 50

Waste Paper-Case for Government Action (Whiting P L, Thames Board Mills) 1975 **8** (5), 23

WATER POLLUTION

The Control of Industrial Discharges to Tidal Rivers and Estuaries (Beavis B, Rowley C, Newcastle-upon-Tyne U) 1974 **7** (6), 53

WATER RESOURCES

Planning for Water Resources (Perret D, Thames Water Authority) 1977 **10** (2), 65

WATER SUPPLY INDUSTRY

Economic Analysis of Public Water Supply in the Piscataqua River Watershed (Forste R H, Christensen R L, Water Resources Research Centre) 1971 **3** (4), 75

Strategic Planning for Water—A Case History (Mohanty R P, Nat Inst of Training in Industrial Engineering) 1984 **17** (4), 79

Water Supply—The Case for Joint Planning (Dam A van, Soc for Intl Devel) 1978 **11** (1), 69

WEST GERMANY *see* **FEDERAL REPUBLIC OF GERMANY**

WHALING INDUSTRY

Whales and the Whaling Industry (King A, Friends of the Earth) 1975 **8** (2), 89

WHISKY

Marketing Strategies for Scotch Whisky (Targett D, London Business Sch) 1983 **16** (2), 65

WOMEN

Narrowing the Gap—Equal Pay in Britain 1970–1986 (Tzannatos Z, U of Buckingham) 1987 **20** (2), 69

Working Women in the European Community—The future Prospect (Davidson M J, Cooper G L, Manchester U) 1983 **16** (4), 49

WOMEN EXECUTIVES

Accelerated Development for Women Managers (Beck J) 1988 **21** (3), 75

The Female Manager—The Pressures and the Problems (Cooper G L, Davidson M J, UMIST) 1983 **16** (1), 10

WOMEN MANAGERS

Accelerated Development for Women Managers (Beck J) 1988 **21** (3), 75

WOOL INDUSTRY

The Future for Wool (Clarke K C, Intl Wool Secretariat) 1975 **8** (6), 70

WORK STRUCTURING

Effective Planning and Control of Large Projects—Using Work Breakdown Structure (Lanford H W, Wright State U; McCann T M, ANALYTICS) 1983 **16** (2), 51

WORLD ECONOMY

Are We Taking the World Development Problems Seriously?—An Overview of Recent Reports and Publications—Book Review Article (Lloyd B, Bank of Credit and Commerce Intl SA) 1979 **12** (3), 97

Energy and the Economy—A Global and National Analysis (Smil V, Manitoba U; Kuz T, U of Winnipeg) 1976 **9** (3), 65

Energy Resources and World Economic Growth (Brookes L G, U.K. Atomic Energy Commission) 1973 **6** (3), 39

International Security and the World Economy (Schmid G, Inst for the Future) 1981 **14** (3), 21

Joint Planning for an Interdependent World (Dam A van, Consultant) 1975 **8** (6), 8

National Policy Making in a Global Economy: The Case for U.S. Economic Planning (Bolling R, Boston Coll; Krauthoff L C, U.S. Government) 1983 **16** (3), 25

Towards a Global Economy (Hetrick J C, Hetrick Associates Inc) 1972 **5** (3), 46

The World Food Prospect (Brown L R, Worldwatch Inst) 1977 **10** (1), 26

Y

YOUTH TRAINING

National Programmes to Promote Youth Training (Atkinson K N, Manpower Services Commission) 1985 **18** (3), 26

YUGOSLAVIA

Business Planning and Employee Democracy in Yugoslavia (Milisavljevic M, Belgrade U) 1983 **16** (4), 84

Z

ZERO-BASE BUDGETING

Zero-Base Budgeting—A Technique for Planned Organizational Decline (Pearson J V, Henley; Michael R J, London Borough of Bexley) 1981 **14** (3), 68

Zero-Base Budgeting—Dealing with Conflicting Objectives (Lee S M, Nebraska U; Shim J P, Mississippi State U) 1984 **17** (4), 103

THE BEST OF LONG RANGE PLANNING

Series Editor: **Bernard Taylor,** *Henley - The Management College, UK*

The Best of Long Range Planning brings together the best articles on particular topics previously published in *Long Range Planning* so that readers wishing to study a specific aspect of planning can find an authoritative and comprehensive view of the subject, conveniently in one volume. *The Best of Long Range Planning* builds into an invaluable reference library, covering all important aspects of Strategic Planning.

STRATEGIC PLANNING

The Chief Executive and the Board
Volume 1
Edited by **Bernard Taylor,**
Henley - The Management College, UK

This first volume is about the place of strategic planning or strategic management in the leadership and direction of major businesses. The authors deal with three issues: 1) What should be the role of the chief executive and the board in making and implementing strategy? 2) How do most chief executives and directors behave in practice? 3) What happens when major companies adopt strategic management or strategic leadership as a management style?

297x210 mm	122 pp	1988
0 08 0365663	flexicover	US$24.75
0 08 0374042	hardcover	US$52.00

ENTREPRENEURSHIP

Creating and Managing New Ventures
Volume 2
Edited by **Bruce Lloyd,**
Independent Consultant, UK

The management of change and new business development is central to corporate survival and success but is far from easy to achieve. This selection of papers offers a number of guidelines for the transition from the initial opportunity to the move into the new market and the effective management of the new venture. The authors highlight the important place of entrepreneurial initiative and motivation in the implementation of product development and diversification policies. An extensive introductory article provides a detailed overview and analysis of the literature in the Long Range Planning journal relating to this crucial area.

297x210 mm	192 pp	1989
0 08 0374077	flexicover	US$30.00
0 08 0371086	hardcover	US$64.00

MAKING STRATEGIC PLANNING WORK IN PRACTICE

Volume 3
Edited by **Basil Denning,**
The Strategic Planning Society, UK

Few large firms today fail to include planning as one of their key management systems. Yet the design, integration and successful implementation of strategic planning is a complex procedure. This volume, by focusing on the organizational process which a company uses to help managers develop effective strategy, offers guidance and warns of pitfalls to avoid. Three key areas are examined: 1. The design and structure of a planning process; 2. The development of a suitable framework for the integration of strategic planning within the company; and 3. The active implementation and execution of strategic plans. The articles selected offer a little guidance along a difficult path, in the hope that some of the well known pitfalls may be avoided.

297x210 mm	130 pp	1989
0 08 0374085	flexicover	US$24.75
0 08 0371213	hardcover	US$52.00

PLANNING FOR INFORMATION AS A CORPORATE RESOURCE

Volume 4
Edited by **Alfred Collins,** *Coopers & Lybrand, UK*

This volume deals with the problems associated with the use of information within companies, both for competitive advantage and within strategic processes. The book is in three parts: 1) Information Technology as a Strategic Resource, 2) Information Technology in the Strategic Planning Process, and 3) Managing Information Technology for Strategic Impact. The volume provides an excellent framework and specific cases illustrating how leading organisations are planning for information as a corporate resource.

297x210 mm	118pp	1990
0 08 0374093	flexicover	US$24.75
0 08 0372708	hardcover	US$52.00

PERGAMON PRESS
Member of Maxwell Macmillan Pergamon Publishing Corporation

Oxford   New York   Beijing   Frankfurt   Sao Paulo   Seoul   Sydney   Tokyo   Toronto

DEVELOPING STRATEGIES FOR COMPETITIVE ADVANTAGE

Volume 5

Edited by **Patrick McNamee,**
University of Ulster, Northern Ireland

How can an organization use strategy to achieve a competitive advantage over its rivals? This book addresses this fundamental issue in strategic planning with a selection of exceptional articles covering two complementary areas: 1) techniques for developing competitive strategies, and 2) case histories showing how these techniques have been applied to particular situations. The authors pinpoint the crucial factors which help companies, whether smaller firms or major multinationals, successfully build sustainable and profitable competitive advantage at the Strategic Business Unit and Corporate level.

297 x 210mm	140pp	1990
0 08 0377696	flexicover	US$24.75
0 08 0372716	hardcover	US$52.00

STRATEGIC PLANNING FOR HUMAN RESOURCES

Volume 6

Edited by **Sheila Rothwell,**
Henley - The Management College, UK

The need for strategic planning for human resources has become ever more pressing: intensified international competition requires employees to adopt change rapidly within their organization, and competitive 'cutting edge' is increasingly derived from the way people manage and use their potential.

In this volume the authors examine the critical issues and options facing top management in the areas of manpower planning, matching business needs, personnel policies, communication and corporate culture, and industrial relations.

297 x 210mm	155pp	1990	
0 08 037770X	flexicover	US$24.75	approx
0 08 0372724	hardcover	US$55.00	approx

STRATEGIC SERVICE MANAGEMENT

Beyond the Moment of Truth
Volume 7

Edited by **Denis Boyle,**
The Service Management Group Limited, London, UK

Strategic Service Management is a new approach for competitive success which embraces the major developments in service management thinking over the 1980s. In this volume case studies from a wide variety of industries, both in the private and public sector, focus on the main areas of this approach: 1) creating competitive strategies for a service oriented business, and 2) the process of successful and accelerated strategy implementation. The authors provide valuable ideas and techniques for the service business aiming for market leadership and profit growth, and for all companies where adding value with service and motivating employees towards business goals is vital.

297 x 210mm	140pp	1990	
0 08 0377513	flexicover	US$24.75	approx
0 08 0377521	hardcover	US$55.00	approx

FORTHCOMING TITLES

STRATEGIC MANAGEMENT IN MULTINATIONAL COMPANIES

Edited by
Nigel Freedman,
Philips, Eindhoven, Netherlands

STRATEGIC MANAGEMENT FOR HIGHER PERFORMANCE IN JAPANESE COMPANIES

Edited by
Toyohiro Kono,
Gakushuin University, Tokyo, Japan

CREATING SHAREHOLDER VALUE THROUGH ACQUISITIONS AND DIVESTMENT

Edited by
Christopher Clarke,
Wallace Smith Strategic Financial Planning Ltd., London, UK

STRATEGIC MANAGEMENT OF SERVICE BUSINESSES

Edited by
Ken Irons,
KIA, London, UK

How to obtain articles, issues and volumes referred to in this Index

Long Range Planning is published bi-monthly.

Long Range Planning is available on subscription. Details of current subscription rates and sample copies are available from: *North America*: Pergamon Press Inc., Maxwell House, Fairview Park, Elmsford, NY 10523, U.S.A., telephone (914) 592–7700, facsimile (914) 592 3625. *Rest of the World*: Pergamon Press plc, Headington Hill Hall, Oxford OX3 0BW, U.K., telephone (0865) 64881, facsimile (0865) 60285.

Back Issues, Back Volumes

Back issues of previously published volumes are available from Journal Sales, Pergamon Press plc, Headington Hill Hall, Oxford OX3 0BW. Complete volumes are available from Vol 1 (1968) to date, single issues from Vol 19 No 1 (First issue 1986) to date.

Single articles from Long Range Planning

Photocopies of articles from Long Range Planning are available from Information on Demand Inc, 8000 Westpark Drive, McLean, Virginia 22102, telephone (800) 999 4463 or (703) 442 0303; facsimile (703) 442 0907.

Per article
(up to 20 pages including copyright fee)   US$19.00

By special arrangement with the Publishers U.K. customers may obtain single copies, subject to availability, from the Strategic Planning Society, 17 Portland Place, London W1N 3AF. Telephone: (071) 636 7737.

Per article
(including copyright fee and postage)   £8.00

Reprints of single articles are available for large-quantity purchases. Prices may be obtained from the Reprint Department, Pergamon Press plc, Headington Hill Hall, Oxford OX3 0BW, U.K., telephone (0865) 64881.

ORDER FORM

To order any publication listed, please fill in the details below and mail this form to your regular supplier or, in case of difficulty, to the appropriate Pergamon office. Requests for sample copies of journals should be sent directly to your nearest Pergamon office.

☐ Please enter my ONE YEAR SUBSCRIPTION to
LONG RANGE PLANNING at   DM 730.00

☐ Please enter my TWO YEAR SUBSCRIPTION to
LONG RANGE PLANNING at   DM 1387.00

☐ Please send me a FREE SAMPLE COPY of
LONG RANGE PLANNING

BOOKS - Please send on firm account
(Indicate hard or flexicover)   Price   Qty

____

____

____

____

Name ____

Organization ______________________________________

Address ____

_________________________ Post/Zip Code ___________

Invoice my Pergamon account no. ___________________

Please bill me ☐

Cheque or money order enclosed ☐ Total value ________

Save postage and handling charges: send your payment by cheque/money order made payable to Pergamon Press.

Credit Cards
Pergamon welcomes payment by credit card. The following cards are accepted: Visa, Mastercard, American Express and (only outside USA & Canada) Diners Club.

Please charge my _________________________ credit card

Issuing Bank (MasterCard only) ___________________

No. _________________________ Expiry Date _________

Signed _______________________________ Date _______

Pergamon accepts UNESCO coupons.
Prices and proposed publication dates are subject to change without prior notice.

JOURNALS: Prices include postage and insurance.
German Mark (DM) prices quoted apply in Europe, Africa, Asia/Australasia (with the exception of Japan). For the rest of the world apply to the nearest Pergamon office. Advertising rate card available on request.

SAVE 25% ON JOURNAL BACK ISSUES WHEN ENTERING A CURRENT SUBSCRIPTION.
Back issues of all volumes of Pergamon journals are available in hard copy from Pergamon Press. Please send for a separate price list. Subscribers ordering a current subscription may order back issues at a 25% discount.
Back issues in microform are only available from University Microfilms International, 300 North Zeeb Road, Ann Arbor, MI 48106, USA.

BOOKS: US Dollar prices are valid for all countries except Australia, Austria, Germany (BRD), New Zealand, UK and Eire. (Prices for these countries are available from the appropriate Pergamon office.) In addition, on some titles, the US Dollar prices may vary for customers in other regions.

PERGAMON OFFICES

BOOK ORDERS ONLY
USA & Canada:
Pergamon Press,
Order Dept,
Front and Brown Streets,
Riverside, NJ 08075,
USA

COMBINED BOOK & JOURNAL ORDERS & REQUESTS:
Pergamon Press Inc,
Maxwell House,
Fairview Park, Elmsford,
New York, NY 10523,
USA

Australia & New Zealand:
Pergamon Press (Australia)
Pty Ltd, P O Box 544,
Potts Point, NSW 2011,
Australia

Germany & Austria:
Pergamon Press Gmbh,
Hammerweg 6,
D-6242 Kronberg/Taunus,
FRG

India:
Pergamon Press,
20B/46 Tilak Nagar,
New Delhi 110 018,
India

Japan:
Pergamon Press, 5th Floor,
Matsuoka Central Building,
1-7-1 Nishishinjuko,
Shinjuko, Tokyo 160,
Japan

Korea:
Pergamon Press,
RM 711-1, Hanaro Building,
194-4, Insa-Dong,
Chongno-ku,
Seoul 110-290, Korea

People's Republic of China:
Pergamon Press,
Qianmen Hotel, Room 4037,
Beijing, PRC

UK & all other countries:
Pergamon Press plc,
Headington Hill Hall,
Oxford OX3 0BW, UK